WAR STORIES OF D-DAY

WAR STORIES OF D-DAY

OPERATION OVERLORD: JUNE 6, 1944

MICHAEL GREEN & JAMES D. BROWN

ZENITH PRESS

▲

To all the Allied soldiers,
sailors, and airmen who took part
in the invasion of Normandy, France,
on June 6, 1944.

▼

First published in 2009 by Zenith Press, an imprint of
MBI Publishing Company, 400 First Avenue North, Suite 300,
Minneapolis, MN 55401 USA.

Zenith Press titles are also available at discounts in bulk quantity for
industrial or sales-promotional use. For details write to Special Sales
Manager at MBI Publishing Company, 400 First Avenue North, Suite
300, Minneapolis, MN 55401 USA.

To find out more about our books, join us online at
www.zenithpress.com.

Design Manager: Brenda C. Canales
Designer: Helena Shimizu

Front cover image credit: *U.S. Navy*
Maps: *Patti Isaacs, recreated from U.S. Army source maps*

Library of Congress Cataloging-in-Publication Data

Green, Michael, 1952-
  War stories of D-Day : Operation Overlord : June 6, 1944 / Michael
Green and James D. Brown.
    p. cm.
  Includes bibliographical references and index.
  ISBN 978-0-7603-3669-4 (hb w/ jkt : alk. paper)
  1. World War, 1939-1945--Campaigns--France--Normandy. 2.
World War, 1939-1945--Campaigns--France--Normandy--Personal
narratives, American. 3. Operation Overlord. 4. United States--
Armed Forces--Biography. I. Brown, James D. II. Title.
  D756.5.N6G75 2009
  940.54'21421092273--dc22

                                        2008044748

Printed in the United States of America

CONTENTS

ACKNOWLEDGMENTS

THIS BOOK WOULD NOT BE POSSIBLE WITHOUT the assistance of Martin K. A. Morgan, the historian in residence of the National World War II Museum, located in New Orleans, Louisiana, who provided the authors access to its impressive collection of oral interviews.

The National World War II Museum, formerly known as the National D-Day Museum, was designated in 2000 by Congress as the country's official World War II museum.

For those who are inspired by this book to learn more about D-Day and the locations in which it took place, the National World War II Museum offers a variety of educational travel programs, hosted by world-class historians, which include a tour of the Normandy battlefields.

INTRODUCTION

We are but warriors for the working-day;
Our gayness and our gilt are all besmirch'd
With rainy marching in the painful field.
But by the mass, our hearts are in the trim.

—Shakespeare, *Henry V*

MILITARY PLANNERS SELDOM KNOW THE EXACT DATE an operation
will commence. This is particularly true for large, complicated operations. The planners of the Normandy landings
therefore sequenced the operation with respect to "D," short-
hand for "whichever day the operation begins." Thus, a piece
of the operation that needed to take place three days before
the landings was referred to as happening on "D–3," and one
that would occur five days after the initial landing would
be specified for execution on "D+5." Technically, every military operation begins on D-day. However, for the millions of
soldiers, sailors, and airmen on both sides of the Normandy
landings, there is only one D-Day: June 6, 1944.

The rightful preeminence of this one D-Day over all
others in wars before and since is a consequence of its
criticality not only to the course of World War II but to the
flow of geopolitical events to this very day. The operation was

so large in scale and its outcome so important that both sides knew that it would be the most important single battle of the war. General Erwin Rommel (one of the few realists left in the German high command) and the Allied leaders knew that the landings would be repulsed on the beaches or they would not be stopped at all. Both sides knew that there would be only one chance to get it right. Both sides knew that failure of the landings would result in an extension of the war by years and could even reshape the war's ultimate outcome. And because both sides had carefully weighed the battle and understood the consequences of losing it, they knew that casualties would be heavy. Both sides were right.

The Normandy landings combined the two most harrowing kinds of military operations: a seaborne landing on an opposed beach, and a night airborne assault. Preparations began years earlier as the gravity of the task was realized. The technique of division-size parachute and glider landings had to be learned. Floating ports had to be invented. Amphibious tanks were developed. Rocket barrage ships were constructed. An ingenious method of unrolling a fuel pipeline from a gigantic floating bobbin was utilized, and even built and used. For all this scientific and military cleverness, though, one of the most important pieces of military hardware proved to be a stamped steel "froggy" clicker available at any five-and-ten-cent store.

In most military operations, individual soldiers, noncommissioned officers, junior officers, colonels, and generals each have their role to play. The confusion of both the amphibious landing and the airborne assaults wrote new chapters in the leadership manuals. Division commanders jumped from low-flying C-47s to land seconds later as rifle squad leaders. Privates charged down the ramps of landing craft and arrived mere minutes later at the high-water line as platoon leaders. The fog of battle hung low and thick over hundreds of square miles of battlefield in the predawn hours of June 6, and roles and missions that had been rehearsed for months devolved into a series of individual struggles just to understand what was going on.

The motivation of many soldiers caused them to remain fixated on their original missions, regardless of how the preconceived situation might have changed. For others, individual initiative drove them to extemporize new missions based on whatever fellow soldiers could be gathered up and whatever enemy forces could be found. The most remarkable common factor, though, is how uniformly motivated individual soldiers were to pick up the pieces of their intended battle and continue to take the fight to the enemy. Soldiers who might have been expected to hunker down "until the Brass gets this sorted out" did just the opposite. Despite all the years of planning and unprecedented marshalling of combat forces and logistics, the true story of the success of the landings comes down to the individual heroism of the soldiers, sailors, and airmen who were there.

The accounts that follow are transcriptions of oral histories. The sentence structure and syntax tend to be those of the speakers rather than writers. The editors have striven to preserve the voices of these men as much as possible. Editorial changes have been limited to those instances where clarification is absolutely necessary to understand the story. We hope to provide the reader with an opportunity to hear these men in their own words, to see the battlefield through their eyes. Most importantly, we hope to convey even the barest fraction of the emotions these men felt as they entered battle as *warriors for the working-day*, and emerged as the heroes who saved Western civilization.

1 | PARATROOPERS

Jack R. Isaacs (U.S. Army)

The job of the 82nd Airborne Division on D-Day was to seize areas around the Merderet River and a small French town. Paratrooper Jack Isaacs did his best to fulfill that mission with the forces at hand.

ON JUNE 4, 1944, WE MOVED TO the airport from which we would take off for the invasion of France the following day. We were confined at the airport after being told of our destination, the village of Ste. Mére Eglise in France. Our mission was threefold: take and hold the village, deny the Germans the use of roads through the area, and prevent a counterattack toward Utah Beach. The one-day delay in the invasion of France is well documented. We spent the extra day doing what we could for rest and relaxation and making final preparations—checking equipment, receiving instructions on sand tables and aerial maps, studying aerial photos, and rehearsing what we were going to do and how we were going to do it.

Takeoff was somewhere around eight in the evening. It was still full daylight in England at that time of year. The intended drop time was to be after midnight, but it took a great deal of time to form aircraft serials in the limited airspace. It took 108 planes to fly a regiment of parachute infantry. Three regiments (the 505th, 507th, and 508th) were going in with the 82nd Airborne Division, and two regiments with the 101st Airborne Division, plus the British Sixth Airborne Division. In addition, artillery, medical, engineer, and support personnel were to be transported. There were hundreds of planes, and they needed space and time to be formed.

G Company, 3rd Battalion, 505th Parachute Infantry Regiment, was to be the lead-in company. Since Ste. Mére Eglise was such a pivotal town to the Utah Beach landings, our job was critical. As the 3rd Platoon leader of that company, I was in a Dakota C-47 [twin-engine transport plane] holding position in the left V on the run-in for the drop.

Landfall was in the general vicinity of a French village on the west coast of the Cherbourg peninsula. Unfortunately, as we approached the coast, we hit an area of reduced visibility, which forced the planes in the formation to scatter. I knew that my flight of three planes was veering to the left (north), and I would probably be off target. This was to be my third combat jump, and it was my twenty-eighth parachute jump. Breaking free of the fog, about three to four miles in from the west coast, I saw no other planes, only a few floating clouds. There was a goodly amount of German antiaircraft fire, including light machine gun, 20mm, and 88mm high-explosive stuff. Whether you looked north, south, east, or west, you could see black puffs of antiaircraft fire. I didn't feel that my own plane was being fired upon directly, and I know that we weren't hit. The red light came on at approximately the right time for the drop, and when the green light came on, I took that stick of eighteen jumpers out. We were over land, and my next thought was simply getting onto the ground safely.

I could see as I approached the ground in the dark that I was coming into a fairly good-size field for Normandy, approximately 150 by 250 yards. I subsequently learned that it was bounded on the east by a blacktop road, on the south by a gravel road, on the west by a country lane, and on the north by a common hedgerow. All sides had hedgerows. I could see cows in the field as I came down. That was reassuring because where there were cows, there would be no mines.

I landed without harm and, after getting out of my equipment, commenced to find my men, take command of them, and move to our objective. I found one man immediately. I didn't know him, which indicated that there were probably other planes in the area, but I hadn't seen them. Shortly after finding this man, we heard an approaching motor vehicle and set out to find it, wanting to ambush it and use it for our own purpose.

The vehicle was faster than we thought and it passed us on the blacktop road before we could get there. We took up a position in the weeds beside the road anticipating that another vehicle might come along. Our thinking was that since it was a blacktop road, it would carry quite a bit of traffic and we might get another chance.

No other vehicles came by, so I set out to gather what men I could. I heard an identification cricket and, following the sound of it, came upon a man who was badly injured. The Germans had staked out the large fields in Normandy to prevent glider landings. They had set poles in the ground, about the diameter of a telephone pole but only ten to twelve feet off the ground. The poles had been sharpened and looked like large pencils sticking in the ground. Unfortunately, this man had landed right on one of the poles and had broken his leg about midway between the knee and the hip and had fractured his thigh. He was in great pain and was effectively out of the fight. There was no way I could take him with me. Each man in the parachute units carried a first-aid kit, which contained morphine. I took this man's morphine and gave him a shot, then put a bayonet on his rifle, stuck it in the ground, and put his helmet on top of the butt of the rifle. This was somewhat of a universal symbol that a man was out of action and did not intend to fight. Then I went on to find additional men.

Moving to the north side of the field, I came across other American parachutists, none of whom I knew. Moving farther along the hedgerow on the north side of the field, I eventually came upon Lt. Pat Ward, who had been in G Company back in Fort Benning and Fort Bragg. He was now the S-3 (Plans and Training officer) of the 3rd Battalion. He had found a few men, and we combined forces, the idea being to gather up what we could and immediately make our way to Ste. Mére Eglise. We had learned in Sicily and Italy that if you missed your drop zone, you took command of whomever you could find and moved to your objective, fighting if you had to in order to get there, and just doing whatever you could to help carry out the mission.

We found a few equipment bundles and gathered them to augment our supplies. At the break of day we discovered a small house in the northwest corner of the field. We ultimately used the yard of the house as an assembly point as two-man details were sent out to find other jumpers in the area. We had assembled about thirty-five men, the bulk of whom I did not know. I did have from my own platoon Cpl. Quentin Echols from Tulsa, Oklahoma. Corporal Echols had a broken ankle and was unable to do anything except hobble along, but he had great determination. There was Private Whistler from my company. I found my own runner, Pvt. Robert Treet. One man I found who was to stay with me for a long time was an artilleryman from the 101st Division. Finding this man told me that the drop had been badly scattered because I knew that the 101st was supposed to be in the vicinity of Carentan, miles to the south of where we were. I knew that the 101st was to be south of the 82nd Division, and I assumed I was on the north flank of our projected landing site.

At about dawn, while we were around this small French house, the owner came out and was surprised to find his farmyard occupied by Americans. There was a great deal of consternation on his face, and I'm sure alarm, too, regarding his own personal safety. We subsequently learned that his wife was in the house with his early teenage daughter. It was at this point that the French phrases we had been studying would have come in handy, except neither Lieutenant Ward nor I could remember a single phrase. With sign language and a great deal of pointing and looking at maps, the Frenchman helped us find our location; we were about six miles north of Ste. Mére Eglise. Our immediate task was to get organized and move to Ste. Mére Eglise.

Also about this time, the gliders started coming in to Normandy, and one of them chose our field to make his landing. He managed with unerring accuracy to hit one of those anti-glider poles, demolishing the glider and his load of equipment and injuring every member of the crew. We managed to get the wounded glider men to our little French house. Shortly thereafter, we noticed a German soldier step into the field and approach the injured man that we had left next to the anti-glider pole. He looked him over then shot him. This infuriated us, and we made sure the German didn't survive his trip back to the hedgerow.

By now it was about seven in the morning of June 6, 1944, and the Frenchman told us by sign language to go down to a large farmhouse, which was actually only a few yards from where I had landed, although I had not seen it in the dark while coming down. The Frenchman indicated that he was going there. I trusted him because he left his wife and child with us in the small house. I was sure he would come back and not bring the enemy down upon us, although later I had my doubts. I grew apprehensive and decided to go to the large farmhouse myself to see what was up. I picked Pvt. Henry Voges, from my company, and another man to go with me. I decided that just the three of us would go down there on reconnaissance and see what there was to be found. We went down the small lane on the west side of the field, and as we approached a T intersection with a gravel road I saw our supply sergeant crouching in a ditch. I directed him back to where I had left Lieutenant Ward and the other men and told him to report to the lieutenant and do whatever duties his job called for.

We then turned east and walked up the gravel road. I was in the lead on the north side of the road. Private Voges was about five yards behind me on the south side of the road, and the other man was about ten yards behind me.

We were nearing the house when Private Voges threw a pebble at me to get my attention. Turning toward him, I saw that he was motioning for me to come quietly over to his side of the road. I got on that side of the road and, looking through the hedgerow, saw the house and the Frenchman, who was talking to some German officers. There were thirty-five to forty German soldiers standing around in the farmyard. From my experience in Sicily and Italy, I realized I was looking at a battalion headquarters or the equivalent. It was my immediate intention to get back to Lieutenant Ward with the news. We would attack this group. We had recovered two light machine guns, a BAR [Browning automatic rifle], and a 60mm mortar, and each of us had his personal weapon. Furthermore, the element of surprise would be with us, and we could do that group of Germans some great harm.

Unfortunately, at just about this time, a German guard stepped out of the farmhouse gate and discovered us. I fired first and he went down, but the fat was in the fire. There would be no surprise in this thing now. We decided to beat a hasty retreat back to the lane, which would give us cover. Somehow we made it without anybody being hurt. We got back to Lieutenant Ward and reported to him what had gone down. We had come to France to fight, and it was my intention to gather up my own force and immediately attack. The Germans were only 100 to 125 yards away, and even though they knew where we were, they didn't know how many there were of us. Although they were talking to the Frenchman and he might have spilled the beans, I doubted that. He wouldn't direct the Germans in such a fashion that they would attack us where we were because his wife and daughter were with us.

Lieutenant Ward agreed with me that we should attack immediately, and we hastily made a plan and then set out down the road. Suddenly, from the north we were fired on by a large group of Germans other than those at the large farmhouse. I could see about twenty-five Germans, and they had at least two light machine guns. They were aggressively approaching with covering fire and had us pinned down in just two or three minutes. Simultaneously, we were getting fire from the east side of the field near the blacktop road. We knew there was a large German force to the south of us. We were almost surrounded, with only the west open for escape. We returned fire as best we could. I was on the east side of the lane, and the covering fire of the two machine guns was bearing down on me. With me was my runner, Pvt. Robert Treet, and we were returning fire, firing left handed, which we were trained to do. Also, the ditch we were in was so shallow that it was hardly giving us protection from anything. I said to Private Treet, "We will have to get on the other side of the road or we'll be killed right here." He agreed without any hesitation. I crawled across the road, and he started to crawl across the road behind me, but he was hit and killed in the road.

We took several other casualties. We were in a bad spot. After talking briefly with Lieutenant Ward, he agreed that we should evacuate immediately to the west. The Germans would likely bring mortar fire to bear on us, which was a standard tactic. Not having had foxholes dug and not being in a good defensive position, we were vulnerable.

We immediately set out to consolidate our group and evacuate to the west. I was senior to Lieutenant Ward and I directed him to take the point guard, move to the west, then veer slightly to the south to get us through there. I would stay with the rear guard and offer him what protection I could. I had five or six men with the rear guard. We jumped into action and carried out the plan rather successfully. Our rear guard was able to deliver enough fire to slow down the advancing Germans from the north. The ones from the south never put in an appearance. The ones from the east were delivering a covering fire for their comrades coming from the north. But we were able to slow that attacking group and actually drive them to ground long enough for us to evacuate our rear guard. We had just moved to the west several hundred yards when the column stopped. Not being pursued by the Germans at that point, I went forward to see what the holdup was. I came to a man lying in a hedgerow by a field and asked him where Lieutenant Ward was. He simply said, "He's been captured. He went through that gate over there and that hedgerow there with Germans on either side of the gate, covered by the hedgerow. They had him dead to rights. He would either surrender or die right there, so he was taken prisoner." I also lost Pvt. Henry Voges in this action, and I assumed that he had also been captured. Subsequently I was to learn that he had not been captured; he had managed to evade the Germans but had simply become separated and ultimately made his way back to the unit.

This firefight had lasted perhaps three to four hours. I decided to set up a perimeter defense where we were in the field and allow the men to get some rest. They had been up and going for something like twenty hours, and fatigue was a matter to be considered. We deployed to best defend ourselves from any direction.

While in the field and looking back to the east, I determined that we had moved about a thousand yards and gained a little elevation. We also discovered a rather sizable column of German foot soldiers moving toward us. Through my binoculars it appeared that they might number as many as 250, which would be too big a force for us to attack, but we would defend ourselves if they came our way. I moved the bulk of the men to that side of the field, preparatory to fighting if it came to that. But as the Germans got within perhaps 500 yards of us, they took another lane and went in a different direction, bypassing us.

Making a personal reconnaissance, I found another field that I thought was better suited for defense than what we had, so I moved the group to that field. On the east side of it was a country road that passed through a defile, with the depression providing a point of vulnerability for any vehicle traveling in it. I took a position adjacent to the road next to the defile, and put the artilleryman who was with us from the 101st Division on the other side of the road. I had Corporal Echols on that side in the field, and I deployed the other men around the perimeter of the field. With that done, we took up defensive positions. By this time it was approaching dark, and it was our intention to get some rest and defend ourselves, then see what could be done tomorrow about getting to Ste. Mére Eglise.

We had been reduced to about twenty men, having taken casualties in the firefight and lost others as POWs [prisoners of war]. I knew that Private Treet had been killed and that two or three men had been injured. I knew from talking to the men that two or three of those in the original firefight had elected to take cover rather than withdraw with us, and no doubt those men had been captured. One of them was a corporal and one was a high-ranking sergeant, either a first sergeant or a master sergeant. The highest rank remaining with me was the supply staff sergeant. I had one other corporal besides Corporal Echols, but I didn't know him. We had learned in Sicily and Italy that if a man didn't know you, he might not obey you. This presented a problem. The men whom I knew in my platoon and in my company did what I told them to do without any question.

Sometime well after dark, I was awakened by the sound of enemy armor. The tank tracks made an unmistakable noise, and I knew that they were within just yards of us. Looking to the road where we were positioned, I saw that an enemy column was moving up in a close march formation.

The German column was made up of tanks, supply vehicles, half-tracks, trucks, and men all in close proximity to one another, with no interval of any significance. They were moving through the depression in the road. My immediate intention with our weapons and grenades was to block each end of the road by knocking out a vehicle then attack the jammed-up vehicles in the defile. It was a perfect ambush spot. We had the wherewithal to knock out tanks because each of the men was carrying a Gammon grenade, a British sock grenade that was effective at close range against enemy armor. I organized the men I had, but I quickly learned that I had no men other than the artilleryman from the 101st Division and Corporal Echols, with the broken ankle. I was told that all the others had doubted my leadership and had gone off on their own. I subsequently learned that all those men were captured and spent the rest of the war as POWs. With only two men and myself, there was nothing we could do about the enemy column. We spent the rest of the night in that position, watching the column pass silently by.

The next morning we observed in a neighboring field a German Nebelwerfer [rocket] battery moving into position. That was the so-called "screaming meemie" artillery of the Germans. We had to sit helplessly and watch them go into action and fire several volleys before they packed up and hauled away, again in response to counterartillery or naval fire. On the morning of June 8, I made a personal reconnaissance of two or three fields around us and decided that the three of us would be better situated in a different field.

Corporal Echols, with the broken ankle, hobbled along as best he could. At this point, I feel I should commend the unknown artilleryman who accompanied us. I never knew his name, but I would commend him to all artillerymen because of his calm determination in the desperate situation we were in. He stuck with me, helped with Corporal Echols, and did everything I told him to do and more.

Late in the afternoon of June 8, we began to hear small-arms fire, which was obviously both German and American. We couldn't see anyone, nor did we know whether it was another batch of American parachutists engaging the enemy, or ground forces approaching. We had no way of knowing.

We saw an infantry squad moving toward us. They were firing over our heads, at Germans on our flanks, who were retreating before them. We watched the Germans run past us to our rear. The Americans were in front of us, and we were in the field between them, in the line of fire. We took the best cover we could. We managed to avoid being hit by either the Germans or Americans. I heard the squad leader tell his men to "bring that son of a bitching BAR up here." He then laid down more fire, driving the Germans from the area.

We stood up and yelled at the squad leader. The sergeant approached and informed me that he was a member of the 4th Infantry Division, and they had come in over the beaches and were attacking to the north. He directed me to his battalion headquarters, and with the artilleryman and Corporal Echols between us, we managed to get down the hill, onto the road, and down to a farmhouse where the infantry battalion headquarters was located. I reported there and told the battalion commander of our experience. He evacuated Corporal Echols through their medical channels then directed me and the artilleryman to sack out in the barn at his field headquarters. In the morning we could go back to our respective units. They issued us rations and whatnot. So the artilleryman and I ate for the first time in a day and sacked out in the barn, where we welcomed sleep in a secure place.

The next morning, coming out of the barn, I saw my own battalion executive officer, Maj. Bill Hagan, talking to the infantry battalion commander. I reported to Major Hagan, and he told me that the 3rd Battalion of the 505th was just down the road and that as soon as he was through with his discussions with the infantry battalion commander he would take me back to my unit. We passed the artilleryman back through channels so that he could rejoin his own unit with the 101st Airborne Division. Major Hagan and I returned to the 3rd Battalion of the 505th Parachute Infantry

Regiment and subsequently walked into G Company's command post, where I learned what had happened at Ste. Mére Eglise. This was June 9. The bulk of the unit had landed where it was intended, had moved into Ste. Mére Eglise, and had taken the mission's objectives, but it had suffered a good many casualties in doing so. Captain Follmer had broken his hip on the drop and had been out of action at the beginning. Lieutenant Ivan Woods, the executive officer, had taken over command of the company. Lieutenant Orman, Lieutenant Mastrangelo, and I were three platoon leaders who thus far had been uninjured.

On June 10, Lieutenant Woods called a platoon leaders' meeting, the purpose of which was to outline our future plans for movement. As I was reporting to this meeting, the other group already having arrived, an 88mm round exploded in a tree near us. The tree burst into flames, and tree splinters and shrapnel wounded several of the men. Lieutenant Woods was wounded severely enough to be evacuated to the United States. I was wounded in the shoulder and sent to the battalion aid station, where I was patched up and returned to duty. Our company mechanic, Corporal Monnie, was severely wounded, having lost an arm. Lieutenant Orman was the next senior officer, so he became the company commander after the wounding of Lieutenant Woods.

The company engaged in several small actions of a defensive and offensive nature, ultimately arriving at the village of Ste. Sauvour Le Vicompte (generally referred to as Ste. Sauvour) on the night of June 16. We were directed to attack through the town and to secure the high ground to the west. The battalion assembled for action with I Company on the right and G Company on the left. We launched our attack without any reconnaissance and very little information about what we might encounter. We were attacked by five German tanks and were fiercely opposed by several German machine gun positions. G Company managed to knock out two of the tanks with one bazooka [antitank rocket launcher] and only three rounds of ammunition. To top it all off, we were strafed by two of our own fighter planes.

Lieutenant Orman was killed just west of Ste. Sauvour, and Lieutenant Mastrangelo was wounded while we were trying to cross a railroad embankment near the town. I was appointed company commander. All our other officers had been wounded or captured or were missing, so I found myself as the sole officer left in G Company. We had started with eight and were now down to one.

Night fell, and we continued the attack in the dark. It continued all night long, dawn finding us actually having worked our way behind the enemy positions. I had only seventeen men left, the others having been lost in the night or been casualties, but we were in a strategic position alongside the road running west of Ste. Sauvour. We were actually 200 to 300 yards ahead of I Company, and when our position became known to the Germans, they started to withdraw. We were in an excellent position to deliver flanking fire, and I Company was delivering frontal fire, so we caused a great many casualties among the retreating Germans. Also, at point-blank range in this position, we observed an 88mm gun being towed down the road toward us. It was accompanied by two or three other vehicles and approximately twenty to twenty-five men. We were lying alongside the road in the hedgerow when this

group of Germans approached. We achieved complete surprise and, with a withering fire, wiped out the entire crew
of the 88mm gun. We destroyed the tow vehicle, the 88mm,
and the two or three vehicles accompanying it. The devasta-
tion discouraged the Germans, who were still attempting to
defend themselves against I Company, and it became a rout.

The company was able to reassemble the next day, and
our seventeen men grew to about seventy-five men who had
become lost in the night attack. From there, we continued
small-unit actions and eventually found ourselves in an
attack position ready to take the high ground surrounding the
French town of Le Haye du Puits. We effectively removed that
town from the German supply train because we dominated
the town and its road junction, which was critical to north-
south traffic. It was in this position that we were ultimately
relieved by the 8th Infantry Division. We then prepared to
return to England, which we did by landing craft, having
spent about thirty-eight days in Normandy. I have often
said subsequent to this action that I entered Normandy as
a twenty-one-year-old platoon leader and in ten days was a
forty-two-year-old company commander.

Len Griffing (U.S. Army)

*German antiaircraft fire was fierce on D-Day. Len Griffing, a
member of the 101st Airborne Division, had a most exciting
introduction to France, which involved a German self-
propelled antiaircraft gun trying to shoot him out of the sky.*

JUNE 5 WAS D-DAY FOR US because the actual invasion started
at about eight in the evening when we climbed into the

aircraft in England. Unlike the previous day, this time the planes took off, and we were actually going. It took a couple of hours of flying around to form up. The steak and the ice cream supper we'd eaten turned sour. Most of us threw it up into the barf bags that were provided for that exact purpose. Anyone who says he was not scared right down into his bones was just not being honest. Someone lit a cigarette, and as he lit it he took three or four fast, deep drags in a row. The flame was over an inch long, but the cigarette had no ash—just fire. Then he passed it on to the next guy, who did the same.

When it was time to stand up and hook up, most of us were so airsick that jumping out seemed a reasonable thing to do. At least it was better than staying. The planes came in over the west coast of France and had to fly twenty miles or so over land to put us over the drop zone. We were low enough so that every guy with a pistol could get off a few shots at us. The bullets and the shrapnel hitting the metal skin of the plane were like heavy rain on a tin roof.

Now that I think back on it, this was a pretty dangerous time. Each of us carried a half dozen hand grenades and everybody carried taped to his leg a land mine that was capable of knocking a track off a tank. We were supposed to use these to seal off the beach so that the beach landings could get ashore before they were hit by the German reserves. Our job was to tie up the reserves until the beach was secure.

But regarding the plane, as soon as we started taking fire, we hooked up and stood in the door, so we could get out of the plane fast if it was hit.

I was pretty far forward in the stick, maybe number four or five, and I could see out the doorway. The sky was lit with tracers. I remember seeing one of the transports a quarter mile away get hit and explode in a big ball of flame. You always hope that the guys get out, but as I think back, that plane had three or four guys aboard as crew, and I know they didn't get out.

The green light came on for us and we started out the door. I remember being in a kind of time warp. Anytime you make a parachute jump, you've got about three seconds when all the things that are supposed to happen do happen. But I remember feeling that I had infinite time to see and do everything I did. I looked at my watch and it was 12:30. When I got into the doorway, I looked out into what looked like a solid wall of tracer bullets. I remember this as clearly as if it happened this morning. I think it's engraved in the cells of my brain. I said to myself, "Len, you're in as much trouble now as you're ever going to be. If you get out of this, nobody can ever do anything to you that you ever have to worry about."

As I stood there with my hands on the edge of the doorway ready to push out, it seemed that we took some kind of a burst under the left wing because the plane went in a sharp roll. I couldn't push myself out because it was uphill, so I just hung on. The rest of the stick tried to hang on to the jump cable, but they either fell or almost fell. Anyway, they were in no position to follow me out the door.

The pilot got hold of the ship, stopped the roll, and started rolling it back the other way. As soon as he got it to where I could push myself out, I did, and I was in the air. As I think back, I can't believe I was that stupid with the plane going maybe a hundred miles an hour. The guy who went out before me was a half mile behind us. And by the time the guy behind me got out, he was a half mile away from me in the other direction. My chute popped open and I was the only parachute in the sky.

We never jumped more than 600 feet, but it seemed to take a hundred years to get down. The moon had gone behind a cloud, and it was so dark that I had no idea what I was landing on. It could have been grass, might have been trees, it could have been water. But I could see four muzzle blasts following me all the way down.

I was coming down on a flak wagon [self-propelled anti-aircraft gun] and I was the only thing they had to shoot at. Tracers went under me, and I pulled my legs up. Then they went over me. As the ground came up, I had to make a decision about what kind of landing to make—a ground landing, a tree landing, or a water landing. If you make the right decision, you walk away. If you make the wrong one, you break a leg or you drown. What I saw below me was so uniform that it just had to be grass or low shrubs. The flak wagon was slightly behind me. So I pulled on my front risers and slipped the chute forward to get as far away as I could from the flak wagon, and landed maybe a hundred feet from it.

Now, these were the old days, and we didn't have quick-release harnesses, and our rifles were in canvas bags. When we hit the ground, we were helpless. The flak wagon kept shooting at me, and the bullets either hit in front of me and bounced over me or they were too high. I guess they had trouble making the gun shoot down. I probably would have been hit anyway through shear Teutonic [German] perseverance if the next flight of planes hadn't arrived. The flak wagon gave up shooting at me to shoot at the planes. I managed to get out of my harness to slip away. I had guessed right about the grass.

I think about this incident quite a bit. If I'd had any combat experience at all, I'd have gone in and taken out that flak wagon. But if those guys had been more experienced, they would have taken me out before I got out of my harness. I often wonder if today there are a couple of guys sitting in Stuttgart or wherever who remember this incident the same way I do.

The drop zone was like a scene from a dream. Guys appeared from the darkness then disappeared back into it. There must have been some Germans, but they weren't wandering around like we were.

As new guys came down, the field was getting populated. Someone either knocked out the flak wagon or it pulled away, because it was quiet. Guys were walking around trying to link up, and everybody had a cricket. There were so many clicks and counterclicks that nobody could tell who was clicking at whom. I didn't run into any of my own 501 [101st Airborne Division] guys. The guys who came in after me were 506 [101st Airborne Division].

A fighter plane with its throttle wide open was hit and started on fire. It went straight up screaming until it exploded.

There was a very fluid situation on the drop zone. I seemed to be with maybe six to eight guys all night, but not the same guys. Some guys would drift off, new guys would come in. None of us knew where we were because we couldn't match up with any landmark that we were told about when we were briefed. I guess all of us were beginning to suspect that this thing wasn't coming off as planned, and all we could hope to do was stay out of trouble as best we could until daylight.

We cut all the phone lines we came across to sever German communications. And some guys set up roadblocks whenever they came to a crossroad. A glider pilot was wandering around trying to attach himself to somebody who would take care of him. Once he landed he was infantry, but he hadn't thought of that.

Finally, first light came and I saw my first Luger. One of our guys managed to pick one up during the night. I also looked at my own carbine and saw that the magazine was missing. I checked in the chamber, and it was empty. I'd spent the first night of the invasion with an empty weapon. I bet that in all the excitement, I threw back the bolt to chamber the piece and forgot to put in a magazine. I'm told that during the Civil War, rifles were found after the battles that had as many as ten charges shoved into them, but the guy with the rifle had forgotten to pull the trigger even once.

Early in the morning, I remember a huge flight of bombers coming directly overhead. They were maybe 5,000 feet up, maybe a dozen planes wide. They came on as a low, distant rumble that increased in level until it overpowered everything. They just kept coming and coming. As far as I could see in both directions was solid aircraft coming in and going out. God knows how many planes, but it sure was impressive to a nineteen-year-old foot soldier.

Eventually, by pure chance, I stumbled onto my own company. I don't remember exactly what we did or where we did it, but in retrospect it seemed that we marched all night and stayed awake all day. We got our sleep ten minutes at a time. I found that I could actually sleep while I was walking in column down the road. I got so thoroughly exhausted that one day I was sitting, leaning against a big tree, and a sniper was firing at me. I wouldn't move. I just sat there and watched the bullets chipping away at the bark of the tree. This guy came close, but he never hit me.

One night, three of us had a machine gun set up at the end of a hedgerow that extended out 90 degrees from our main line of resistance. This is the kind of thing that kept us from getting much sleep. Three or four times during the night, we saw movement or at least thought we did. In the morning, we saw a couple of German paratrooper helmets. They probably came in with one of the patrols. This was a new development, and we knew that the Germans were throwing in the good troops. I recall that from then on it got a little tight. This was hedgerow country, where every field was bounded by a pile of dirt with a hedge on top. The Germans had been there for years. They could drop a mortar round in your back pocket just by knowing where you were standing. They defended each field by punching a hole in the hedgerow and sticking a machine gun through it. We were occupying Europe one field at a time, mainly by chasing out the guys defending it. Then the paratroopers came in. I believe it was the 5th Parachute Division. We didn't gain ten feet unless we walked over bodies to do it.

One day when we were looking at a field about a quarter mile wide that seemed to be well defended, suddenly from the direction of the beach a whole bunch of new guys in clean uniforms appeared at the dead run. They weren't wearing jump boots, so I knew they weren't our guys. Besides, they didn't look tired. They ran right through where we were as if we weren't there. This was the first time that someone else was between them and us since we'd left England. To us this was the rear echelon—the same as if we'd been back in London.

One day I was hit. One moment I was talking with three guys from Company F and the next moment all four of us dived into a ditch in an 81mm mortar barrage. One of the mortar rounds came into the ditch and got us all. I was the only one conscious. I remember wondering if I should take the morphine that we all carried, but then I recall saying, "No. If these guys follow up the barrage, I'm going to have to be conscious." But the barrage let up and our medics came out to take us out of there. If I could thank those guys now, I would, because they were brave men. The stretcher bearers were the guys from the regimental band, and they made up for all those mornings they woke us up to stand out in the cold.

James Eads (U.S. Army)

Due to weather issues and intense enemy antiaircraft fire, the airdrops of the 82nd Airborne Division were widely scattered on D-Day. This resulted in paratroopers such as James Eads fighting either as individuals or in small groups.

ON JUNE 1, 1944, OUR OUTFIT [THE 82nd Airborne Division] was secretly trucked to Salt Bee Army Air Corps Base, outside of Nottingham, where we were housed in hangars under strict military secrecy. The invasion was postponed twice because of weather. Then on June 5, 1944, our orders came.

We boarded, sixteen men to a plane, at 1900 hours and took off for France at 2100. We took an evasive and circular route and rendezvoused with our correct units in preparation for our mission objective. We were also receiving heavy anti-aircraft fire. We jumped out sometime close to 2400 hours.

Our C-47 had been hit at the worst time by flak and machine gun fire. We were off target. The green light came on and the troopers started out of the plane. The fifteenth man had equipment trouble. After some delay trying to fix his rig, I—being the sixteenth and last man to go out—bailed out on a dead run. My opening shock was terrific. First, I saw all the tracers coming my way. Second, I tried to guess how high I was. Third, I checked my chute. I saw flame from a fire that was reaching as high as I was in the air. A tracer had gone through my chute canopy like a cigarette hole in a silk handkerchief, smoldering and fiery red. The hole was getting bigger by the instant. I grabbed my front risers and brought them to my waist. I was in a hell of a hurry to get down before my chute became a torch. Incidentally, the bullets, in which tracers intermingled, were still snapping all around me. It seemed as if they would curve to one side just as they were going to hit me. I became so fascinated by this that I forgot to release my risers and I was plummeting to earth extremely fast. Just as I checked the burning hole in my chute and saw that it was now about eighteen inches in diameter, I hit the ground, after plowing through the limbs of a medium-size tree. Now, when I say I hit the ground, I mean to say I bashed into the ground. My feet slid forward, and I took most of the shock with my hind end. My chute then draped lazily over the tree, which I saw now was only about twenty feet high.

I could hear shooting and yelling all around me, and saw a glow of light from a huge fire to the front and left of me.

From this glow, I could see troopers coming out of the C-47s only 300 to 400 feet high. As I started to sit up to get out of my chute, I promptly slid flat again. After two or three more attempts and a sniff of the air, I finally discovered that I was lying in cow manure. I recall that I even snickered at my own predicament.

Suddenly from my right front, three men in a line about ten feet apart came running toward me, the first one about a hundred feet away. I could see the coal bucket style of helmet and thought, Oh hell, out of the frying pan, into a latrine, now this. As my Tommy gun [M1 or M1A1 Thompson submachine gun] was strapped to my chest, I immediately gave up trying to get it out and reached for my .45 automatic pistol, which was strapped to my right thigh. I always kept a round in the chamber and seven in the clip. I thumbed back the hammer and started firing. The third man fell with my eighth round right at my feet.

I gave a huge sigh of relief and tried again to get up. This made my chute shake the tree. Then from my direct right about seventy-five yards away, a German machine gun nest opened up at me. I could hear the rounds buzzing and snapping through the leaves of the tree and into the ground beyond me. Again I thought, damnit, is the whole Kraut army after me, just one scared red headed trooper? I tried once again to rise, and bullets ripped into my musette bag and map case strapped to my chest, rolling me onto my left side.

I rolled back under my cushion again and tried to unstrap my Tommy gun. Just then, a loud boom came from the area of the machine gun, and all I could hear was the shooting and yelling coming from the direction of the glow of the big fire about 300 yards away.

I finally sat up, got out of my harness, grabbed my Tommy gun, and started moving toward the action. All this took place within five minutes. Hearing a sound behind me, I dropped flat and tried to see what or who was there. Taking a chance on a hunch, I snapped my cricket. An answering two clicks came back at once, then up crawled a trooper. I didn't know him, but I could have kissed him for just being one of us. His first words were, "I got those over anxious Kraut machine gunners with a grenade, but it blew off my helmet and I can't find it. . . . Holy cow! You stink!"

Moving to the edge of the orchard, we came to a hedgerow typical of the whole area. As we were attempting to get through this grove, we heard a click and answered it at once with two clicks; another trooper, ready to go. Assuming a hedgerow to be (as described in our briefing session) about four feet high, I slid through and dropped and slid about ten feet down to a narrow roadway.

After assembling, the three of us prepared to move across fields to the fight going around the fire about 250 yards away, straight on from us. We figured it to be quicker than trying to follow the road and undoubtedly running into a roadblock.

Just then, to my left, coming down the road toward us, was the sound of hobnailed boots running. We crouched down along the bank, and I could hear the other two moving to my left and fanning out. I told them to wait for an opening burst before firing. The runners had to come around a slight curve in the road, and I wanted to make sure all of them rounded the curve before we fired. We then saw three of them strung out, the first one now only about forty feet away. I started firing short bursts at the last man, then the second one. All three fell.

We then scurried over the hedge into another orchard. A large two-story house was to our right, so we circled around it and moved closer to the action, now only a short distance away. One of the men with me had an M1 rifle; the other had a Tommy gun, same as mine.

Hearing running and shouting to our left, we dropped down as about ten Krauts came crashing through what looked like a garden. They were almost on top of us when we opened fire. All fell. Our surprise was complete. Also, the trooper with the M1 fell. We then moved on.

Suddenly, two figures loomed out of the shadow of a building. I almost fired before I recognized them as wearing civilian clothes. The man with me could understand and speak French, so, crouching low, we held a hurried consultation. I could understand some of the talk, and the trooper told me the rest. All of us had bailed out right on top of Ste. Mére Eglise when the townspeople were trying to put out a fire and were being "chaperoned" by a hundred or more Krauts. Our planes were so low that all of the troopers bailing out were perfect targets and were being slaughtered. We thanked the townspeople, told them to get back in the building, then continued on.

About seventy-five yards ahead, the trooper and I entered the edge of a large square with a church at our left side. Troopers were lying everywhere, almost all of them still in their chutes. One was hanging from the spire on the church. There was a stone wall around the church about four to five feet below the level of the courtyard. We dropped behind this just as a troop-carrying vehicle came down a street toward us. We were sitting ducks, so we both started firing, hoping to take as many of them with us as we could. I also noticed, out of the corner of my eye, fire coming from a building across the street at point-blank range. One of us got the driver of the truck. It stopped, and out of it came the Krauts. I had to put in another clip. I had just accomplished this and begun to fire again when I heard my buddy grunt and saw him fall. Suddenly, the firing from the vehicle stopped. I shot out the building's window area and raced back behind the church, circling around it to a spot where the museum now stands. I reloaded with just one clip, as I had no more taped together. I had started out with twenty clips, ten on my belt, seven in my knapsack, and three taped together, staggered and reversed. At thirty rounds to a clip, I had six hundred rounds. The three taped together gave me ninety rounds for speedy reloading. I had already emptied six clips.

Starting out again down the opposite side of the square from where we had met the troop carrier, I almost tripped over a Kraut lying on the ground facing a church. He had a burp gun [submachine gun]. As he rolled to bring his gun around, I fired. Then, in the building behind me, a Kraut carbine let go and numerous Kraut voices began to yell something. Somehow, the man lying on the ground had missed me; his bullet hit the K ration in my right pocket.

I emptied my clip at the front of the building and moved out fast, reloading as I ran. It was now about one hour and thirty minutes since I had bailed out.

Hearing some firing immediately ahead, I ran on, figuring on being able to help someone in need, plus I wanted the company of my own people. I came upon four Krauts under cover, firing in the opposite direction. Sporadic fire came from the direction they were firing. As I looked, one fell, so I dropped the other three. One thing about a Tommy gun—it's just like a garden hose. You aim it in the general direction of your target, hold onto the trigger, and wave the gun back and forth. You waste some ammo, but you can hardly miss with some of it.

I yelled for the troopers to stop firing, then raced over to them. As I was running low and still looking everywhere, I noticed a sign saying "Chef du Pont" with an arrow pointing up the way I was going.

There were eight troopers behind a low stone wall and among some bushes. I held a hurried conversation with a sergeant and was told there were six members of the 505th Regiment [505], also one from the 508th, and one from the 101st Division. Two of the 505 men were seriously injured. One man had some TNT. I then explained my mission to this sergeant, and asked him to help. We checked the two wounded. One had died and the other was past help. We made him as comfortable as we could and moved out toward Chef du Pont. The sergeant told me it was only a couple of miles away. It was then somewhere around 0300 hours.

We skirted a road, keeping to the second hedge from the road, three men to the left side of the hedge and four to the right. We saw eleven dead troopers, all in their chutes and four hanging in trees. Somehow, we managed to reach the edge of Chef du Pont with only two short battles and without losing a man. We ran into a group of Krauts at the edge of the village. There must have been a platoon. For some reason, they must have thought we were at least a company, because they broke and ran after about a five-minute heavy gunfight, maybe because of our numerous automatic weapons—two BARs, three Tommy guns, and two M1s. I was now down to nine clips.

We passed a building on the left side of the street with lots of German writing on it. A heavy machine gun opened up from behind a short, low stone wall ahead and on the left. One 505 man circled behind and threw two hand grenades and cut loose with his Tommy. The nest was silenced.

Across the street was some kind of important building and it was flushed out by three of the men, two from 505 and the other 508 trooper. Then one of the men peeked around the corner and reported a train depot just to the left of a long, narrow courtyard. He took off for it, with a word to cover him. At the far end of the courtyard or square, a machine gun cut loose and he fell almost in the middle of the court. Then directly ahead of us along each side of the road and across the track, more Krauts opened up. One more man fell.

We concentrated our fire on them and then dashed toward them. They ran, going on down the street, house to house, room to room. We proceeded toward the river. When we got to the edge of the town, there were only three of us. I had two and half clips left, so I took the remaining clip from the last man to fall who had a Tommy gun. I picked up four more clips. Of the three men left, one was from the 505, one from the 101st, and me, from the 508. When I jumped, being a demolition man, I had ten pounds of TNT. The man from the 101st had six pounds, plus his BAR. Each one of these TNT quarter-pound blocks are tremendous, if set right, packed right, and detonated correctly. The trooper from the 505 had an M1. That was our firepower. It was now about noon.

Starting across the causeway, I noticed it was flooded on both sides. Suddenly from our right, from an old factory building about 400 yards across the flooded area, heavy firepower poured on us. We dove to the left of the offside of the causeway for protection. We immediately drew fire from across the bridge in the middle of the causeway. The 505 man fell. The other man and I moved on, firing in bursts at the men ahead of us. When we came to the bridge, no more fire was coming from that direction. However, heavy fire was still coming from the old factory. We then noticed some rifle fire from the other end of the causeway and to our right. I directed the 101st man to give me his TNT and keep firing at the factory.

I dropped below the left side of the bridge. I laid my gun down and set my eight pounds of TNT, then hand-walked under the bridge to its opposite end and set the other eight pounds, and promptly was knocked into the water. I came up and swam back to the starting point, with fire from the factory hitting all around me. I retrieved my gun, then noticed that my side and my head were bleeding. It was then that I noticed that my BAR man wasn't firing. He was dead. At the same time, I heard firing going on again in Chef du Pont.

Crawling along the offside of the causeway, I set the short fuses to my charges and connected them with primer cord for instant detonation to the end of the regular two-foot fuse, then continued along the offside of Chef du Pont. I had gone about fifty yards when the roadway vibrated terrifically from my charges. I went on into Chef du Pont and met up with fourteen paratroopers, most from the 505, a couple from the 101st, and three from the 508. I told the officer in charge what had happened, and he sent six men back to set up a roadblock. One of the paratroopers had a bazooka, and I was sure the officer was glad to have him stay with us.

The others headed back to Ste. Mére Eglise. Within five minutes, they were shooting at all kinds of vehicles trying to come through Chef du Pont, get over the bridge, and get away from the invasion of the paratroops. We knocked out a big truck just as it reached the causeway and another small one that tried to get by him. We now had an effective roadblock.

Within the hour, about twenty more troopers came up from behind us, and almost the same number entered the scene from the Chef du Pont side. In the meantime, I lost three more men, as almost that whole hour had been one continual roar of guns. I had fifteen rounds left.

I joined the troops in Chef du Pont and sent eight men back to the causeway to keep the roadblock active. Not seeing any of my men, we returned to Ste. Mére Eglise. I ate, drank a bottle of wine, had the blood washed off my minor wounds, and joined in the civilian celebration that was going on. I was so happy that they were happy. I cried with them. It was now late in the afternoon and almost dark. The people were celebrating, so glad to finally be relieved.

An officer from the 82nd came up and told me my group was assembled at Hill 30 and I was to join them. He had another mission scheduled for that evening. I joined what was left of my people at the edge of Hill 30, and after one hell of a battle we captured it. This lasted until the wee hours of the morning. After the hill was secure, we set up a perimeter defense, and by morning light on June 7 had beaten off four counterattacks. We had started with thirty men for this particular mission; six were left. I said a silent prayer and slept for two hours.

Edward Barnes (U.S. Army)

Despite being dropped so far off course on the morning of June 6, 1944, that his maps were useless, 82nd Airborne Division paratrooper Edward Barnes and friends decided to make life miserable for the German troops in their area.

ON MAY 28, 1944, THE REGIMENT [507TH Parachute Infantry Regiment, 82nd Airborne Division] left Tolerton Hall for the marshalling areas of Fulbeck and Barkston Peak, preparatory to the Allied invasion of the Continent. While at the marshalling area, we spent the time getting our equipment ready, doing calisthenics, and writing letters home. Each battalion in the regiment viewed sand tables of their drop zone and viewed our objective.

To prepare for a stay of at least three days in Normandy, I wore a wool shirt and a pair of wool pants under my jump suit, as I figured it would be cool at night. In our musette bag, we carried extra socks, a mess kit, insecticide powder, a candy bar, plenty of cigarettes, and a Gammon grenade, which is plastic explosive. We were issued invasion money in case we needed to buy our way out of a tight spot, which proved helpful to me later in the invasion.

From our musette bag harness hung two grenades, one on each side. Our gas mask bag helped carry some of our candy and cigarettes besides the gas mask itself. I carried a folding-stock .30-caliber carbine and about sixty rounds of ammunition. We were issued K rations for three days. As I was the battalion wire chief, I had a sixty-pound switchboard strapped across the front of my thighs. My normal weight was 170 pounds, but with all the added equipment I must have weighed in at about 250 pounds.

We assembled at our planes on the evening of June 4, 1944, preparing to take off, when orders came down that the drop was postponed for twenty-four hours because of bad weather over the Channel.

The next night, June 5, 1944, we again assembled at our planes, and this time we got the word to go. We climbed in and with a little push from the crew chief I was able to make it up the ladder, as I could not climb because of the switchboard strapped across my legs. As we sat there, the full impact hit as to what was about to take place. Most of the men tried to be jovial, including me, but the atmosphere was a little subdued.

We took off from Barkston Heath and Fulbeck, England, at 11:50 p.m. on June 5, 1944. We flew out to the west coast of the Continent (the Cotentin Peninsula), then east between the Channel Islands, and made landfall at 2 a.m. on June 6. The trip across the Channel was uneventful, so I dozed off.

We were alerted about ten minutes before jump time that we were approaching the coast of Normandy. As we approached, we were given the signal to stand up and hook up and check one another's equipment. We were all standing there poised, and looking at the door at the red light waiting for it to turn green—the signal to go.

As we peered out the door, we could see the flak and tracer bullets coming up out of the darkness. Then the light turned green and we started to pile out the door into the darkness. There is no sweeter feeling than the rude jerking that lets you know your chute has opened.

On the way down, I was straining to see the ground below so I could prepare myself for the hard landing I expected because of the additional weight of my equipment. But to my surprise, the canopy hung up on a tree in the field, and I never had a softer landing in all my nineteen jumps.

As soon as I touched ground, I unstrapped the switchboard from my legs and started to take off my chute. As I was in the process, I heard someone approaching out of the darkness. Not knowing whether it was friend or enemy, I grabbed my carbine and spun around. In the darkness, I could see nothing, so I again started to take off the chute. Again I heard the same sound of footsteps. I grabbed my carbine and peered into the darkness, but this time I could make out a figure approaching. I lay on the ground, ready to fire, trying to make out the number of men in the party, when to my amazement the footsteps turned out to be an old brown cow. I guess she was just curious to see who had invaded her domain. I was so relieved I just had to sit there and chuckle to myself.

After I removed my chute, I started off in the direction of some small-arms fire, as I did not recognize any of the landmarks that we had viewed on the sand tables back in England. By the time I got to the spot where I thought the firefight was taking place, there was silence and no one about.

After a few more false excursions like that, I decided it would be better to hide the switchboard in a field so as to travel a little lighter. Rather than walk on the roadway, I took off across the field, looking for some friendly faces. A feeling of loneliness closed in on me as I pictured the whole German army trying to locate and exterminate me.

After about an hour or so of this, I decided to lie in a ditch alongside the road to wait for daylight so I could see just where I was headed, and see anybody coming down the road before they could see me.

At the first light of dawn, I took off again toward where I thought our drop zone should have been. At about 5 a.m. I was challenged by a voice on the other side of the hedgerow. I gave the countersign, and up popped another trooper. He was in the same spot as I, hopelessly lost.

We continued down the road and finally ran into some more troopers, also lost. By this time, we had a mighty fighting force of six troopers. In the distance, we could see the outline of a church steeple, so we decided to head for it and maybe get some information as to our whereabouts and the whereabouts of any other troopers in the area.

We continued cautiously on our way toward the church, expecting any minute to be fired on by the Germans, when we heard a challenge from the ditch up the road in front of us. We gave the countersign and were told to come forward slowly. When we got to within about fifteen yards of the spot where we heard the challenge, we could see that they were troopers from the 82nd Airborne.

We all went up to the church in the village, which turned out to be the village of Graignes, and reported to the commanding officer in charge, Major Johnson, who was a battalion commander in the 507th Parachute Infantry Regiment. It seems that the major was just as lost as the rest of us.

After questioning some townspeople, we found we were twenty miles from our designated drop zone, which left us twenty miles farther behind the German lines. We were completely off the maps we were carrying. We spent most of the day going out on patrols, harassing the enemy and rounding up any other lost troopers. By day's end, we had accumulated about sixty troopers.

On one of our patrols, as we proceeded down the road, I could see a body lying in the roadside. As we approached, I could see that it was one of our Airborne troopers. I rolled him over and there was a round blue hole in the middle of his forehead. I figured he must have been dead about two hours. I don't think I can express my feeling at sorrow, as this was the first dead American soldier I had seen. I got his name and serial number from his dog tags and turned them in to our headquarters.

On the afternoon of June 7, we got word that a column of Germans was headed our way, not as reinforcements for their defenses but retreating from the direction of the invasion. We were told to mine the concrete bridge that spanned a twenty-five-foot-wide stream that flowed right outside of town. Two troopers were sent down the road as outposts. They climbed the tree to get a better view of the road. The rest of us were deployed on our side of the stream.

Soon the outposts came running out of the woods and reported that they had been spotted. We lay in wait. It was our intention to wait for them to get three-quarters of the way across the bridge, then blow the bridge, and the Germans on the bridge, to smithereens. But the well-laid plans of mice and men often go astray. The Germans had worked their way up to their side of the bridge, undetected, and opened fire. It was a ruse to draw our fire to estimate our strength. By this time, the membranes in my throat were drying out, as this was my first firefight.

We returned the fire with rifles, machine guns, and mortars, and the command came down to blow the bridge before we were overrun and lost control of the bridge. The bridge went up in a million pieces. The German column started to retreat in the direction they had come. They would have to look for another crossing farther downstream.

It would be ten days before we worked our way back to the main force, which was now around Carentan. We were relieved after thirty-seven days in Normandy.

Back in England, at a pub, I happened to run into the pilot of the plane that dropped us in Normandy, and he told me his radar went out over the Channel. As he crossed over the Channel Islands, he knew how many minutes of flying time it was from there to the drop zone. (The pathfinders who had preceded us had in many cases found it impossible to mark the drop zones. The pilots were puzzled by the failure to see marker lights, causing the pilots in some cases to overshoot the drop zones.) So after our pilot's calculated time, he flipped the green light, and out we went.

To repeat the title from General Eisenhower's book, this was certainly "The Longest Day."

Parker A. Alford (U.S. Army)

The 101st Airborne Division was air-dropped near the French town of Carentan and assigned the job of seizing causeways for use by American seaborne landing forces. It fell upon officers such as Parker Alford to successfully complete that mission.

FINALLY, WE WERE TOLD WE WERE TO invade Normandy, on the Cherbourg peninsula, and would drop into Ste. Mére Eglise and take the locks and the bridges over the Douve River, which ran through Carentan, France. The purpose of securing the locks was to keep the Germans from flooding the beaches at Utah, which would stop our seaborne forces who were to come in later in the day on June 6.

Our beachhead was Utah Beach in and around St. Marie Dumont. The 82nd was committed to take Ste. Mére Eglise and the high ground beyond. The Germans had moved in some panzer divisions beyond Ste. Mére Eglise and were commanding the high ground there. We studied mock-ups of the area until we were familiar with all of the Utah Beach area. Reconnaissance planes would fly each day and bring back news of the movement of enemy troops, and it would be transmitted to us through our commanding officers.

On June 5, 1944, we were visited by General Eisenhower and his aides. The general talked to our pathfinders, who went in early to put out smoke pots so that our airplanes had some signal to fly in on and would not be too disoriented. We were later to see General Eisenhower at the Newberry airports or air terminal.

After blackening our faces, sharpening our knives, and checking our equipment—which we carried on us for the hundredth time—we got in formation and walked to the air terminal. This was about 10 p.m. on June 5. On the way to the terminal we were swinging along, some singing, when a little old Cockney lady ran up and said, "Give 'em 'ell, Yank." A lump came into my throat of fear, pride, and a dreadful hope that I wouldn't let these young men or my country down. This was my third D-day invasion and their first.

We waited in the air terminal for thirty minutes before we got the order to go to our respective airplanes. At about 10:30 p.m. Colonel Johnson, our regimental commander, came roaring into the hangar on his jeep to see us. He had pearl-handled .45s on each hip and a knife in his teeth, knives in his belt, and many hand grenades on his person. He gave a short pep talk. I recall his concluding remarks as he grabbed a dagger from his boot: "Before I see the dawn of another day I want to stick this knife into the meanest, dirtiest, filthiest Nazi in all of Europe." As he returned the knife to his boot, a great roar came from all portions of the hangar. As these young men applauded their commanding officer, we knew that this invasion had to succeed. After this speech we were ordered to board our airplanes. My plane carried eighteen men. My position was next to the door. Each man had a cricket: one mash, a double-click challenge; mash twice was four clicks, which meant friend. This was to identify friend or foe in the dark. You are both the hunted and the hunter when you go on before schedule, as we were.

We taxied out, took our position in line with the other C-47s, and were finally airborne. We rendezvoused over southern England for a period of time. We passed over Portsmouth, England, and could see the seaborne forces and the ships, as they had already left port. I could see numerous white-caps from my position in the aircraft, and the whole armada unfolding around me. The moon was bright and the feeling was lonely.

We were at last on our way to Fortress Europe, and God knows what awaited us. Our approach was to fly low and come in from the rear of the Cherbourg peninsula, dropping on our drop zone beyond Carentan and the Douve River. Our pilots were to drop us and then head back to England, where they would become the pilots for the gliders. We were over land for twelve minutes. From my position by the door I was watching flak as it came up to the planes. I looked around the airplane and saw some kid across the aisle who grinned. I tried to grin back but my face was frozen. Suddenly the pilot gave the orange light, which meant to stand up and hook up. In a C-47 you have a static line pull with no free fall, and it was too low to use the reserve chute.

About twelve minutes over land the green light came on and my watch read 1:10 a.m., June 6, 1944. My radio operator and I kicked the radio out and I followed after it, yelling, "Go!" The sky was full of exploding flak, and even a Billy Rose [Broadway musical] extravaganza could not have competed with the numerous colors. I floated down, and to me it seemed an eternity. I tried to go faster by pulling on my risers; this put me in a dive and I was very grateful when the ground came up to meet me. As I landed I heard much running toward me and around me. I was sure I was completely surrounded by the enemy, and in the cold and darkness I eased out of my parachute and got my Tommy gun (which we called a "grease gun") in shooting position. Now the running was coming straight at me, and whatever it was snorted. It was a herd of milk cows that had been disturbed by the noise of our invasion. I relaxed and could actually laugh at myself. I was able to get up on very shaky knees, gather up my chute, check my weapons, and head out in search of the radio and my operator. I found my operator but we could not find the radio. We did find a trooper who said he was from the 506th who had broken both legs when he crashed into a tree on landing. We gave him an additional Tommy gun, extra ammunition, and some morphine. We told him we would be back later with a medic to get him. We pushed on farther and encountered Gen. Maxwell Taylor, commanding officer of the 101st Airborne, and his radio operator.

These two men challenged us with their crickets, and when we made the proper reply we were able to get close to them for conversation. General Taylor said we were the only people he had encountered and we should push on for our objective to see if we could find any other men and officers.

We were pretty well scattered all over the drop zone. We had lost some of our men of the 1st and 2nd battalions of the 501 in the marshes along the Douve River. Because our mission was to take the locks and dams on the Douve River, General Taylor picked a point on his map and said we would meet there. This point was close to a small town called Pouppeville, near where the 4th Infantry Division was to enter Utah Beach. After we pushed on, we came to a crossroads, where we met several other officers and men of various battalions, including some of our own men. On June 6 at this crossroads, which we later named "Hell's Corner" for the fierce fighting we encountered there, we made a head count of one general, one full colonel and three lieutenant colonels, four lieutenants, several NCOs [noncommissioned officers] who were radio operators, several other NCOs, and other paratroopers—in all about thirty. It was at this point that General Taylor made his classic remark, very similar to the remark Churchill made to the House of Parliament.

He was able to look around at all the brass we had and he remarked that "Never before in the annals of warfare had so few been commanded by so many." This lessened the tension. We discovered that General Taylor was exactly the type of fearless warrior you needed to run an airborne division.

General Taylor dispatched Lieutenant Colonel Ewell and myself and several other officers and men to head toward Carentan. At this point Lieutenant Colonel Ewell explained to General Taylor that I was to furnish naval gunfire support when it became light enough to be able to adjust the fire. It was decided that I was to stay with the 3rd Battalion, commanded by Colonel Ewell, to bring naval gunfire up on Carentan or any other resistance.

This was what we called hedgerow country, and the Germans were entrenched in the hedgerows with machine gun nests and numerous pillboxes, mostly in the corners of the hedgerows. While at the crossroads we had begun to get enough troops to look like a battalion, and we pushed on to Carentan. We encountered some troops who were coming back to the crossroads at Hell's Corner. Colonel Ewell stopped them to ask about the locks and dams over the Douve River. The men told Colonel Ewell that the locks and dams had been secured, and that the Germans were eliminated and had had very little time to flood the beaches. However, they did flood some of the low country around Carentan. The Douve River had five causeways leading from the highway where we were to cross the river into Carentan, which was held by German paratroopers and grenadiers [infantry]. The German paratroopers were one of Hitler's elite corps, as were the American paratroops. This turned into quite a battle for Carentan, but it did not occur on D-Day.

On the road to Carentan we were held up around 5 a.m. by heavy artillery and mortar fire at a crossroads coming from the town of Beaumont. A part of the 502nd and 506th regiments was held up there due to intense mortar and artillery fire. They had attempted to dig in to the hedgerows. At this time, a naval gunfire officer of the 506th decided to try to contact our naval shore party. He had both his 609 radio and a 327 radio. Colonel Ewell had taken a French farmhouse as his HQ [headquarters] and we were in the basement, which had a wine cellar. Some barrels of wine were still in there and our troops took advantage of their generosity by filling their canteens with wine.

Colonel Ewell wanted naval gunfire power brought on Beaumont at daylight, and we used a 327 radio to try to go direct to the crew of the *Quincy*, which was our command ship, with grid coordinates that the colonel wanted. The Germans kept jamming our frequency, so we were unsuccessful. We then decided to go through our shore party with our 609 radio and were able to transmit by voice. Lieutenants Osborne, Roberts, and Carn were on the beach with their radio people awaiting our instructions as to where to lay the gunfire. We used our voice transmission about this on the 609 radio. Each time, the navy wanted verification as to who we were. I finally, in desperation at 6:30 a.m., told them that I knew a naval officer who played linebacker with the Nebraska team in the 1940 Rose Bowl game. The navy sent back an inquiry as to whether or not I could name the player. I replied that it was K. C. Roberts, who was part of the shore party. The navy came back, "Roger, Roger, where do you want the fire?" We got the navy to completely obliterate the small town of Beaumont, dislodge the enemy, and put them in retreat. They fell back some four or five miles. Much of the credit should go to Lieutenant Ferrell for his bravery and dogged persistence on finding his radio, whereas I was unable to find mine.

Later that day the poor fella had some shells fall short, killing approximately thirty men of another company that we were unaware was in front of us. This put a damper on our whole party.

We captured Pouppeville on the way to Carentan, and the 4th Infantry Division was able to come ashore with very little resistance. However, they encountered considerable resistance off the beaches later that day.

At the airport before we left, I mentioned our encounter with Colonel Johnson and his fierce declaration about sticking a dagger in the meanest Nazi in Europe.

Guy Remington had fallen into a swamp area near the Douve River where the Germans had flooded the swamps. We lost many men to drowning in the swamps, some never able to get out of their parachutes. I was to run into Remington later that day near Carentan, and he told me of an experience he had coming out of the swamps. It concerned the cricket story. He was pulling up to the bank of the river out of the swamp and he heard a noise in front of him. He froze and of course pulled out his Tommy gun and his hand grenades and clicked his cricket. He heard nothing. He was prepared to drop the hand grenades when he heard a whisper, like someone saying "pssst" to him. He parted the hedgerow and there was Colonel Johnson with his machine gun across his lap, ready to spring. Colonel Johnson said, "I lost my damn cricket."

We thought we did a good job on D-Day. It was a long, tiresome day and we were worn out. We had to fight until relieved since paratroops are not required to stay in a long campaign; in fact, we weren't equipped to do so. Our officers and men were certainly brave and fearless. Our generals were fearless warriors and certainly deserved the names they acquired at being the elite troops of Uncle Sam.

David E. Thomas (U.S. Army)

One of the most respected men in most combat units is the medic. David Thomas, a medic for the 82nd Airborne Division in the invasion of Normandy, found out in combat that one must be very flexible in his job description to survive.

AS PART OF OUR PREPARATION TO BE medics for the D-Day invasion, each medic was given a canteen of alcohol, which we thought we would use for sterilization purposes when we got to Normandy. I doubt that a drop of it ever got out of England. That's a fact. And while we were in this enclave, we were briefed and re-briefed on sand tables. I didn't pay all that much attention. I had been in the Airborne long enough to know that night jumps never went off as planned. And I'll guarantee you that this was the way it was in Normandy. It certainly did not go off as planned.

While we were locked up I wasn't doing very well in the poker game, so I thought I better go and listen to the chaplain, not wishing to miss touching all the bases. About the time I was sitting down on a cot in the last row and the only seat left in the house, Chaplain Elder said, "Now, the Lord is not particularly interested in those who only turn to him in times of need." I thought, "Gee, he must have seen me come in." So I got up and left again. I still didn't do very well in the poker game, which didn't do my morale any good for what was coming up for us.

The first jump on June 5 was canceled and we jumped on June 6. We took off, oh, I don't know, eleven something. Something like that. We headed out over the Channel and all you could see were C-47 aircraft, and fighters escorting them. It looked like we had the whole damn army coming in airborne.

Well, this lasted for a while. We had passed the islands of Alderney, Jersey, and Guernsey and we got some flak, but nothing got hit that I know about. Then we turned into the coast in all that stream of aircraft. We hit clouds over the coast and when we came out of those clouds we were all alone in the sky. We could not see another airplane. The pilot had no idea where he was. So we were looking and looking trying to find something we could recognize and finally we recognized the Merderet River, which flows into the Douve down by Chef du Pont. That was where we were supposed to rally around and hold the bridge over the Merderet to keep reinforcements from reaching the beaches. We figured that was as close as we were going to get, so we jumped and landed. I had an uneventful jump and landing.

After I landed in this field, I saw something white and I crawled up to it and I met my first cow in Normandy. I got up and started walking in the direction of the stick looking for the other jumpers. The first fellow I ran into was Bill Ekman.

Bill was all alone too. He just happened to be an old friend of mine who was the commanding officer of the 505th Parachute Infantry [82nd Airborne Division]. While we were standing there we could see the troops descending on Ste. Mére Eglise by parachute. Ste. Mére Eglise was the first town liberated by a battalion of the 505th Parachute Infantry. We exchanged a few pleasantries, and Bill said, "Well, why don't you come with me?" And I said, "Gee, I'd like to go with you, Bill, but I am due down at that bridge by Chef du Pont and I better head in that direction."

So we parted, and as night wore on I scarfed up a few more people here and there, and there were eight to ten by dawn. We crossed the Merderet River, which was flooded. They dammed up the thing and the flood plain was covered with water. A lot of troops who landed in there drowned, actually. But we made it across and we joined a group that had maybe a hundred troopers in it. We were surrounded. We had hedgerows all the way around. It was a typical roundup—wagons and a cowboys and Indians sort of an affair—with the Krauts on the outside and us on the inside. We had a lot of prisoners. We pre-empted the ditches and the hedgerows, and we gave the prisoners a few shovels and let them dig their own ditches out in the middle of the enclave.

What I remember most about this was a soldier who had his leg blown off right by the knee and the only thing left attached was his patellar tendon. I had him down there in this ditch and I said, "Son, I'm gonna have to cut the rest of your leg off, and you're back to bullet biting time because I don't have anything to use for an anesthetic." And he said, "Go ahead, Doc." I cut the patellar tendon and he didn't even whimper. We were able to take him into a cottage with a thatched roof that was being used as an aid station, although what we medics could do was minimal because we had only what we carried in our packs. All of our medical bundles that were dropped from the planes were somewhere else. So we could only give the wounded some morphine with morphine ampoules as long as they lasted, bandage their wounds, and give them some nursing care.

Then I got burned out of my aid station. The Germans put tracers through the thatched roof and set it on fire, so I had to bring the troops out and put them in the open. I mean the wounded troops. But when we moved out that night, we took anything we could put a wounded man on who couldn't walk, and we had six Germans carry it and one soldier with an M1 rifle to keep the Germans in line. We made a night march to a bigger group, where it was more of the same but more people. They had, oh, I don't know, two to three hundred people in this group. But again we were surrounded with no place to go. We stayed there for a couple of days. What I remember most about this was having a lot of wounded in a shed, and a soldier brought in a lightly wounded German who had killed his buddy on a machine gun; this soldier had shot and wounded the German and captured him and brought him in. We had all kinds of sick people, and the German was making a nuisance of himself. He kept hollering for *wasser* [water] and the soldier kept telling him to shut his mouth. And when he didn't the soldier said, "The hell with it." He rammed his bayonet in the German's guts, threw him over his shoulder, dumped him in the ditch outside, and went back to his machine gun.

I have no idea what happened to those wounded. When we moved out that night, I left them there because we couldn't take them with us in any way, shape, or form. I left them in the shed with a couple of wounded medics to take care of them until they got captured.

That night we were supposed to move out and join a larger group. No one had gotten any sleep for about three days and we had a single column. We would get a break, the column would stop, and somebody would fall asleep. The column was not policed properly and it broke up into many fragments. I don't know what happened to the rest of them. I do know that I wound up on the edge of the Merderet with about twenty other people. The Germans knew where we were, and we weren't moving very much. We were right on the edge of the flood plain. They had a machine gun to our left front, and anytime anybody tried to get into the water they would shoot at him. Some people made it. Some people didn't.

While I was there, I was digging deeper into the ditch in the hedgerow when a bullet plunked the bank right by me. I could look back and see where it barked a tree. By sitting there and shooting back azimuth, I could figure out what tree it came from. I looked and I looked and finally I could make out a set of German jump boots or jack boots. I tried to get a couple of the infantrymen with me to see it and none of them could. I guess the statute of limitations applies and they are not going to get me for the Geneva Convention, so I bummed an M1 from one soldier. The thing wouldn't fire, it was so dirty. So, after giving him a few appropriate comments about what I thought of him as a soldier, I got a carbine from another fellow and put a quick clip into where this German was. I got my head down real quick. I got back there about ten days later and he was still lying dead under that tree.

As the day wore on, we finally wound up with just two troops, Maj. Dave Thomas and SSgt. Roy Perkins out of the 507th, who was also a medic. Our thought was, "Let's try and keep low and keep quiet and get out of here when darkness comes." That was a long day. One time I was lying in a ditch with an M1 rifle, and out in front of me, within fifty yards, were four Germans just lolling around taking a break. I thought, "My, I could kill all of them." Then I thought, "Boy, if I do they'll know where I am." So I just let them live. That was a prudence call.

I also remember seeing a German coming along a hedgerow where there were several dead Americans. I was crouched down, so I just lay down and played as if I were dead. The German came around and he stopped and he looked at me and looked at me and then he reached under my ankle with his foot and pulled my foot up and let it go. I just let it flop down as if I were lifeless and I breathed shallow breaths. Finally, I guess he decided I was dead so he moved on.

Come nightfall, Roy and I had a little conference. We contemplated hitting the Merderet again, but neither of us was very anxious to get wet. So we decided that we would just hit the country road and head in the direction that we wanted to go and see what happened.

We got into a little town called Abrefontaine. This happened to be a German strongpoint. When we tried to get out of the town, we hit a wire or a rope that was apparently attached to a machine gunner's wrist, and we got grazing fire from machine guns. No matter how we tried to get out of town, we got blocked. So finally I said, "Roy, the hell with it. Let's walk out of town the same way we walked in." He said, "Why not?" So we started out, but we got challenged by a German rifleman who had listened to basic training instruction. He was under a tree where we couldn't see him and we were in the middle of the road. That was the end of the ball game for us. We were taken prisoner and were broken up soon after that.

Roy escaped twenty days later and had lost a lot of weight. He was on an involuntary diet because they didn't feed him very much. They put me in a *kampfgruppe* [battle group]. I got there the next morning and the boss came along in a Volkswagen. He got up and raised his hands and said, *"Heil, Hitler."* All the rest of them raised their hands and said, *"Seig, Heil."* I thought, "Christ, it's just like they told me." Anyway, they put me to work as the *kampfgruppe* surgeon. They also put a soldier with a Schmeisser pistol (MP38/40 submachine gun) on me to make sure that I didn't take a walk. We were stationed in a solid stone barn that was in defilade. We were opposite the 90th Infantry Division, and we got an awful lot of artillery fire coming in. The *kampfgruppe* headquarters was in a house at a Y in the road, maybe a hundred yards from this barn where we were taking in the patients. The *kampfgruppe* headquarters got pretty well beaten up because it was not in defilade.

My entire staff consisted of one *feldwebel*, a staff sergeant of the German army. This guy had been shot at too often. He'd been in the Afrika Corps, and every time incoming rounds were heard he would dive under a stone spiral staircase that went to the upper floor. He and I were the entire medical staff for this *kampfgruppe*, which amounts to a regimental combat team.

We didn't get fed very often. About midnight, they would bring up a horse hauling a cart loaded with noodles, and that was about it. We would get a lot of wounded patients and some deaths. When that happened I would sneak the dead men's rations and stash them away. Evidence that the 90th had good training was when I tried to get information from wounded American prisoners about which way the front line was and that kind of stuff. They figured that I was just a trap, a plant, and none of them would tell me anything.

We were here for a couple of days. But the horse that hauled the noodle cart was shot, and we ran out of noodles. Then we fell back to a stone chateau. An old Frenchman who was there saw me and said, "*Bonne*, American." The Germans were saying, "*Schwein*" [pig]. The Frenchman handed me a big glass of milk in which six dead flies were floating. I thought, "Gee, I can't let the old man lose face," so I drank the milk through my teeth and spit the flies out.

It was getting along toward dusk and the fellow who was on me with the Schmeisser was very busy digging his slit trench. On top of it he would put bundles of branches from the bushes in the hedgerows. He would put the branches (usually used for cooking and heating) across the slit trench and then throw the dirt back on top to protect him from tree bursts. While he was doing this, I unobtrusively stepped through a gate into a pasture and urinated and nobody said anything. So I slowly ambled away down one side of the pasture, where they could not see me. When I got to the corner of the pasture, which was beside a road, I dove into the ditch adjacent to a hedgerow. As I was crawling in it, along the road came a company of troops riding bicycles. They just happened to choose that place to take a break. So I just lay there and stayed quiet until they moved on. By that time it was dark and the stars were out, and I could tell by the stars which way to go. If you try to do this at night and you don't have a reference point, you're going to walk in circles. So whenever it clouded up and I couldn't see the stars, I would lie in the ditch and catnap a little bit. But when I could see the stars I just kept heading in the right direction using the North Star for reference.

I almost walked up on a German sentry. He wore a flashlight with a little red glass, so you had to get pretty close to see the illumination through the red glass. He must have been standing there sleeping. When I saw him, I backtracked a little ways, then took off on another tangent.

Then I almost fell into a mortar pit. It must have been a big mortar because it was an awfully big hole. There was even a stepladder to get down into it. But apparently everyone inside was asleep. They didn't know I was there.

Then I got mixed up in a fire direction center or headquarters of some kind with lots of wires coming into it. I thought, "Well, I could cut those wires and put them out of business for a little while. Yeah, but then they'll know I'm here."

One other thing you might be interested in knowing. When we jumped in, we had patches on our elbows. I recall that under the patches were forty dollars' worth of French francs and a little compass. One of the first things I did after I got away was pick this patch open and fish out the compass. But I had landed on it, and it was broken and useless to me.

Dawn came and I thought, "Well, I better hole up

somewhere." I saw a hedgerow and I got in the shallow ditch in front of it. I spent a very interesting day in the ditch. At one end was a guy with a Schmeisser. At the other end was another guy with a Schmeisser. Every once in a while they would fire a few bursts. On the other side was a machine gun, and every once in a while they would walk that machine gun down the hedgerow. They would get just over my butt. And that's where I found out about "nervous polyurea." It seemed like I was piddling every fifteen minutes, making mud and smearing mud on the red crosses on my helmet. I had lost faith in those red crosses at this point.

This is where I spent the day. When it got dark, I started out again. I knew I had to be near American lines. I hadn't gone far when I could see a slit trench with spoil scattered around; the trench seemed very poorly constructed. I crept up on it and found C rations, a blanket, and a rifle, but no troop. I thought, "Well, all right, I'll get something to eat." So I ate a can of C rations and lay there waiting. I figured some squad leader was going to check the position sooner or later, but nobody showed. So I just kept working my way to the rear. Come dawn I could see what looked like a 105mm howitzer. So I sneaked up on it, and it turned out that some alert boy from Arkansas who was guarding this thing pointed a carbine at me and told me that he'd like to hear what the password was. I said, "Look, I've been out of touch. Don't tell me the password stuff. Just take me to your leader." So I wound up with the artillery of the 90th Infantry Division. They passed me back to division headquarters. They passed me back to the 82nd Division headquarters, where I gave a thorough report to the division G-2.

While I was waiting there for transportation to the 508th Parachute Infantry, we got a lot of incoming. Being a careful sort, I dove into the ditch. I looked up and here was the commanding general, nonchalantly leaning against the tree and ignoring the incoming. I looked at him and I thought, "Well, he's making more money than I am. I'll stay in the ditch. He can stand up there and play hero if he wants to."

2 | GLIDERS

Richard H. Denison (U.S. Army Air Forces)

Lacking the prestige of a fighter pilot or even having any armament to defend one's own plane, as bombers did, the C-47 aircrews did the unsung job of dropping paratroopers over Normandy or towing gliders, as did Richard Denison.

AT THE TIME OF THE NORMANDY INVASION, I was a second lieutenant in the Air Corps and a navigator in the 84th Squadron of the 437th Troop Carrier Group. We were flying C-47 Gooney Birds, which were a military version of the DC-3 civilian airliner.

For the D-Day invasion, we flew out of Ramsbury, where there was extensive training with paratroops and glider troops. Most of these training flights, especially with paratroops, were at night. The navigation conditions were almost unbelievable. In many cases there was no horizon and no lights, and in the background you could hear a terribly weird, almost goose-bump-causing sound from the barrage balloons. And of course, as you got closer to Bristol or any of the other cities that had these barrage balloons, the sounds became more intense, and you were always wondering if you would blunder into one of those cables at night and shear off a wing, and that would be all she wrote.

We had many glider training missions using both the American CG-4A—a metal-frame, fabric-covered glider—and a British Horsa, which we jokingly called "hearses." It was a glider that was actually larger than the Gooney Bird. I remember that part of the control rods were wood. It did have landing gear, and it had a flap, which was about three feet wide. When that flap was dropped, you felt like you were heading into the ground at about a 90-degree angle. Upon touching down, you either had all brakes locked or no brakes at all. There was an air bottle with a green knob, which we called the green apple, and if you pulled the green apple, the wheel simply locked. Although in theory these gliders were to be used one time, we used them many times in training.

On a lot of the training missions, we would go out and do all the navigation, then return to our home base and drop the gliders. This training avoided the difficulty of trying to retrieve the gliders.

At that time America had so much wood, these gliders came in large wood boxes. I remember flying over one of the bases at Greenham Common and seeing what I thought were cottages on the ground, but it turned out that these were glider boxes that the ground crew on the base had used for sheds, and some of them were even living quarters.

The CG-4A had what was called a Griswald nose. Once this glider cut loose from the airplane, it was on its own and the pilot was committed to go down with it. If the glider held a jeep or any other heavy equipment, and if the pilot lined up for a field but went between two trees or encountered some obstruction that caused the glider to stop, inertia made the heavy contents of the glider come straight forward and in many cases it crushed the pilot and co-pilot. The Griswald nose was an attempt to solve this problem. It had a large hinge at the top of the fuselage so that the entire nose could swing upward. A cable ran back over a pulley at the rear of the aircraft, then came back around and was fastened onto the tank gun or the jeep—whatever happened to be in the glider. When the glider made a sudden stop, the jeep or any heavy object would tend to come forward but at the same time would pull this cable taut, which would swing the nose up and the jeep would go shooting out under the nose. Then the nose would descend again, and the pilots would be safe. This was the theory, but I don't know whether or not it worked.

It's quite a spectacular sight to be at a base when all the aircraft are coming in, releasing gliders. We never did a double glider tow to my knowledge. They were all single, but when thirty-six airplanes released their gliders, they were going to come down. In some cases, there were accidents on the ground. I remember seeing a Horsa land; the crew got out, looked around, and immediately started running away from the glider, for just about this time an American glider came by and sheared the nose right off the Horsa.

We did have a way of retrieving gliders, and some of them were retrieved later on from Normandy in this manner. Each group had one or two aircraft that had a large winch near the rear of the cabin. A cable went from the winch onto the end of a wood boom that was about ten to fifteen feet long. At the end of the boom, which could be extended below the aircraft, was a hook that was attached to the end of the cable, which was on the winch in the airplane. The hook was very loosely fastened to the boom.

For a glider to be "snatched," as we called it, it was sitting in a field. Out ahead of it at the end of a tow rope was a large loop that was held off the ground on two poles about ten to fifteen feet in the air (similar to football goal posts). The tow plane, or the snatch airplane, would come down and lower his boom, and the hook would catch in the large loop that was supported by the poles. When this happened, the winch in the aircraft let out the cable, but then began braking and eventually stopped. By this time, the tow plane was pulling the glider into the air. I saw this used only one time; however, I did see movies where this type of operation went on in Normandy, bringing gliders back following the invasion.

As June approached, there was more and more push on training. We were training in some weather when we certainly should have been on the ground. On one night flight with a load of paratroopers, our formation went completely to pieces. Every airplane was on its own, and we landed at a RAF [Royal Air Force] base. It was one of the most terrible landings I have ever seen in a Gooney Bird. Due to the structure of the landing gear, I thought that the landing gear struts would probably come up through the wings. But after getting on the ground, paratroopers were laughing and saying, "Boy, what a great landing! It sure beats coming down in that damn parachute!"

It was raining, but the paratroopers were a rough, tough bunch. Many of them just lay down under the wing of the aircraft. We crewmen ended up sleeping on a billiard table in the officer's club at the RAF base. If you ever tried to sleep on a piece of slate—well, that's hard sleeping.

Early in June we got a strange project. We were given white and black paint, and shown where we were to paint stripes on the aircraft. We had no idea what this was, and in the absence of any logical directive, we did a tremendous amount of bitching and complaining about why we were doing this. Since there was no great interest in this, you can well imagine that these were not the neat and tidy stripes that you see on today's models of aircraft that took part in the D-Day operation. This was for positive identification of our aircraft, and any plane not marked could be shot down.

Tension continued to build up, and in late May or early June a barbed wire compound with lots of concertina wire was set up near our aircrew area tents. Eventually, members of the 82nd Airborne moved into this area. I do not remember which subdivision of the division we had, but these were glider-borne troops. Our living area for aircrews was also surrounded by barbed wire. Once this happened, we began to get our briefing, and we were not permitted to speak to anybody on the base other than our own aircrews. We were marched, in formation, down to the mess hall, where we ate with no conversation with anyone else, then were marched back to our living area again.

The briefing was for the landing on June 5, which didn't happen because of the weather. We were out at our aircraft, hooking up with our gliders, all ready to go. One of the other concerns at this time was the possible use of "butterfly bombs" on airports that were going to be used to carry troops in the invasion. To prevent this, our base soon received two half-track armored vehicles and a large cable, which would be strung between the two half-tracks. They would go down the runway, sweeping it clear of any butterfly bombs that might have been dropped. The butterfly bomb scare was a false alarm. I never heard of any butterfly bombs or any German efforts to prevent the invasion.

On one of our training missions, we were in trail, towing gliders at night, north of Portland. A German intruder [aircraft that penetrated enemy territory seeking air or ground targets of opportunity]—at least we were told it was an intruder—dropped a flare, and of course our formation was vividly outlined. There was nothing we could do other than watch the flare burn and hope that it was not an intruder who was going to come in and simply wipe out our formation. Along with the threats of the barrage balloons and the weather, it was enough to keep anyone on the edge of their seat.

We were out at the aircraft waiting to go on June 5. Aircraft were hooked up to the gliders that they would be towing. We waited, and the flight was canceled. I don't think anyone slept the rest of that night. There was simply too much tension and too much edginess for anybody to get any sleep. It was a terrible letdown. The tension could be cut with a knife.

We had lined up on the flight line again on June 6 after another briefing for the takeoff. I would be flying in a C-47 Gooney Bird. To take off in your glider, a jeep in line with your aircraft was connected with a cable that ran out the same distance as the glider; the cable was the same length as the tow rope on your glider. As you pulled out, the jeep pulled out beside you, and when you saw that his line was taut, you knew that your glider was taut and you could pour on the fire and get the glider airborne. It was a little more difficult to get these gliders airborne than it had been in practice, for the troops were given the option of picking up as much ammunition as they could carry. This tended to overload some of the gliders. Our glider was carrying a 57mm antitank gun. My crew consisted of First Lieutenant Worst; a pilot, Lieutenant Carter; the co-pilot, Lieutenant Denison; myself as the navigator; Staff Sergeant Jennings, the crew chief; and Staff Sergeant Beugger, the radio operator. I do not recall the aircraft number. Ours was one of the aircraft that went through the invasion without a scratch.

Our entire trip into Normandy and back out was only three hours and forty-five minutes. We headed in a generally south and southwest direction to Portland Bill, and from there to various points established in the English Channel by latitude and longitude.

Generally, our course was southwest, then it turned to go between the islands of Jersey and Guernsey, coming into the Cherbourg peninsula on the west side. We crossed the peninsula for the glider drop, came out on the east side, and returned to England.

We were towing the glider at 120 miles per hour. As we began to go between the islands of Jersey and Guernsey at an altitude of 1,200 or 1,500 feet, we received our first flak. We could see heavy shell bursts in the air, but they were not reaching our formation. As we approached landfall we began a let-down to 800 feet, flying straight and level with the glider behind us. As we approached our drop zone, we flashed a green light from the navigator's astrodome back to the glider pilot, telling him that he was to cut off. The glider pilot did not have to cut off at that time if he did not think that this was his drop zone. In our case, our pilot, I think his name was McCann, chose not to do so. And from what we could see below us, I certainly did not blame him for not wanting to cut off. The flak was coming up, with many tracers, and we were at 800 feet and flying at only 120 miles per hour. For every tracer that came by, we knew that there were a great many bullets and shells that we did not see. Since our glider pilot had chosen not to cut off, we then made a 360-degree turn, continuing our low speed at the same altitude, and brought the glider back to the area again.

At this point the glider pilot had no choice, for if he did not cut off from the tow plane, we would disconnect him from the tow plane itself. This could be disastrous, for the tow rope would then not fall loose from the glider and the glider would be left with this tremendous nylon tow rope in the front with very heavy brass fittings on it. So the glider pilot cut off. This was in the vicinity of Ste. Mére Eglise. When the glider cut loose, we put the throttle to the firewall, went down to the deck, and increased our speed to about 220 miles per hour, coming down as low as we could get. A tree loomed up ahead of us, and I yelled, "Watch out for the tree," so loud that I was hoarse all the way back to England.

We came out over a point called the Isle of San Marcouf. We had been told that all flak batteries would be neutralized. As we came up on the island, we could see the gun emplacements, but fortunately we received no gunfire. Our glider cut loose at 4:08 a.m. on a Tuesday morning in June. (How peaceful that sounds now.)

The copilot on the airplane that I had taken overseas, and one of my roommates, Donald Handegard, never returned from the mission. We lost one airplane, and they were part of the crew. To this day they remain forever young. I remember them as they were.

Heading out to sea from the coast was an unbelievable assemblage of ships. I looked down at the ships as we were going over them, almost at deck level, and on one of the ships I saw the crewmen scattering to our right. I looked up, and saw that the C-47 on our right still had his tow cable dragging. He had not released it. This obviously was causing some concern for the sailors. However, when we called the pilot on the radio, he immediately released it.

We returned uneventfully to England. There is no way to describe the feeling, the exhilaration, of knowing that you are still alive. We got very little sleep, and the next day I went back again into Normandy with our second glider mission. This one was also three hours and fifty minutes. We came directly in over the beachhead. One of the gliders ahead of us—a Horsa—had cut loose for landing. He evidently hit a land mine upon landing, and was absolutely destroyed by the ensuing explosion.

Regarding the mission into Normandy, we had been told that pathfinders would be ahead of us. There would be landing zones marked. This was not the case. We were also told that we would have access to the radar system called Rebecca Eureka. The aircraft carried an antenna on each side of the airplane, and a signal that was transmitted and returned to the aircraft would tell you how far you were from the beacon, which was on the ground. The beacon was supposed to have been dropped or be in position with the pathfinders. However, there were so many aircraft involved that we were not permitted to turn on the Rebecca Eureka system, for it would, in fact, overload the ground station. So, here again, all these great plans with electronic aid did not work, and we did the best we could to spot the landing zones. Locating one field that was designated as your drop zone turned out to be much different with heavy ground fire when the field was surrounded by a lot of other fields. I guess it's one of those things about war; the best-laid plans don't always work out. I'm not really sure that our glider got into the field all right. He returned. The way my group operated was that glider pilots going out to the coast were picked up and brought back to England. They gave up their weapons to infantrymen coming in, many of whom had lost their weapons in the water. The glider pilots were threatened with court-martial, or they would be charged for the weapon if this happened again.

Glider pilots were an unusual breed of men. Every time you made a glider landing, it was a controlled crash, and you were committed; there was no return. Some of the glider pilots who had been brought in had been involved in operations in Sicily where they were badly shot up by their own navy. They then came up and made the landing in Normandy. They later made a landing in southern France. They were then involved in the Market Garden operation (about which the book *A Bridge Too Far* was written), landing in Holland on a German armored division. They were then faced with another landing across the Rhine. Upon talking with these people later on, I found that they were bitter, difficult to manage, and simply had no compunction about telling the commander or any officer to go to hell. They would say, "Okay, court-martial us, and you may save our lives." They were a tough bunch of what I consider very brave men. Following the invasion, we flew into the hastily prepared strips on beaches to haul out wounded. We were not under enemy fire, but we had a low priority. Fighters had the right of way, taking off and landing, and each fighter landing and taking off created a tremendous cloud of dust. It was very hot for the wounded in the aircraft, and there was a tremendous smell of fear mixed with the smell of wounds. I saw flight nurses become ill.

I was later reassigned to the 9th Bomber Command. I joined the 386th Bomb Group. I flew twenty-eight missions in the Martin B-26 Marauder, often called the "Widowmaker." I then flew twelve more missions in a Douglas A-26.

Robert Butler (U.S. Army Air Corps)

American paratroopers were supposed to clear landing zones for their glider infantry reinforcements to come in on. Robert Butler, who volunteered to be a glider pilot, survived D-Day.

I WAS INDUCTED AT FORT CUSTER IN Battle Creek, Michigan, in 1941, and ended up in the Coast Artillery, in a barrage balloon battalion in Seattle, Washington, where the Japanese were expected to invade at any moment. We lived out in the country on this barrage balloon site and all our meals were brought to us by truck. We had to stay there twenty-four hours a day, seven days a week, and weren't allowed to leave.

I did not enjoy this type of service, and when I found out that they were looking for volunteer glider pilots, I immediately applied. The qualification for becoming a glider pilot at that time was having a pilot's license in civilian life, which I did have, at a rather tender age.

Our training started in Victorville, and we promptly became staff sergeants in order to get higher flight pay. We graduated as flight officers, which was a new designation and rank alongside a warrant officer. Although we were accorded the privileges of going into officers' clubs and eating in the officers' mess, we were never totally accepted as full-fledged officers.

Our training after graduation from Victorville was in various areas of the United States, from Arizona to Texas to Louisville, Kentucky. One of the first was at Tucumcari, New Mexico, where the Air Corps had taken over a dude ranch that had a landing strip. About twenty of us lived very exclusively in the dude ranch facilities with its French chef.

Our instructor was a German defector who was a world-famous glider pilot and had trained many German troops and pilots prior to their entering World War II. The Germans were not allowed after World War I to have any power planes, so they instead became very proficient in gliders. We learned a lot from this German instructor, who was very strict and taught us a great deal about clouds and thermal activities.

Our training aircraft were Sweitzer gliders, which were the finest soaring glider at that time. They could stay up for literally hours, gliding from thermal to thermal, cloud to cloud, and mountaintop to mountaintop. Flying them was a great experience. However, we were to find out later that this soaring-type glider had little or nothing in common with military gliders.

Eventually, we got into the CG 4 military gliders, which carried fifteen fully laden Airborne troops. We practiced for many months throughout the country under every condition imaginable. I eventually became an instructor in North Carolina for nighttime training, which was as exciting as combat duty in that we had to land by smudge pots at night in very small areas. Of course we instructors had to wait until the very last second to take over in case of emergencies, and there were many. It was a nerve-racking job, and I was almost elated when I received word that I was being transferred to England. Although I was newly married (as of June 6, 1943), and of course I hated to leave my new bride, I knew it was inevitable.

We traveled to England aboard the *Mauritania*, a passenger ship that had been taken over to carry U.S. troops. We officers were allowed much better quarters than the rank-and-file troops and enjoyed having dinner in the luxurious main dining room, although I'm sure our food was the same as that served to everyone else.

I joined the 434th Troop Carrier Group at Aldermasten, England, and was in the 74th Squadron. Our training there was varied over several months. We initially used the English Horsa, an enormous glider that carried thirty-five troops. The glider itself was made mostly of plywood and had hydraulic flaps and a tricycle landing gear. It was so large that it could not be flown very successfully at night and was meant to land in France in the daytime.

After becoming quite proficient in the Horsa glider, it was decided that my group would go in at night, and we went back to the CG-4 glider and trained for many weeks to land in exceptionally short spaces between all sorts of obstacles.

We were on many alerts in preparation for going in on

D-Day, but we were continually stalled because of weather and one reason or another. We were on alert about twenty-four hours a day, and the last week or so we didn't get much sleep, concerned as to when we would be jerked out of bed with the words, "We're off."

Finally the time came. That night as we gathered in the fields in preparation for takeoff, General Eisenhower suddenly appeared and gave us a short pep talk. I can't say we were too exhilarated by his appearance; it simply added to our anxiety, realizing that we were in for a very exciting time.

We finally took off, and I had fifteen troops in my glider, plus my copilot, Tim Homan. We glider pilots were prepared to fight with the rest of the Airborne troops and were equally laden with burp guns and M1 rifles, .45 pistols, hand grenades, and lots of ammunition, plus our food rations. We were well supplied.

We were also given a pair of large, extremely dark goggles to wear when we started getting into flak. We didn't really know what to expect in that regard, but it wasn't very long before we found out. Well out into the English Channel, we met phosphorus shells that lighted the sky just like daylight, and then we started receiving lots of flak. Reaching the shores of France was a harrowing experience. We kept on going past the shoreline into Ste. Mére Eglise, which was well behind the lines—particularly the invasion lines. The main objective of the troops we carried was to cut off communications and roads so the invasion troops could break through to us.

Nearing our landing zones at Ste. Mére Eglise, the tow planes kept getting higher and higher, which was our largest worry because when we released, we had to circle and circle in order to come back to our proper landing area. A lot of this was caused by mass confusion, and too many planes coming in at pretty much the same time, and an exceptionally large amount of ground fire coming up at us. Many gliders as well as the tow planes were shot down. At my release time we circled several times, and I landed by moonlight between two large hedgerows. The paratroopers were supposed to land a couple of hours before us and plant smudge pots for us to land by, but they didn't make it, so we landed by moonlight. I had a parachute on my tail that I directed my copilot to activate about fifty feet off the ground, so I was able to plop between four huge hedgerows, which contained trees fifty feet or more in height.

The glider directly ahead of mine was piloted by Col. Mike Murphy, and the glider contained General Pratt as well as several other occupants. General Pratt was killed in the air, and Colonel Murphy did not make a successful landing between the hedgerows. He crashed into one and severely crippled his legs. I'm not sure what happened to the rest of the occupants of his glider.

It was still dark when we landed, and our instructions were to hide as quickly as possible where we wouldn't be seen, and communicate if necessary by activating a brass cricket, which we all carried.

Upon daybreak, we rendezvoused with other troops. Of course, there was mass confusion as to what to do and where to go. We were gathered around in a group when all of a sudden General Gavin appeared. He had an objective in mind over the hill and took the Airborne troops with him. He directed us glider pilots to stay where we were until we could be evacuated because we were too exhausted to be of much help to him.

Leonard Lebenson (U.S. Army)

Glider infantrymen formed an important part of the U.S. Army Airborne forces that landed in Normandy on June 6, 1944. It was soldiers such as Leonard Lebenson who were supposed to help organize the airborne forces once they were on the ground.

THE ASSIGNMENT PROCESS AT CAMP UPTON HAD not only assigned me to the 82nd Airborne Division, but I was earmarked before I got there. I think this was done on the train on the way down. I was earmarked for service in the G-3 (Operations) section, and after taking a short basic training within the division, I received my assignment. Along with me, the total of the group was six hundred men from Camp Upton. Most of them went to the 326th Glider Infantry. Thirteen of us were assigned to the division headquarters. I was the only one to be sent to the G-3 section. I think the assignment was made because of two skills I had as an engineering draftsman: I knew how to hold a pencil and make lines with it, and I knew how to type, which was self-taught. Both skills were helpful to an operations sergeant.

We originally were in Ireland for about four to six weeks, and then we were sent to England. We were stationed in the Midlands, and our headquarters was in Leicester. The other American Airborne division in the UK [United Kingdom] at that time was the 101st, which had come directly from the States to England. They were in the south of England, relatively close to the Channel. When the plans were made for the airborne lift to France, the 101st of course left from where they had been training, and the parachute elements of the 82nd also left from the area where they had been training, which was in the Midlands. However, the glider elements of the 82nd could not fly that long a distance from the Midlands to Normandy, so they were transferred to the south of England, relatively close to the 101st. The glider elements, including myself, left from that area, so for the last few days before the invasion, we were separated from the bulk of our division.

Apparently, in the first glider serial, there were some fifty-two gliders in the D-Day lift. Most of them were taken up with antiaircraft or antitank guns of the 80th Battalion, which was part of our division. There were some radios and a couple of command jeeps, some trailers carrying map material, and some 75mm pack howitzers. Actually, the part of that original glider serial contained only a few members of our headquarters, including myself, representing the G-3. There were a couple of enlisted men from G-2 (Intelligence section). The principal staff officers were included one way or the other, either as part of the parachute element or part of the glider element. Basically, only a small fraction of the headquarters was included in the initial lift.

I was assigned to a certain glider, and when I didn't show up or when I wasn't there, they said, "We'd better put someone in there," because there was probably a map trailer in that glider. So they assigned another draftsman to go in my place. When I finally showed up, for whatever reason, it was decided to let that be and not change the arrangement. They found a place for me to go in another glider that did not carry any equipment, just men. Among them were General March, who was the division artillery commander; a number of men from the 80th Antiaircraft Battalion; and some men from the headquarters of the division artillery. I knew who these men were, but they were not men with whom I normally operated. But that worked out okay.

We had originally expected to go the night of June 5. It meant that there were two nights' sleep missed, the night of the fourth and the night of the fifth. By June 6, I hadn't slept since June 3. That was about fifty-six hours without sleep. By the time D-Day night came around, it was well over seventy-two hours without sleep. Of course, I wasn't the only one with that problem. If you think about the guys who came in over the beaches, who in some cases had been in small landing craft for a long time in terrible conditions, I'm sure they didn't have any sleep either. I guess adrenaline keeps people going. It was kind of a tired army that landed because of the conditions of getting there.

Having come to the sealed-in area on the afternoon of June 5, and all systems being go, I had to draw ammunition, which included some bandoleers, clips, and various kinds of rifle ammunition, as well as grenades; a first-aid kit; rations, which included one ration of D (three chocolate bars, each one supposedly enough for a meal) and one ration of K (three packaged meals—breakfast, lunch, and supper); a small map case; an acetate sheet; and of course a mess kit, shaving articles, and a canteen with water. We went in with two days' worth of rations. I filled up as many pockets as I had with cigarettes, because at that time I was a heavy smoker. I decided that I wasn't going through this operation without a photographic record, so I was carrying a Brownie camera, which I fit into the back pocket of my field pack. I also carried a blanket, a shelter half, a little shovel, a bayonet, a knife, and a length of rope that I had taken from a navy ship before going into Sicily; it stood me through the whole war. It was about a hundred feet long and about an eighth of an inch in diameter. I also carried a half roll of toilet paper, which I found out was about the most important thing you needed. It was a pretty heavy load.

We ate a meal, and then we had a formation just before leaving. What made my experience a little different from that of all the other guys was that they had done this earlier, and I was doing it at the last minute. So I didn't have too much time to think, worry, or be concerned about what was going on. There was a formation at which Eisenhower's message to the troops was read, and each of us was given a printed copy of it. There was an opportunity for prayer for those who wanted it. Then we went on trucks to the airfield. When we got there, it was dusk. In June 1944 in England (which was operating on "double summertime"), dusk was around eleven o'clock.

I was extremely nervous. I had to stop three or four times to urinate while we were on the airfield before loading onto the glider. I wasn't the only one, of course, but we were all jumpy and nervous. We smoked a lot. We didn't say too much. Finally, we got loaded. I didn't know the people I was going with. As it turned out, it was very fortunate because there were many, many accidents in gliders, mainly from crashing into hedgerows, trees, or buildings.

Many times the load in the glider (which could be a jeep or trailer or gun) broke loose, creating a great deal of damage among the personnel. We had none of that because we were just fourteen people seated in two ranks, one on each side of the glider. We stowed our packs and rifles as securely and neatly as possible under the seats. Of course we had the Mae West, which was an inflatable vest, so that if we had gone down in water, we would have been able to inflate these things. The Mae West is worn over everything. The first thing you took off when you landed was the Mae West, and you just threw it away.

As I recall, the nervousness that I had been feeling and the fear in view of where we were going and what we might expect disappeared as soon as the plane took off and we were in the air.

I also remember feeling feverishly warm prior to taking off. A lot of that had to do with the way I was dressed. It was June and we were wearing woolen uniforms that were impregnated with a foul-smelling chemical meant to protect us in case of a gas attack. I think the feverishness also came from mental agitation and maybe because most of us smoked. At that time there was no anti-smoking campaign. At least nine out of ten of us smoked.

The trip itself was about two hours. In order to avoid our own ships, so we wouldn't confuse them by flying over them, the Airborne elements went out over the sea and down the west side of the Cherbourg peninsula, then flew in the back door across the peninsula. Then they had to drop the two divisions before going over the fleet on the way back to England, making the drop before leaving the French territory, of course. That meant that since the drop zones were relatively close to the invasion beaches, there was a flight over land—the Cherbourg peninsula. The signal had to be given to hit the drop zones, which were close to the beaches on the other side of the peninsula, so navigation was a little tricky. Unfortunately, it was complicated because there was a cloud bank over the peninsula that night. Everything was clear and you could see well, and suddenly you couldn't see anything. It must have been a terrible predicament for a pilot. Many of them, because of the clouds, had to break formation to avoid the risk of hitting another plane. The drops of both Airborne divisions were seriously compromised. The men were scattered all over the peninsula, south of the peninsula, some of them in the water, and some of them on the west side of the peninsula.

As I found out later, we were very lucky to have landed almost where we were supposed to land. And when you do that, you expect that everybody else did too. It wasn't like that, as we found out. Whoever and whatever circumstance made that happen we are thankful for.

We hit the clouds and it got kind of noisy, and you could see flak but you really couldn't see too much. Then we suddenly knew that we were flying on our own. In other words, we weren't being towed anymore; we had been cut loose. That is a very unusual feeling, flying through the air without a motor. It's noiseless. All you hear is the rushing sound of the air, but other than that it's very quiet. But the quiet was punctuated by the noise of some explosions. We knew that we wouldn't be flying that way too long because we were coming in low, so there wouldn't be much time after being cut loose before arriving at the ground. Then there was a sudden up movement on the aircraft—like a little elevator uplift; you could feel it pancaking.

Then we hit something, and then again. We twisted around in a series of very rapid, violent movements. I'm not an expert on automobile crashes, but that seemed about what it was like, only much accentuated. We were wearing seatbelts like those on today's aircraft. There was some movement of various articles of equipment packs, rifles, et cetera, throughout the cabin. We had hit a tree, bounced off the corner of a shed, and landed against another tree. Pieces of the glider were strewn over a relatively small field. But the fourteen men climbed out of the wreckage. Only one guy was hurt. Hurray! We're in France! We didn't know what to do. You have to be quiet, but you can't really be quiet when you're climbing out of something like that. Of course, it must have made a hell of a racket when it hit. We were under the direct command of a general, so there was no question about who was in charge.

We got our stuff together and put on our various packs, rifles, et cetera. A few minutes after all this happened, we were just getting ready to leave when I noticed that I didn't have my helmet. It must have gotten knocked off and I didn't even know it. I ran back, scrounged around, and found it. At the same time that it was knocked off I must have gotten a blow to the side of my head, because I had a severe black eye, which I didn't even know about until people later remarked, "What happened to your eye?" I didn't feel it, which I think was due to everything that was happening.

A wounded parachutist was on the ground in the field next to us, and he called out because he heard us coming in. We saw him and wrapped him in a parachute for comfort. He had been there for a couple of hours and told us that we were right outside a town where there had been some fighting. The fighting had more or less petered out as far as he could tell.

We went to another field (all the fields were surrounded by hedgerows, the famous Normandy Hedges, so that when you were in one of the fields, you really didn't know where anything else was) and saw a house at one end of it. There was a road just on the other side of the hedgerow from the house. It was a narrow country road, which, as we walked on it, we discovered was just a couple hundred yards outside of the town of St. Mére Eglise, our division's initial objective. It was the first town liberated in France on D-Day.

We were lucky, first that we had landed more or less where we were supposed to, and second that we could confirm where we were even though it was dark. It was quiet at that point because the fighting was on the other side of town. The town had already been freed. We walked in, met a couple of our men, and saw a few civilians peeking out of their houses and walking quietly around. Our job was to proceed to the command post (CP), which was a relatively large field near a farmhouse about a mile or so outside of town. It was about four in the morning and still dark, although it got light not long after that.

Led by General March, we proceeded toward the division command post's supposed location. (I went back six days later, on June 12, with my camera, and took some pictures of the crashed glider, which was still there.) General March was followed in file by the rest of us; I brought up the rear. I don't know why I was bringing up the rear. It was a lonesome feeling because we were walking along with about ten yards between each of us. We were spread out over about 140 to 150 yards.

We proceeded cautiously because there was a lot of small-arms fire, which we could hear all around us. It was hard to identify whether it was fifty feet away, half a mile away, or a quarter mile away. There was also occasional machine gun and artillery fire. There was a tremendous amount of noise in the distance from the beaches; the pre-beach invasion bombardment from the naval ships was going on at that time. So the sky was being lit up in that direction with all kinds of flashes. You could hear that artillery, which was probably about eight to ten miles away, or, depending on which ships, maybe six miles away.

However, in our location it was basically small-arms fire. We were fortunate not to run across any directly or be held up by it. As soon as the sky got light, we were able to verify where we were (in a farm area) and could proceed more quickly. Cows grazed in the small fields. It was so peaceful looking, but of course we were in a war, so the situation felt contradictory.

At about eight or nine in the morning, we arrived at the command post. The commanding general, Matthew Ridgway, was there, along with his aide, a couple of the staff officers, and two or three other enlisted men. During that morning I don't think there were more than fifteen to twenty men there. People would come in, walk through, and find out where they were or where they were supposed to go. The command post was trying to be a directional center, but it was really not in control of anything. General Ridgway, a brave and forceful man, was continually on the move, trying to exercise his control. We were just standing there, waiting for things to develop, and waiting until things were in place so the CP could then start exerting its functions. A number of glider pilots were there. Early that day, it was just myself and another sergeant as part of the staff. We were just gathering information about who was there. There weren't any messages because we didn't have any phones or radios; we didn't even have a map set up. I had some folded up sections of a map with me in my pack, but I didn't do anything with them at that point. We dug ourselves in because there was artillery around. We went into hedgerows with a ditch on one or both sides, then enlarged the ditch or deepened it so we were relatively safe, even when later on the artillery became very heavy. As the day proceeded, more and more people showed up. We didn't have any information from the beaches, and we were concerned that the invasion taking place might not be successful.

Yet we were confident, particularly those of us who were together. I can imagine that those who were dropped off by themselves might not feel as confident. We could hear the naval fire. As soon as it got light, our planes were in the sky, which was tremendously heartening. Both American and British planes were flying over very low. There were no German planes that we could see that day. We were ready as individuals. If anything closed in on us, we were prepared to do battle. I have a picture that I had someone take of me that day. I am seated with a hedgerow to my back. My legs were crossed awkwardly because of all the junk I had. My field jacket was puffed up with ammunition and grenades and rations stuffed into my pockets.

As the day progressed, people started to come together, and the noise was building up. By about five or six in the evening on D-Day, there was very heavy artillery fire on us, and we had some casualties from artillery and small-arms fire. It could have come from the next field but we couldn't see enough to be sure. We didn't know at the time the extent that our troops were dispersed. We didn't know that our troops were engaged in desperate battles just a few miles away. But we had confidence in our leadership. We had good officers. At the end of that day, we had smoked a lot of cigarettes and done a lot of talking and just waiting. By about ten or eleven o'clock we probably had about twenty men there. We were not yet functioning as a CP, but the following day we were. Cohesion was developing. More and more was becoming known about troops and battles, and Generals Gavin and Ridgway were in control of things and in contact with each other.

Our location was known to groups around us. Messages were coming in, although we still didn't have any radio or telephone communication. Once it was dark we divided up into one-hour watches while the rest of us tried to sleep. We stopped smoking because we didn't want to light matches. At one point I crept under a big tarpaulin that was part of parachute equipment wrapping in order to take a smoke. The next thing I knew, it was daylight. I had fallen asleep immediately. I was awakened by the crack of artillery. But at least I had finally gotten some sleep.

Clinton E. Riddle (U.S. Army)

The German military, who had long expected the Allied invasion of France, were well aware of the threat posed by paratroopers and glider infantry, as Clinton Riddle found out in his first taste of battle.

OUR TRAINING IN ENGLAND WAS MORE OR less routine—close-order drill, forced march, double timing, hand-to-hand combat training, firing ranges, glider rides, field problems both day and night, inspections, and parades. We became famous later on as the 82nd became the Honor Guard in Berlin.

On May 29, we packed up and moved by trucks to Leicester. From there, we went by train to near Ramsbury. June 2 was spent in studying sand tables and maps of the French coast. We were also shown the location of some of the gun emplacements. All of our movements were confined to camp. We couldn't talk to anyone except our closest friends.

June 4 and 5 were days of just waiting in camp. The preparations had been made and everything was moving toward a departure in a few hours. My uniform for battle was combat jacket and pants, steel helmet with a first-aid kit tied in the front of the helmet, GI shoes and leggings with a trench knife strapped on my leg, combat pack with rations, shelter half, M1 rifle, ammunition belt, canteen, and a small American flag on the right shoulder of my jacket. I also carried some extra ammunition and a gas mask.

When we were studying the sand tables and making preparations, we were told that the invasion would have to be on June 6 or 7, and no later than June 8 because of the tides. The weather was so uncertain that we just had to wait from day to day.

The paratroopers went before us. Then fifty-two gliders carrying antitank weapons and heavy communication and other equipment went later in the day. The night of June 6 was the first of the light glider landings.

Early on June 7, the 325th Glider Infantry and 375 gliders began to cross the Channel. I was in Company B, 1st Battalion. We loaded in the gliders before daylight. I remember seeing the moon break through for just a moment. Then in a little while we moved off the runway and were in the air. We were using British plywood gliders that carried thirty-three men. This is a lot more than the CG-4As could carry. The British gliders had a three-wheel landing gear rather than the two wheels and skids of the U.S. gliders. There were big white markings on the wings of each one.

Men from our headquarters platoon and the rest of our Company B made up the number in my glider. The pilot and copilot were from Kentucky and West Virginia. I sat in the front seat near the pilot. The ride was not rough and I was sitting and taking it easy. From the very front seat I had a breathtaking view of the many boats and ships in the Channel.

I could see the C-47 tow plane before us traveling approximately 150 miles an hour and about 2,000 feet high. Every man had been coached on what to do in case we went down. We didn't carry parachutes, only Mae West life preservers.

About halfway across the Channel, which was twenty-three miles wide where we were crossing, our tow plane began to miss and sputter, then finally just quit and began to lose altitude. The glider pilot tried to keep the glider riding as high as possible, and we were moving faster than the plane. In the process, the tow rope became slack and the glider overran the plane. The pilot of the plane continued to crank the engine until we were down within a hundred feet of the water. We could see the waves churning up to meet us. All we could hear was the rushing of the wind as it swept past the glider, and the groaning of the men in the glider. "Oooh, something's wrong." When the glider tilted up on one wing, almost in a half roll, we knew what was going on. The slack in the tow rope had become tangled in the landing gear. But the glider pilot was able to maneuver the glider enough to get the rope from around the landing wheel.

The order was given to stand by for a crash landing. Each man checked his life preserver and laid down his equipment and rifles. Six cases of tank mines were thrown out, also six GI cans of water and anything else that would lighten the glider before contact with the water. The sergeant was standing by with an axe ready to chop a hole in the top of the glider so we could get out on the wings, which were filled with thousands of Ping-Pong balls to keep the glider afloat.

When it looked like all hope was gone and prayers were said, at the last minute one of the motors fired up with a roar and a cloud of smoke. Then the other motor fired up. Boy, what a good thing it was to hear the roar of the airplane engines. When the plane's motors began to operate, they tightened up the slack in the rope, although we had no way to tell the pilot of the plane what was happening. It was a miracle that our glider pilot was able to get the rope unfastened without having to hit the tow rope release lever. If he had hit the lever, we still would have gone down into the Channel, having been cut loose from the mother plane.

Soon we were flying again, and everything was all right until we got over the coast of Normandy. The fighter planes were three layers thick overhead, and the train of C-47s and gliders reached as far as I could see. Word had been received back from England after we left that we would not be able to land in the area we had planned. The pilot of the plane could pick up the news on the plane's radio, but we did not know about it back in the glider. We were over the coast for approximately two and a half to three minutes before being released from the tow plane. We wanted to get down as quickly as possible because of the small-arms fire, yet we had to pick out a place big enough to land on the way down.

It didn't take long to see that the Germans had dug holes in the field and set posts upright and placed mines on every post. The German forces had been cut off by the landing of the parachute units ahead of us, so the men who had been sent out to place posts in our landing zones had not yet received new orders to stop work, and some of them were still there digging when we were trying to land.

As I raised up to look out the front, the pilot pointed toward a small garden-like spot completely enclosed by hedgerows, some with trees growing out of them. The pilot brought the glider in low over the first hedgerow, cutting the top out of some of the trees with the wing. The glider hit the ground, bounced a time or two, then rolled to a stop. The pilot had done a great job in bringing the glider down without crashing into the hedgerow.

We were the only glider in the company that landed without mishap. Others either crashed into a hedgerow, or the front wheel of the tri landing gear in the nose of the glider came up through the floor and cut many of the men's legs.

We lost 11 percent of the men of the 325th on landing alone. One reason we were using the British-type gliders was that it was so hot in Africa that the sun warped the wings of the CG-4A gliders, and they were unfit to be used in the invasion. Another reason was that they carried more men than the American gliders.

Upon landing, we climbed out of the glider and assembled ourselves. Because we were not able to land in the planned spot, we started the long hike to our positions.

About that time, two German fighter planes came over with guns blazing and spraying us with machine gun fire. I was down on my knees, trying to put a makeshift antenna from a walkie-talkie radio onto the big field radio that I was carrying because all of the radios had been damaged in landing. The makeshift antennae worked. It was all we had to keep us in touch with the battalion until we got another radio.

A news reporter came along about that time and took my picture while I was down on my knees working with the radio. I saw the picture a little later in the *Mightiest Army* magazine.

There was very little ground fire in the area where we landed. But as I started through an apple orchard, a Frenchman was milking a cow, and that particular area was being shelled. Later, as we were slowly moving in single file on either side of the road, the old Frenchman came by with his bucket of milk. I stopped him and got me a canteen cup of warm milk for my breakfast. This was less than fifteen minutes after landing.

Our mission was to block all roads and blow the bridges so the Germans could not counterattack at once. We landed within sight of Ste. Mére Eglise, which was the first town taken in Normandy by the 505th Parachute Infantry of the 82nd Airborne. In this town, lying in a doorway along a street, was the first dead German I saw after landing.

I slept just a little the first night in a gully in a briar patch. We passed through Ste. Mére Eglise and to a holding position on June 8 and 9 before going on.

On June 10, we began our mission of attack soon after midnight. We went into attack in the early morning and ran into a trap. Many men of my company were killed, wounded, or lost. When B Company entered a small orchard where the Germans were dug in, the Germans waited until we were pretty close before they opened fire. The whole company was caught in the crossfire. I was battalion messenger at the time, and the battalion unit followed the line companies in the attack.

Before I knew it, we were caught under fire from a tank and pinned down. The captain and the major I was with told me and a few men with us to make a holding force until they started back. I stayed, all right, until they got a head start. I found a little gully and crawled back far enough to get under the cover of some bushes. Then I passed the captain and a major running as hard as I could.

We retreated back to our old lines and dug in. While I was digging, a shell almost dropped into my foxhole. One did drop into the hole next to me, and a small exploding shell almost cut the soldier's arm off. We stayed there taking all that the Germans could throw at us until almost nightfall, then we moved across the meadow and dug in.

I went back by myself the next morning to where the men had been killed. One of my best friends and eighteen others lay dead in the little orchard. You could almost cross the orchard by walking on the bodies. They were all in a line, just as they had entered the orchard in an attack. I don't want to cite any names, because someday their people may chance to hear or read this. So I will say "one of the boys," as he lay there, had his hand extended straight up in the air as though he was reaching for someone or something. I can see that picture in my mind today as plain as I did on that morning as I stood alone and looked over the battle area. He was wearing a pair of black gloves that somebody had probably sent from home. I could not bring myself to wear gloves in combat for a long time after that, and even now I never pull a pair of gloves on without thinking of him.

E. Schroeder (U.S. Army)

The ability to air-drop vehicles and towed weapon systems was not present during World War II. This forced the U.S. Army's Airborne divisions to use gliders for the job. Glider artilleryman E. Schroeder found that the process was far from perfected.

EARLY IN 1943, WHILE I WAS UNDERGOING basic training with a new division at Fort Jackson, South Carolina, someone in the War Department got a bright idea. The 82nd Airborne Division was set to go overseas, and the potential for a high casualty rate made them decide to send the division overstrength. At a battalion officers' meeting at Fort Jackson, our CO [commanding officer] put out the request for volunteers. It was at that moment I made the mistake of reaching up to scratch my ear.

I think it was the last week of May that we packed up everything necessary for a trip to the Continent and headed for an airfield in the south of England. I don't recall the name of the nearest town because there were no passes anyhow. It was surrounded by barbed-wire fences and patrolled by military police, just in case one or more of us decided that the upcoming party was not exactly our cup of tea. Here we were, in a concentration camp, without having even faced the enemy as yet.

My unit was the 320th Glider Field Artillery Battalion. Unlike the infantry, we had a lot of heavy equipment, such as jeeps, 105mm howitzers, and ammunition. Those last days were busy ones as all of that stuff had to be properly loaded and chained down. We had received many large British Horsa gliders on reverse lend-lease. They were actually larger than the C-47 tug planes. They were also built completely of plywood, and to this day I am still picking splinters out of my ass from my crash landing in Normandy.

Early on the morning of June 5, on the way to the mess hall, it was noticed that all the aircraft had a new look. It seems the Air Corps boys had spent the entire preceding night painting the big black and white invasion stripes on wings and fuselages. We concluded that someone was trying to tell us something. This was a busy day of tying up all loose ends. For example, the issuing of anti-gas-impregnated clothing. This stuff was like bacon grease, stiff and dank when the weather was cool and irritating to one's sweaty skin when it was warm. Soon after the landing, I cut a piece of nylon from a parachute to ease my badly chafed neck. I still have that scarf, and by now it's in better shape than the neck. We also got the little sleeve flags to sew on, in case we might forget what country we were from.

Sometime around midday, all officers and key non-coms were ushered into the briefing tent, where a sand table held a three-dimensional layout of the Cotentin Peninsula. The division's drop zones were in the area of Ste. Mére Eglise, about five miles inland, the mission being to secure the town and prevent enemy reinforcements from crossing the Douve and Merderet rivers. Individual battle maps were handed out for further study. A famous photo of Ike greeting a unit of the 101st Airborne on the afternoon of June 5 was taken in an adjacent field while we watched through the fence. This was their first time in combat, so it was quite appropriate that they receive the coach's pep talk. That evening we were treated to a movie. I have forgotten the title, but it was about the life of Ted Lewis and featured a member of his band who had an arm shot off in World War 1. Rather appropriate, I guess.

My unit did not go in with the initial lift, but rather with the second of the day. This sounds like the easy share, but such was not the case, as I explain shortly. For one thing, we had the pleasure of seeing the returning aircraft bearing jagged holes of various sizes. At some time in the early afternoon, we strapped on the field equipment and headed for the airstrip, with that feeling of "Thank God, the waiting is over." There stood a neat line of tug C-47s with the two lines attached to an equally neat row of previously loaded gliders. Apparently, we were expected. So we loaded up as engines were started up, and shortly, with a bit of a lurch, we were on our way. There were a few minutes of circling as the lift formed up because the planes were rising from several airstrips throughout the area. My craft contained a jeep and trailer loaded with three round clusters of 105mm howitzer ammunition, plus several clusters on the hood of the jeep. Personnel consisted of the glider pilot and co-pilot, the ammunition corporal and two of his men, and me. Shortly, after everybody was on course over the Channel, the pilot informed me that the glider felt a bit nose-heavy, and could I maybe shift a little weight. I promised to try, so we spent a good part of the crossing transferring the ammo on the jeep hood back to the trailer, and I told my men to "get to the back of the bus." From time to time, flights of American fighter aircraft appeared above and on the flanks. They were a welcome sight. We did not fly over the invasion beaches, but rather approached from the other side of the peninsula, this being the shortest distance, except that it meant more time over hostile terrain.

As we approached the coast, we saw a burning building to the right, and to the left a naval vessel, probably a cruiser, firing some big stuff inland. We were now over land, and clusters of tracers started coming up. It was always pleasant to realize that for every one you could see, there were probably five or so hunks of metal you couldn't see, and the fact that when they appeared up ahead, you knew that in a matter of seconds that's where you'd be. I recall vividly my first sight of green tracers. I have no idea what kind of gun it was because most of the tracers were red or pink.

It was now time to prepare for landing, or, as the glider gang calls it, "a controlled crash." Fields of any good size in the area had been planted with the large poles known as "Rommel's asparagus." The standard landing technique was to aim the nose between the poles, shear off the wings, pray, and hope for the best. All the smaller fields were surrounded by hedgerows and trees, so, slap it down, pray, and hope for the best. Shortly before cutting-loose time, we sat down and buckled up the four-way safety harnesses. Our pilot selected one of the smaller still-clear fields, having very little choice because the heavily loaded, ungainly craft, once cut loose, had a glide ratio of something like minus. I was seated directly behind the pilot's compartment and over the area of the nose landing gear. I had heard somewhere that on a hard landing the nose-wheel strut tended to come up through the floor and could be hazardous to one's health. I found out the hard way that they were right. We banged down hard in the middle of the field and bounced into the hedgerow trees. For a few moments I thought I might have a broken leg; however, after shoving aside a ton of debris from my prone position, I managed to crawl through what was left of the nose section and get on my feet. Of course, there were many bruises and contusions, plus a slight concussion that put me into a rather happy state of mind. I have been that way ever since. Incidentally, my four-way harness was pulled out by the roots and was still hanging on me.

Unfortunately, the copilot was badly smashed up, and the corporal suffered what appeared to be at least one fractured vertebra. My unit's designated area was southwest of the town, but I arrived on the northeast side. Oh, well, at least it was the right county.

Getting back to why the second shift isn't exactly a bed of roses. We didn't have the advantage of darkness and surprise. The reception party was ready and waiting. The first shift had secured the town of Ste. Mére Eglise, the first to be liberated on the mainland of Europe. It straddled the main highway to Cherbourg, and Jerry thought he would like to have it back. We landed right in the middle of a fierce enemy counterattack.

My first friendly contact, after emerging from the wreck, was a trooper who was wondering if we had any machine gun ammunition. I had to tell him "only if your machine gun is 105 millimeter." Several men of my battery, in another glider, were captured shortly after landing, the sergeant receiving several Schmeisser holes in one sleeve of his field jacket. Their captors, after reviewing the situation for a while, decided this was no way to run a war and turned their weapons over to the captives. In military terminology, this is known as "about face." This was the day that I became a firm believer in the fact that "if it ain't your time, you ain't gonna get it," no matter what!

One of our battalion staff officers took a rifle bullet in the side of his helmet. Instead of going on through his head, it went up and over between the plastic liner and the outer steel shell, clipping his ear on the opposite side. This same guy, on the same night, had occasion to toss a hand grenade. It hit a tree branch and bounced right back into his lap. It turned out to be a dud. There was also the case of a couple of guys in the ammunition section in a jeep with the usual trailer load of 105mm rounds, plus the stack on the hood. A direct hit on the trailer by an enemy shell blew all of the propelling charges, which in turn blew all of those on the hood. The occupants suffered nothing more than scorched eyebrows and possibly soiled laundry. Then there was the Southern boy riding in the back of a gun-section jeep when it ran over a small mine. He said, "Man, when that thing went off, my asshole sucked up about three yards of that camouflage net." Although the attacks continued sporadically, the defenders had enjoyed a brief breathing spell and now had much needed reinforcements.

By the end of the day, we figured we were here to stay. The gliders were constructed so that a large tail section could be unbolted and pulled aside to remove heavy equipment. That, of course, was according to the book and under normal conditions. D-Day was not exactly a normal condition. Although my vehicle had survived the crash in reasonably good shape, strain on the bolts, even with their built-in wrench handles, had made them absolutely unbudgeable. After grunting and swearing for quite some time, and so mad and frustrated that I was even oblivious to enemy fire, I finally gave up, cocked my carbine, and joined in the defense of the area for the rest of the night. D-Day did not automatically shut down at midnight. Some of the bloodiest confrontations took place the following day, and for many days thereafter, but of course that is another story.

3 | OMAHA BEACH

Kenneth P. Lord (U.S. Army)

Omaha Beach was one of the two assigned American invasion beaches in Normandy, France, on June 6, 1944. Kenneth Lord of the 1st Infantry Division, nicknamed the "Big Red One," describes the big picture of the landing.

THE 1ST DIVISION HAD ITS HEADQUARTERS AT Blandford, in the southern part of England. We received two plans in December 1943 and January 1944. They both proposed that our air force would blast the Germans to surrender. We were to make two landings in France, one at Cherbourg and the other at Brest. Our mission in each was to rapidly deploy our troops and prevent the French from slaughtering the Germans as they pulled back to Germany. We did not believe it would happen. It was about the last week in January that we finally received plans for Overlord, the landing in Normandy.

The normal course of events that would appear logical would be estimating the enemy forces we would have to overcome, determining the type and equipment necessary to defeat the enemy, and making a shipping list of the type to get our forces successfully landed. We soon found out that we were wrong and that the first thing we would get was the shipping list and then we would have to work backwards.

We were also advised that the list of ships and craft was not ensured to be accurate.

On D-Day the 1st Division was designated as the command unit. We would have the 29th Division less its headquarters attached to us. We would also have a Ranger group under Colonel Rudder comprising the 2nd and 5th Ranger battalions. SHAEF [Supreme Headquarters, Allied Expeditionary Force] had given them the mission of scaling the cliffs at Pointe du Hoc and knocking out the big guns that could effectively destroy our navy. We also had assigned to us an engineer shore brigade under the command of General Hoge. In addition we had corps troops and special British equipment. In spite of our warnings, they had to go close to H hour (the time set for the beginning of the attack/operation). We also had a group of reporters and photographers who had to land at H hour. We refused to give them permission at division level, but told them if they could sell their idea to the regimental commanders we would have no objection. They landed at H hour with Don Whitehead and Frank Capra.

After the plan of attack had been made, we had to figure out how we would load our ships and craft. This had to be done in reverse order. The first to land would be the last to load. We had to closely examine all of our vessels to determine what space was available. Then every vehicle and gun had to be measured and a template drawn to make sure that when we loaded, the vehicles would fit. This took days of planning and then assigning the troops to use these vehicles as proposed.

The British and American service personnel had established well-distributed encampments in southern England.

Since the roads were very narrow and many of our vehicles quite large, it was necessary to build freestanding parking areas that were parallel to the road itself. We called these "hards." They played an important part in the scenario that follows. During our practice landings, named Fabius and Fox, there was one reception point as the troops came in for the exercises. At this point they were broken into craft groups that would be called down for loading. They were assigned to a particular camp and would be called when their craft was ready for loading.

Just before we practiced, we received an awful blow. We had been closely examining the beaches at Omaha and were quite happy that the hedgehogs and element C were piled on the beaches and the Germans appeared to be concentrating on other beaches. One of our bombers happened to jettison some bombs before landing in England. We saw a picture of his bombs exploding but also saw a series of sympathetic detonations of underwater mines. We then realized that something would have to be drastically changed. We went to the navy and pointed out that the official landing operations manual gave the navy responsibility up to the high-tide mark. They did not disagree but simply said they did not have the troops to clear the mines. We appealed to SHAEF, and they sent us two engineer battalions, one training at Woolacombe in England and the other training in Florida. These troops would lead off the division attack. Now we had to change our entire loading plan. We went to the underground headquarters at Plymouth and worked around the clock for three days until we had it finished. We imagine it was a great shock to those engineers to find that they were the first wave. We had planned to support these battalions with a top-secret weapon, the duplex drive (DD) tank. We would drop the tank ensconced in a shroud with a water propeller sticking out the rear of the shroud operated by the tank's engine. When the tank hit land it would drop its shroud and we would have an M4 tank that could maneuver and fire directly at the target. It worked beautifully during our two practice exercises, Fabius and Fox. During the invasion, the English Channel had very high seas with heavy waves that washed over the shrouds, and the tanks sank an entire battalion on the left side of the attack. The battalion commander on the right flank decided not to drop his tanks. However, his tanks took a long time to be unloaded and did not help the engineers on his flank. The engineers had a mission of destroying the underwater mines and opening up paths in the hedgehogs. They were successful with the mines, but with no fire support they made only two or three channels and were unable to mark them. Under the circumstances they did a great job.

When we received the naval gunfire support plan, we were really upset. We had heard of the tremendous support given by the navy for the landings in the Pacific. But we were going to have the support of only one battleship, two cruisers, and six destroyers. The HMS *Rodney* would assist when they were not busy supporting the Canadians and the British. We surely did not feel we would get much support from them, and we did not. The navy had two rocket LCTs [landing craft, tank]; however, we had to have them cover our flank because it was unsafe to fire over the heads of our troops since the vertical dispersion was not predictable. The six destroyers, with their hulls nearly scraping the bottom, gave them point-blank range, which made it possible for us to break through the exits from the beach.

We wanted to find out what air support we would get. We went to see General Quesada, who commanded the Ninth Air Support Command and coordinated all air support. Since we had a long, flat beach where the tide came in very rapidly, we wanted to know what size bombs the Eighth Air Force would be using on the fortifications. He indicated that they would be using 500- and 1,000-pound bombs. We knew that at a high altitude some of their bombs would hit our beaches. Their craters would rapidly fill with water, and many of our laden foot soldiers would drown. We asked them to use a smaller bomb, but Quesada felt that it would not be effective against the fortifications.

We agreed that this heavy bombardment would be limited to targets behind the beaches. The amount of air support we received was amazing. Besides the big bombers, we had high cover, medium cover, low cover, dive-bombers, and spotter aircraft. Every plane had been painted with black and white lines. Not one German plane penetrated into our air space during daylight hours.

We had several battles with our corps, V Corps. This landing would be our third. We made the invasions of Africa and Sicily. During the invasion of Africa we did not get our artillery until nearly two days after we landed. During the invasion of Sicily we put our 105mm howitzers on top of a DUKW [amphibious truck]. Some also had a derrick that would unload the howitzers. The DUKW would act as a prime mover until the two- and two-and-a-half-ton trucks unloaded. As a result we had artillery support almost immediately. V Corps personnel objected with no apparent reason, probably because they did not think of it. After quite a long battle, we won. There was another battle that we did not win but also involved SHAEF. Just a few weeks before we began to assemble for the invasion, they told us that the map distribution would be by units, rather than use our method of the separation of the troops to camps ready for loading. We had used this method for both practice invasions. What we wanted to know was, wouldn't it be a lot easier to shuffle some maps rather than 40,000-plus troops? We had done it twice our way. Where were they when we put together the Fabius and Fox exercises? We lost. Because many troops had been briefed, we feared a break in security. We knew that a great effort was being made to determine where we would land. We did not have any empty trucks to move our foot troops. We went into a marathon with only coffee to keep us awake. We had great help from the English and American service organizations. We finally came up with a solution. After all the troops had been briefed, we started the foot soldiers marching to their new camp at midnight after all the pubs had been closed. Some had to march as far as fifteen miles. When they arrived they were served a hot breakfast. Those going by vehicle would either have a hot meal before they started or shortly after they arrived at their loading camp. Obviously, the timing of the transport movements had to be phased to avoid overcrowding the road net. We also had to be sure that there were available hands when the vehicles arrived. The entire move only took eighteen hours.

We were now ready for loading. When a craft or ship docked, we would send word to the one camp where the contingent was assigned. This was completed without a hitch.

We had originally planned for D-Day to be June 4. A severe storm came up and the attack was postponed for twenty-four hours. The storm did not abate the next day so the attack was postponed again until June 6. We knew that any further postponement would have to be a fortnight since the tides would be at the lowest point in the early morning. We were greatly concerned about the condition of our soldiers who were bobbing around in the rough sea in Weymouth Harbor. We were also concerned that German air might pick us up and send submarines to stop us before we started. They did not come, and on June 5 we set sail. The Channel was rough but we were glad we had started.

Omaha Beach was cut into two pieces. The 1st Division elements were on the left with the 16th Infantry leading off. The 29th Division elements were on the right with the 116th leading off. We realized right from the start that there were a lot more Germans defending the beach than our intelligence had indicated. We did not know at that time that the German 352nd Division had moved up the night before for a practice. When they woke up in the morning they could not believe their eyes. They were seeing the largest fleet ever assembled, with the ominous barrage balloons flying above many of the ships. It made the landing extremely tough, but the Germans were destroyed on the beach. Since they were the counterattack force for that sector, after the landing we quickly moved deep into France as far as Caumont.

When the attack started, the command post for the entire landing force, 1st Division Headquarters, was on the USS *Ancon*, a beautiful ship designed for an excellent command post to command a landing. There was one big problem that morning. We simply were not getting enough messages to know what was going on.

Our advance command post did send a message to stop sending anything further to the 29th Division beaches. We were concerned that we might cut off some vital equipment that the 29th might need. Furthermore, there was no easy way to change our plans, for we had no communication with the LCTs and the LSTs [landing ship, tank]. We had radio silence with the big ships until H hour. We were able to communicate after that time, but a landing operation was so immense that it was quite rigid. We were able to divert the 115th (the reserve regiment of the 29th Division) to the beaches where the 1st Division had broken through. They were ordered to attack the rear of the fortifications holding their division on the beaches. Unfortunately, some mortar positions targeted on their beaches were firing napalm. They were burning up a lot of personnel and vehicles. That division never got many compliments, but in spite of having had no previous combat they did a great job. Our division had fought in Algeria, Tunisia, and Sicily. It makes a tremendous difference.

The Ranger battalions did a marvelous job climbing the cliffs. They were opposed and suffered heavy casualties. The real final blow was when they got to the top and found that there was no big gun. The Germans had obviously moved it, but had surely made it look as though a gun was there.

We were victorious, but we paid dearly with the lives of our close friends and associates. There are a lot of U.S. cemeteries in France, but one of the largest and most beautiful is the one close to Omaha Beach.

Harry Parley (U.S. Army)

To increase the manpower available to the 1st Infantry Division in its intended seizure of Omaha Beach, the 116th Infantry Regiment was detached from the 29th Infantry Division to serve alongside it. Harry Parley went into Omaha Beach with the 116th.

As a private first class of the 29th Division, 116th Regiment, 2nd Battalion, E Company, I came ashore on Omaha Beach on D-Day with the first wave of the assault troops as a flame thrower.

There was some humor to being a flame thrower. While waiting to be loaded onto the ships at dockside, I would often light a cigarette using the flame thrower. Let me explain. Being experienced with my weapon, I, of course, knew all the safety factors. I could, without triggering the propelling mechanism, light a cigarette by simply producing a small flame at the mouth of the gun. In doing so, it produced the same hissing sound as when the thrower was actually being fired. Anyhow, when my team would hear the terrifying sound, I would immediately be the only one on the dock. They later retaliated by hitting me with whatever they could find.

Our point of embarkation for the Channel and, of course, for the actual invasion was the Port of Plymouth. Before these embarkations, we would be transported from Bridestowe to some staging area close to the Channel where we would make ready for action, write our letters, care for our equipment, et cetera. While in these staging areas, and a day or two before embarkation, I would be notified to carry my flame thrower to some central point where the large drums of petroleum had been delivered, and there we would pump, by hand, the necessary liquid to fill our tanks. The liquid used in the flame thrower had always been pinkish red in color, with a consistency similar to warm or hot Jello. As we made ready for what we thought would be just another practice run, and as I filled my tanks, I saw that the liquid was not the usual Jello-like substance. What I was pumping was a mucous-like liquid both in color and consistency. I realized that morning that we would not return to Bridestowe. The invasion was on.

Onboard the troopship *Thomas Jefferson*, loaded with personnel, landing craft, and equipment, time was spent in quiet conversation and contemplation. Humor was infrequent and somewhat forced. My thoughts were of home and family and, of course, what we were about to experience. It saddened me to think of what would happen to some of my fellow GIs, whom I had grown to love. I recall a quiet talk with my Lieutenant Ferguson one evening. He had asked my feelings about facing death, and we exchanged philosophies. I did not envy him his position. He had come to know the men quite intimately as a result of having had to read and censor our outgoing mail. The loss of any of his men would be a two-fold tragedy for him. I've often wondered if he had discussed death with the other men. I never found out. The lieutenant was killed on the beach.

The first-wave E Company consisted of six landing craft, each with an assault team of thirty men. Each team was a complete fighting unit: automatic weapons, riflemen, flame thrower, demolitions, et cetera. Historians are well aware that each man, in addition to his regular weapons, was burdened with extra equipment that in many cases was equal to his own weight and more: satchel charges, Bangalore torpedoes, communication equipment, reels of telephone wire, extra ammunition, cumbersome life belts, and such. Even our uniforms had additional weight. We wore traditional OD [olive drab] clothing that had been impregnated with an anti-gas substance, which, in my opinion, doubled its weight. I carried a pistol, holster, shovel, self-inflating life belt around the waist, raincoat, canteen, block of dynamite, and, of course, the eighty-pound flame thrower.

Leaving the transport was accomplished in two ways. Some of the landing craft were lowered into the Channel empty, and the men then climbed down the rope nets into the boats. Other boats were loaded on deck and then lowered into the water. I was lucky enough to be in one of the latter. I don't believe I could have made it down the ropes carrying the flame thrower with the boat below tossing up and down against the ship in the rough Channel. I never found out how the other flame throwers made it while climbing down the nets. I never found one to ask. I was the only flame thrower to come off the beach unscathed.

Once in the water in the early dawn, the boats began the endless circling, waiting for all the other boats to be lowered from nearby ships. That accomplished, the first wave would be lined up and given the signal to approach the beach. I remember as we hit the water, one of our officers lost his helmet, and we had to stay nearby until a line was thrown from above and the helmet lowered. I recall the shouting above the roar of the engines to some sailors on deck, getting them to hear our request for another helmet.

I cowered in the boat with the others as we circled, waiting for our signal to approach. The Channel was unbelievably rough that day, and many of the men in all the boats became terribly ill. Strangely enough, although I had in the past exercises become seasick on occasion, I was not affected on D-Day. By now, the enemy artillery was coming at us from shore, and as we neared the beach it became heavier, and the boats around us were being hit.

I cowered even lower in the boat, knowing that if we were hit, I didn't have a chance with the load I carried. I remember looking back and seeing the navy coxswain at the controls of our boat standing high above us completely exposed to enemy fire, doing his job as ordered. Although some of the coxswain positions were protected by waist-high armor, many coxswains were hit because they had to stand above the armor to keep sight of their landing zone.

As our boat touched sand and the ramp went down, I became a visitor to hell. Some boats on either side of us had been hit by artillery and heavy weapons. I was aware that some were burning and some were sinking. I can't recall if there were cries from the wounded. I shut everything out and concentrated on following the men in front of me down the ramp and into the water. Ahead of me was a stretch of beach at least a couple of hundred yards deep. I read the actual yardage somewhere many years ago, but I no longer remember it.

The air was thick with smoke and the roar of exploding shells. I stepped off the ramp into a deep, water-filled pocket in the sand and went under completely. With no footing whatsoever and with the weight on my back, I was unable to come up. I knew I was drowning, and made a futile attempt to unbuckle the flame thrower harness. Inadvertently, I had raised the firing arm, which is about three feet long, above my head. One of my team saw it, grabbed hold, and pulled me up out of the hole onto solid sand. Then slowly, half drowned, coughing water, and dragging my feet, I began walking toward the chaos ahead.

During that walk (I was unable to run) I got my first experience with enemy fire. Machine gun fire was hitting the beach, and as it hit the wet sand, it made a "sip sip" sound, like someone sucking on their teeth. That was new to me. Also, enemy fire had a popping sound, not at all like the bang of our rifles or machine guns. It took me a while to get used to that.

Ahead of me in the distance, as I came across the sand, I could see high bluffs rising above the beach. I knew, of course, that enemy fire was being directed down onto the beach from those bluffs, and I could see survivors of the landing already using the base of the bluffs as shelter. Due to my near drowning and exhaustion, I had fallen behind the advance. I could see some of the men running ahead of me being hit by enemy fire. I was also aware that the incoming tide was fast catching up to all of us. To this day, I don't know why I didn't dump the flame thrower and run like hell for shelter. But I didn't. And thereby hangs another tale. Months later, trying to analyze why I was able to safely walk across the beach while others running ahead were hit by automatic fire, I found a simple answer. Evidently the enemy gunners had, as a trained gunner should, directed their fire down onto the beach so that the line of advancing attackers would actually run into the beaten zone [the area between the first catch and last graze of a burst from a machine gun], and, being far behind, I was ignored as a target. In short, the burden on my back may very well have saved my life.

What I found when I finally reached the seawall at the foot of the bluffs is difficult to describe. I can only call it disorganized chaos. Men were trying to dig or scrape trenches or foxholes for protection against incoming fire; others were carrying or helping the wounded to areas of shelter. We had to crouch or crawl on all fours when moving about. To communicate, we had to shout above the din of the shelling from both sides, as well as the explosions on the beach. Most of us were in no condition to carry on. All were trying to stay alive for the moment. Behind us, other landing craft were attempting to unload their equipment and personnel in the incoming tide, and were coming under enemy fire as well.

Along the beach, I could see burning wreckage and equipment, damaged landing craft, and, of course, men trying to come off the beach. The enormity of our situation came as I realized that we had landed in the wrong beach sector, and many of the people around me were from other units and were strangers to me. What's more, the terrain before us was not what I had been trained to encounter. Years later, I was to learn that for some unexplained reason or error, most of my company's boats had come into the wrong sectors, some as much as 500 to 1,000 yards east of target. As a result, in our immediate area were elements of my battalion; men from the 16th Regiment, 1st Division; remnants of the Engineers; and others—all disorganized, all trying to stay alive. I remember removing my flame thrower and trying to dig a trench while lying down on my stomach. Failing that, I searched and found a discarded BAR to use if the occasion arose. We could see nothing above us to return the fire. We were the targets.

By now, about seven or eight in the morning, we were being urged by braver and more sensible noncoms and one or two surviving officers to get off the beach and up the bluffs to higher ground. More men from other landing craft behind us were making it across the beach and joining the congestion at the seawall. I had also learned, sadly, that both my lieutenant and my commanding officer, among others, had been killed. Without proper leadership and under the disorganized conditions, it would be some time before enough courage returned for us to attempt movement up the slopes and off the beach. Scared, worried, and often praying, I had been busy helping some of the wounded. Most of the time, moving in a crouched position, a few of us helped move the helpless to secure areas. One or two times, I was able to control my fear enough to race across the sand to drag a helpless GI from drowning in the incoming tide. That was the extent of my bravery that morning.

By now, clear thinking was replacing some of our fear, and many of us accepted the fact that we had to get off the beach or die where we were. Word was passed that a small draw providing access up the bluff had been found and attempts were being made to blow the barbed wire with Bangalore torpedoes and find a way up through the mines. As I worked my way toward the draw, I could hear the Bangalores blow, followed by other explosions. By the time I reached the opening in the wire, I found that a few men had already gone through. I could see them picking their way up the slope. As I started up, I saw the white tape marking a safe path through the mines, and I also saw the price paid to mark that path for us. One or two GIs had been blown to death, and another, still alive, was being attended to. As I passed, I could see that both his legs were gone, and tourniquets were being applied by a medic. In the weeks that followed, I was to see much worse, but that particular memory remains with me still.

Anyhow, before I could reach the top, word was shouted that we were to come back down because the navy was about to shell the area above us. Evidently, a navy observation team had made it onto the beach and had established communication. For some unexplainable reason, we didn't come all the way down. Maybe it was the fear of triggering some undetected mine. I remember foolishly standing about forty feet below the top of the bluff and watching in amazement the power and accuracy of the navy fire landing just above me. It was like sitting in the very first row of a movie looking up at the screen. I could even look back across the water and see the ship firing its guns. I think it was the USS *Augusta*. The shelling ceased in about fifteen to twenty minutes and we continued our climb to the top. During the delay, I had traded my BAR with another GI for an M1 rifle and extra ammunition. He wanted more firepower and I wanted less weight to carry.

Finally reaching the top, I found an area entirely devoid of vegetation, marked by shell craters and covered by a maze of trenches, dugouts, and firing positions used by the Germans earlier in the morning. Also, I saw the enemy for the first time. Two German prisoners, hands on head, were being passed back down the slope. I recall two things about them. One, they were smiling, and two, they looked more like

Asians or Orientals, not at all like Caucasians. Word reached us later that they actually were Orientals who had been forced into the military. I guess that explains why they were happy to be captured.

A few of us spent a brief period carefully examining the dugouts, hoping to flush out more of the enemy, but without success. The Germans had apparently withdrawn from the area, and we could already hear the sounds of combat reaching us from inland. By this time, which was between eleven in the morning and noon, it had become a hot summer's day and we were on our own—a mixed bag of GIs from different outfits, one or two noncoms, and no officers. We knew we had to leave the area because common sense told us that the Germans would be shelling the bluffs and possibly even mounting a counterattack. It was decided to separate into groups and move forward in different directions, hoping to "hang in" and stay alive until more people came up from the beach.

I am unable to recall chronologically what happened to me from noon almost through the end of June 6. The rest of the day is a jumbled memory of running, fighting, and hiding. We moved like a small band of outlaws, much of the time not knowing where we were, often meeting other groups like ours, joining and separating as situations arose, always asking for news of one's company or battalion.

My particular group consisted of four or five men from my company, one of them a capable noncom, and a few riflemen from the 16th Infantry of the 1st Division. I recall that during one brief firefight we were joined by a small band of paratroopers, British infantrymen, and a few referring to themselves as commandos. They went their own way after a while, and so it went all day.

I remember one time earlier in the afternoon, while moving along a road, suddenly coming under fire from some sort of artillery piece around the bend. I could also hear the clank of a track vehicle and realized that it was a tank or half-track of some kind. Terrified, I turned, ran like hell, and dove into a deep covered roadside ditch, characteristic of that French countryside. Already in there was a tough old sergeant from the 1st Division lying on his side as one would relax on a sofa. Knowing that the 1st Division was combat experienced, I screamed at him, "I think it's a tank. What the hell can we do now?" He stared calmly at me for a few seconds, poker faced, and said, "Relax, kid, maybe it will go away." And sure enough, it did go away.

The last hours of June 6 are quite vivid in my memory. As darkness came, we found ourselves in a hedgerow-enclosed field. Dirty, hungry, and dog tired, and with no idea as to where we were, it was decided to dig in for the night. We could hear the far-off sound of artillery and even see the path of tracer fire arcing in the distance. We knew someone was catching hell. As we spread out around the field, I found myself paired off with my sergeant. However, the foxhole we started was never completed. The ground was rock hard and we were both totally exhausted by the time the hole was about three inches deep. Finally, standing there in the dark, aware that it was useless to continue, my sergeant said, "Fuck it, Parley. Let's just get down and get some rest." And so, D Day came to an end with both of us sitting back to back in the shallow trench throughout the night.

Robert E. Adams (U.S. Coast Guard)

The U.S. Coast Guard played an extremely important role in operating a large number of naval vessels and smaller boats that delivered the 1st Infantry Division to Omaha Beach. Robert Adams was in the vanguard of that ship-to-shore movement.

AT THE TIME OF THE NORMANDY INVASION, I was twenty-five years old and was assigned to the U.S. Coast Guard. I was aboard the USS *Samuel Chase*, APA 26, as a boat coxswain of LCVP [landing craft, vehicle, personnel] #22.

Prior to Normandy, our boat division and I had participated in landings at Gela, Sicily, and Salerno, Italy, so we were a fairly experienced group. We had often talked among the boat crew about the big invasion and what would be expected, and of course we feared all types of German aircraft because we had experienced that in other invasions, so we really didn't think our chances were going to be all that great, when and if the time came.

Over in Weymouth, England, several days prior to the Normandy invasion, our boat division and key officers and noncoms of the 1st Division—we had the Big Red One onboard our ship—were taken to a church or a school, and there, laid out on several long tables, were topographic layout maps of the Omaha Beach area. As I remember, we were close to Colleville and a town called Port en Bessin. This particular topographic layout showed the valleys and the rivers and the towns, hopefully as they would actually appear to us as we approached the beach.

We were given detailed information about the support effort that we would have. We were told how many battle-wagons, cruisers, and destroyers. We were told how we would bomb the German positions prior to the landing. As I remember, thousands of ships were to be involved. We were told that all these ships would participate in this particular armada, as they called it, and I guess it was really an armada at that time. Most important to us in the boats, our group was told that we would be the sixth wave. My memory may be faulty here, but we were not the assault wave. We were a wave that most of us guys in the boat felt was going to be a comfortable deal.

After listening to all we would have to support us, mentally we went into this operation with more confidence than we ever had in the other invasions that we had participated in, because I remember we were saying, "Hey, man, this will be a breeze. Be no problem at all."

Before I relate my personal experiences during the invasion, I think it's worthwhile to describe the soldier-sailor relationship aboard the ship. The soldiers were always short visitors before any operation. All of the ship's crew had great respect for the soldiers we carried, but those of us in the boat division, the ones who put these people ashore on enemy-held beaches, really knew partly by experience what they would have to go through, so naturally our respect and concern ran a lot deeper.

Again, as in Italy, we hosted the Big Red One Division, and many of us became good friends prior to the Sicily invasion. Now the division was back again, but mostly replacements by this time. The stay was so short that we were unable to develop any real friendships. Nevertheless, we were proud to have the 1st Division aboard. We all prayed for our safety.

Now, back to the invasion. On June 5, in the late afternoon, when we got out of the harbor, we formed up in a convoy. As far as the eye could see were all kinds of ships on both sides of us. I can't recall whether or not we saw any gliders, but there was wave after wave of bombers overhead. At that particular moment, I believe it was the captain of our ship, over the public address system, who read General Eisenhower's message to all of the people who were going to participate in the invasion, and I can tell you, it was a great moment. Goose pimples came out on almost everybody who listened.

That evening went on without incident as we sailed toward the Normandy beach. All I can remember is that while we were sitting around, we'd say, "What will that first Kraut or that first German think when he looks out and he sees all of us, all of these ships? What on earth are they going to think?"

On June 6 at 5:00 a.m. or thereabouts, we dressed, and those of us who had not already written home did then—the last-minute note as to whether or not you were going to make it.

We had three members and an officer on one of the lead boats. An officer was required. I had probably twenty-five to thirty soldiers in my boat. I do remember that all the soldiers had condoms over the muzzles of their guns and metal equipment; we thought that was pretty funny.

When we reached the point of our debarkation, practically all of these ships were approximately twelve miles from the beach. The first thing I noticed when we got down in the water was the rough sea, and I recall I was well dressed for it. I had good foul weather gear, and so did my crew.

I was thinking to myself, my God, these soldiers will all be seasick before we get them to the beach. Whose side was God on anyway? Ten miles of rough seas, and in our position as a coxswain we were standing, steering the boat. Everyone else was down except the officer and one crew member. We were searching for land and the landmarks that we were told we could see. I don't know how close we were to the beach when we saw the haze and smoke, and we could smell the cordite. It was like going into a new world. A few of our soldiers were seasick, and I suspect that they were anxious to get out of the boat.

As I recall, we went with our usual procedure. We moved in a circle routine, and then broke off into a line, what we called a line of departure, and commenced directly to the beach. I don't recall any German 88 shells, and we knew that noise only too well. We could hear the chatter of what had to be machine guns, and then other types of mortar fire. We were now getting ready to hit the beach. There is almost always a sandbar out from any beach, and our routine was to cut the motor for a second and let our backwash carry us over. I must have unconsciously done this because I was able to get my boat right up to the edge of the beach.

At this time, all was confusion, and it seemed like all hell was breaking loose. In coming in, we chose not to get too close to our other landing craft, and that was a wise decision. We saw hedgehogs made of big telephone posts, and train rails in a tripod formation, placed so that if we came in at high tide, they would damage or rupture our boat. I've always thought that we came in on an ebb tide, an outgoing tide. I read someplace where that was not the case, but I really think it was.

As I recall, the time was between 8 and 9 a.m. because even though we were supposed to have been the sixth wave, we ended up being a much earlier wave than that. There was one ship whose boats just didn't go in; whether they were inexperienced or what, they were circling around and evidently thought the conditions should be a lot better, but by God we did plow in.

We had to maneuver between obstacles to get to the beach, and I recall that the army had an amphibious vehicle that we called "ducks" but was spelled DUKWs. They were a disaster. Already I could see bodies of soldiers with their rumps sticking out of the water because their life belt was just a belt around their waist and not their chest. Obviously they couldn't keep their head up when they hit deep water, so they drowned, and all the belt did was to keep their ass out of the water.

I suspect that the waves engulfed all of these army vehicles very easily, as they did not appear to be all that seaworthy. I remember seeing soldiers lying on the beach up ahead. We saw these guys fall right in front of us. When we were shown the plans earlier in the church, we were told that soldiers were expected to be in about eight miles, and we could see that this was not happening. Right away we knew something was wrong. Soldiers seemed to be huddled in groups.

Our ramp opened, and our brave group from the Big Red One bounded out. I recall looking to my left and seeing two soldiers holding up another between them, and they were yelling words of encouragement. The third man looked half drowned. I suspected he had escaped from one of those sunken army ducks.

About the maneuvering of an LCVP boat, when you hit the beach, you keep your boat in forward gear at low speed because you must keep enough steerage so your boat will be perpendicular to the beach, particularly at Normandy where the high waves were washing in behind you. If your boat got just a wee bit broadside, you would be broached—in other words, washed up sideways on the beach. Too much forward motion was touchy because the tide, in my opinion, was out-going, and if you didn't broach, you could end up high and dry on the beach. Backing the LCVP away from the beach could be just as perilous. You had to keep your boat as straight as possible, perpendicular to the beach, as you backed up. If you went just a little bit sideways, you stood an excellent chance of being washed up on the beach.

Fortunately for me and my crew, I backed out without mishap. While doing so, I saw something I will remember all my life: my boat grazed a telephone post placed by the Germans as a hazard, and on top of it—I could almost reach out and touch it—was a teller mine. It could have blown us all to bits.

So our first landing was successful. Our orders then were to seek out any support boat and take whatever directions they gave us. We approached a support boat and picked up a one-star general and about four or five people on his staff, officers, and a couple of sergeants. And I recall he said to me, "Son, how is it on the beach?" And I guess at this time we were a couple of hundred yards off the beach, and I responded, "Pretty hot, sir." And he said, "Well, take us in as close as you can." I remember as a kid reading cowboy and Indian stories as to how the enemy, whichever side, liked to kill the leader, the man in control, usually obvious by his insignia or whatever. I kept thinking, here I've got a man and his helmet has one star, which I recall was white or silver. Anyway, it was extremely visible. I just kept thinking, why don't I have the guts to ask him to turn around? I'm gonna get killed just because they know he's a general and they'll try to blow this boat out of the water.

Well, neither happened. I didn't ask and we didn't get hit. I put him so close he and his group hardly got their ankles wet.

Even at this time, everything was stagnant on the beach, and we saw those poor bastards topple over—some of them not the ones we let out, but we could see it. All the noise that's going on, you just know, you're just reacting.

While we were on the beach, we were summoned by an army provost marshal to take three men on stretchers back to our ship and two or three others who were standing but evidently shell shocked, because they were like dead guys. They were walking, but they didn't say anything. The order to go back to the ship was received by all, but for the three of us in the crew it was "boy, how lucky can you get."

The seas were still rough, but we made it back to our ship. We had an electromagnetic compass, so we did have a course to steer. The ship was a different world. The gun crews were relaxed, some drinking coffee. Not a shot had been fired. We had not seen one single Luftwaffe plane on the beach, and neither had the ship's crew. Our boat was lifted aboard. Someone took care of the men who were wounded. I think one or two had died en route to the ship.

Alongside our ship was an LCI [landing craft, infantry] that had received several direct hits but had somehow made it back out to the safety zone. The people on our ship were in a rescue operation. Looking down on this LCI, we saw a terrible scene—dead and wounded all over the deck.

While we were aboard, I thought we had a reprieve from the beach. How lucky to be able to return from all of that smoke and gunfire. Thirty minutes later over the public address system came the announcement: "All available boats return to Red Two beach." At least the name Red Two is what I remember, although I see where it was called Easy Red.

Earlier this morning we had a great deal of confidence heading for the Normandy beaches. Now, it seemed like this was a death sentence. How could we go back and fool around on that beach without getting shot, blown up by a mine, or simply shot?

The crew and I made our way back to what we now know as an inferno, and the next two hours are fuzzy. We took another general and some soldiers to the beach from a larger boat.

By this time, our troops had been able to break out some. The stalemate, I think, had ended by this time, but shells continued to drop around us in the water. Some but not all were 88s.

Finally we lucked out and were given some wounded soldiers to take back to our ship. The sun was out but the seas were heavy. In order to get my boat aboard the ship, a huge hook was lowered. Most LCVP boats have a metal ring at least a foot in diameter, and wire cables from the four corners of the boat meet at this ring. The object to getting aboard safely is to grab the lanyard that is attached to the ship's hook, pull it through the ring on the boat that's attached to the cables, and give a hefty pull. Then you're up and out of harm's way. The problem was, because of the wave action, the ship's hook was slack and loose in the bottom of the boat, and the next second it was ten feet above us completely out of reach. Then all of a sudden the monster metal hook started swinging back and forth like a pendulum. I recall ducking and thinking to myself, "I'm gonna get killed by a half-ton hook." Wouldn't it have been ironic to survive all that we saw on the beach, only to be killed by a hook. Obviously it didn't happen. My crew made the hook connection and we were lifted aboard.

Getting on deck, I saw a sight on the port side aft that I will never forget. Dead soldiers were stacked up like cordwood. Helmets were in a big pile. Most of these dead boys still had their boots on. It was a sight you simply had to turn away from.

In thirty minutes we were under way, headed back to England. It wasn't even dark yet. We were onboard and had a hot meal that night. To most of the crew, those not in the boats, it was almost normal routine. It was the easiest invasion they had ever been through. For myself, I was wondering how the guys in the Big Red were doing now. How many of the guys in my boat were still alive? Where in the hell would they sleep that night? Would their K rations be all wet? How many would make it through the night? Most all of us onboard the *Samuel Chase*, particularly those who had been in the boats, thought about it and prayed for our soldier comrades every night. We saw only a small piece of what they had to go through daily.

John J. Barnes (U.S. Army)

*The U.S. Navy decided that the small boats that would take
the 1st Infantry Division troops from ship to shore would start
their run twelve miles out from Omaha Beach. John Barnes
explains what a miserable experience it was.*

WE WERE GOING TO BE THE ASSAULT force as combat opened on
the northern shores of France. Our training became very
serious. We learned to attack pillboxes as a team.

I was in boat team #2 under Lt. John Clements. Out on
the moors we would practice landings from an imaginary
boat. Men would line up in three columns, ten men each. The
first three off the boat were riflemen. They would fan out
when the ramp went down and take up protective fire positions. Next came two men who carried Bangalore torpedoes,
long lengths of pipe containing dynamite. These were shoved
under barbed wire to blow a pathway. The next men were
designated as wire cutters to help further clear the gap. Then
machine gunners to cover us, and next the 60mm mortar gunners and ammo carriers. Lastly, a flame thrower team and a
dynamite team to get close to the pillbox and blow it up.

The pillboxes were huge concrete structures, two to three
feet thick with a small hole from which guns could be fired.
It was this small hole to which we were to direct our attack.
The last members of the assault team would scramble up to
the target, running the last steps, set the charge and hurl it
inside the hole, and run back, shouting, "Fire in the hole!" A
few seconds later, the dynamite would go off, and our team
would charge forward, firing and shouting success. We practiced this routine every day, over and over. Each man knew

his job. We worked together. It was different than the basic training in the United States. We took it very seriously, and the officers made it more serious when they began to set up groups of sharpshooters to freely fire at us in our dry run.

One time, one of the boys set off a charge that had a short fuse. It blew up in his face. I was glad I didn't see him. They said he still had his helmet strap down below his chin, and after that we never wore our helmet straps buckled except for parades or guard duty.

Several times, we left our battalion quarters at Ivy Bridge to go on a full dry run operation. This involved getting truck rides to marshalling areas in tent cities. We began to feel like guinea pigs. Other people were practicing feeding us, moving us about, housing us, taking care of us. For us, it seemed like fun because it broke our routine. Then we were taken down to some harbor and put on a troopship and carried out into the Channel. We spent two or three days onboard, and we always ate better there. Finally, we would climb aboard a small assault boat designed to carry thirty men and go off to the beaches. I didn't know exactly where we were practicing these operations, but they called it Slapton Sands, and I thought that was a funny name. Gradually, we learned more and more about our real target in France.

I can't remember when we first learned exactly where we were to land, or that we were to land with the 16th Regiment of the 1st Division, but we began to run into men from the Big Red One as early as March. One April day, in a very serious briefing, we were shown maps and pictures of our assault beach. It was designated Dog Green, with a draw leading up through the bluffs. The village was called

Vierville-sur-Mer. The draw was called D-1. In front was a seawall. We saw a picture of a church steeple at the head of the draw. On either side of the draw were German pillboxes and other gun emplacements. Obstacles made of steel and wire topped with mines where built along the beach, exposed at low tide and slightly visible in high tide. We were told we would land at low tide so the boats would not ram into the obstacles. However, combat engineers would land to help us clear the way. That still left 600 yards of beach to cross. The landings were scheduled for about six-thirty in the morning. In thirty minutes the tide would start coming in, and we would have to get off the beach in a hurry. We hoped that we would have no problem. Just in case, we were given a quarter pound of dynamite to blow a foxhole in the rocky shore if necessary.

Our officers showed us aerial photographs of the landscape behind the beach. We came to know every house, pillbox, trench, and crossroad like it was our own home neighborhood. We saw a road running east through several crossroads to a small town called Isigny, located on a small river. This was to be our first day's objective. We were to be on the right flank of the assault. Only the Ranger company would be on our right, landing at a point of cliffs jutting into the sea. It was called Pointe du Hoc. This was a couple of miles to our right.

It was either on a Saturday or a Sunday that we boarded the *Empire Javelin*, a small troopship, in the harbor of Weymouth. We were to sail on Sunday night and arrive off the French coast early in the morning of June 5. Sometime around five on Sunday afternoon, we learned of the postponement. We were not bothered by the delay. It just meant that more money changed hands at cards and dice.

Finally the ship began to move. We went to eat around eleven that night. About three in the morning we were called to get ready. Instead of our regular packs, we had been issued assault jackets, a vest-like garment with many pockets and pull-strap fasteners so we could yank off the vest in a hurry. In the various pockets we stored K rations, a quarter pound of dynamite with fuses, hand grenades, smoke grenades, and a medical kit (a syringe and morphine). Besides our regular M1 [rifle] clips, we had two ammo belts slung across our shoulders. In the back pockets of our jacket we carried an entrenching tool, a bayonet, a poncho, and whatever else we could stuff in. As an assistant to the flame thrower, I carried his rifle and pack. Our rifles were in a protective cellophane wrapper and an inflated tube to keep them afloat. Altogether, our equipment weighed about seventy pounds. It was an awkward assortment, around which we buckled a rubber life belt, inflated by carbon dioxide. The buckle in my belt was defective, but I didn't bother with it since it was a last-minute addition, and I had no thought of using it.

On deck, we were lined up in the boat teams. We checked one another's equipment. I don't remember any famous last words, but many men shouted to friends in other boats. I didn't. I still felt like an outsider, not knowing most of the men more than four months. Since we were going to be first to land, we were first to get off the ship. Our assault boats, which were British LCAs [landing craft, assault], were still on the deck, hung by davits. We didn't have to climb over the rope and down the ladders. We thought we were something special. We climbed aboard the LCAs and were lowered to the sea. Immediately, the boats began bobbing up and down in the high waves. It was still dark as we moved away from the ship. I could not see much around us.

We circled in a holding pattern. One by one, the men began to get sick, heaving their late-night meal over the sides or into their helmets or anywhere. Somehow, the wave motion didn't bother me. I felt the excitement of being there. Gradually, we saw the shapes of other boats—many small ones, many larger hulks—and planes droning overhead by the hundreds, flying off toward the coast. Now we could see the antiaircraft fire lighting up the sky. Tracers arced the night. The seasickness seemed to end as more men watched the glowing light of large flashes on the land. They marked the horizon as the bombs dropped from the plane. Then a flash and a mighty roar came from one of the black hulks. It was the guns of the big battleship we were just under. With dawn the sky lightened, and we could see more and more ships and more planes in the sky. We were entranced by this huge scene. Someone shouted, "Take a look! This is something you will tell your grandchildren!" No one muttered the question, "What if we don't live?" At this point, we were excited, not frightened.

As the day grew brighter, our boats stopped circling and we headed in. Large craft unleashed the massive rockets toward the beach. Smoke clouded the lower coastline, and we could just see the bluffs and, above that, the single spire of a church. We knew it was Vierville-sur-Mer. We were right on target. The LCA roared ahead, buffing the waves. Suddenly, a swirl of water wrapped around my ankles, and the front of the craft dipped down. The water quickly reached our waist, and we shouted to the other boats on our side. They waved in return. The boat fell away below me, and I squeezed the carbon dioxide tubes in my life belt. Just as I did, the belt popped away. The buckle had broken. I turned to grab the back of the man behind me as I was going under. In a panic I climbed on his back and pulled myself up. Our heads bobbed above the water. We still could see some other boats moving off to the shore. I grabbed a rifle wrapped in a flotation belt, and then a flame thrower that was floating around with two belts wrapped around it. I hugged it tight but still seemed to be going down. I was unable to keep my head above the surface. I tried to pull the release straps on my jacket, but I couldn't move. Others shouted at me. Lieutenant Gearing grabbed my jacket and, using his bayonet, cut the straps. Others helped release me from the weight. I was all right now. I could swim. We counted heads. One was missing—Padley, our radio operator. No one saw him come up. He had put the large SCR 300 radio on his back.

Across the water, we heard small rapid-fire shots. Our company in the other five boats had landed. I felt a strange sense of relief. Sergeant Laird wanted to swim toward the shore. We were roughly a thousand yards out—too far, said Lieutenant Gearing. "We'll wait and get picked up by some passing boat." But no one stopped. They were all loaded down in the water with goods passing in toward the shore. They were on their own mission and their own schedule.

Suddenly we heard a friendly shout of some limey voice in one of the LCAs, the same type that we had just been on. The boat stopped. It was empty. We were helped to climb aboard. Seven or eight of us got in one boat, three or four in another, and the rest in another. We recognized the coxswain. He was from the *Empire Javelin*. He wouldn't return to the beach. How did the others make out? He dropped them off OK. The other boat had two dead A Company men lying on the floor. One whom we recognized, Sergeant Draper, would live only a few more minutes. How about the others? He couldn't say. We went back to the troopship, the very same one we had left at four that morning. How long it had been. It seemed like just minutes. When I thought to ask, it was one in the afternoon. We had been gone nine hours, over three in the water.

Gradually, the shock wore off. What could we do? The ship seemed vacant. The British captain wanted us to get off. We had no weapons. Lieutenant Gearing told him we were going to stay onboard, go back to England. He had picked up a rifle and said he would hitch a ride in a passing U.S. craft. He ordered us to stay together. He told our sergeant to return to England, re-outfit us, and come back to the company. Sergeant Stevens, who was our NCO [noncommissioned officer] commander, had a twin brother in one of the other boats. There were two other sets of brothers, all from Bedford, Virginia.

On June 7, we landed in a secret mission in a friendly country—England. We went to "repple-depple," a replacement area. There we were re-armed and sent on our way with orders not to say anything to anybody about the action we had been in, although it was all over the papers. We traveled by civilian train to Southampton, got into a boat across the Channel, and were back in Normandy on June 12.

▲ Painted with invasion stripes on its wings and fuselage to prevent friendly fire incidents is a U.S. Air Forces Douglas C-47 Skytrain transport plane at a base in England prior to the invasion of France. Powered by two radial piston engines, the aircraft could carry up to twenty-seven passengers. *National World War II Museum*

▼ U.S. Army paratroopers board a C-47 Skytrain transport plane prior to their night drop over the French countryside in the early morning hours of June 6, 1944. The men who dropped into France came from the 82nd and 101st Airborne divisions. *National World War II Museum*

◀ Pictured within the fuselage of a Douglas C-47 Skytrain transport plane are two rows of U.S. Army paratroopers. The six regiments of the two airborne divisions that dropped into France on June 6, 1944, numbered over 13,000 men. *National World War II Museum*

▶ The most feared weapon faced by the American paratroopers who dropped into France on June 6, 1944, were German machine guns like the MG42 seen here with its crew. The guns had an incredible rate of fire of up to 1,500 rounds per minute. *National Archives*

▲ Although the standard U.S. Army infantryman of World War II was rarely equipped with the Thompson submachine gun, officially referred to as the Thompson M1 or M1A1, paratrooper units were supplied with a great number of them. *National Archives*

▶ The paratroopers who dropped into France on June 6, 1944, suffered terrible losses, as is evident from this picture of dead American paratroopers. Despite these losses, the paratroopers succeeded in clearing the way for the Allied seaborne forces to move inland. *National World War II Museum*

◀ U.S. Army general Dwight D. Eisenhower was the overall commander of Operation Overlord, the invasion of France. His official title was Supreme Commander Allied Expeditionary Force (SHAEF). Eisenhower is seen here posed in front of a large map of France. *National World War II Museum*

▶ Although many of the German military units engaged in battle by the Allied forces during the early stages of Operation Overload were considered of poor quality, other units, such as the German paratroopers, seen here, were first-class soldiers. *National World War II Museum*

◀ While Allied paratroopers were to be dropped over France in the early morning darkness of June 6, 1944, their glider reinforcements would be brought in at dawn and again at dusk. Pictured are C-47 Skytrain transport planes towing gliders toward France. *National World War II Museum*

◀ This U.S. Navy landing ship, tank (LST) is carrying a U.S. Navy landing craft, tank (LCT). Many of those who served or sailed on LSTs said that the initials stood for "large slow target." *National Archives*

▲ Difficult terrain and German defensive obstacles took a heavy toll on the Allied gliders that descended into France on June 6, 1944. Pictured is an overturned glider with the dead crew and passengers laid out next to it for the arrival of the graves registration personnel. *National World War II Museum*

⬆ Being loaded into the bowels of a U.S. Navy landing ship, tank (LST) through the bow ramp doors is a U.S. Army M4 series medium tank armed with a 75mm main gun. The LST could transport up to eighteen tanks, twenty-seven trucks, or 163 troops. *National Archives*

⬆ Amphibious tanks were needed to provide firepower support to the initial assault. The duplex drive (DD) tanks were Shermans modified with a flotation device consisting of a collapsible rubberized canvas screen, and a system of gears and shafts to power two propellers. *Patton Museum of Cavalry and Armor*

⬆ The DD Shermans could not fire their weapons while in the water, but the flotation screen could be dropped rapidly when the tank reached the beach. Visible are the two propellers connected to the tank's tracks that could push it through the water at five to six miles per hour. *Patton Museum of Cavalry and Armor*

▲ One of the German military counterparts to the M4 series of medium tanks employed by the Allied armies in large number was the Panzer IV medium tank, armed with a high-velocity 75mm main gun. German factories built about 9,000 units of the Panzer IV between 1936 and 1945. *Patton Museum of Cavalry and Armor*

◀ The most potent medium tank employed by the German military in France in June 1944 was the well-known Panther tank. About 6,600 of them were built by German factories between 1942 and 1945. The top speed of the tank was twenty-nine miles per hour. *Patton Museum of Cavalry and Armor*

◀ The landing craft, infantry (LCI) was built in the United States to a British design. It could carry up to 210 infantrymen directly up to a beach to unload them by way of gangways mounted on either side of the bow. *National Archives*

▲ Designed to land a single tank or wheeled vehicles of varying sizes and weights directly on a beach was the landing craft, mechanized (LCM). When used as a troop carrier, the LCM could carry up to sixty passengers. *National Archives*

▲ U.S. Army infantrymen enter a landing craft, vehicle, personnel (LCVP), also popularly known as a Higgins boat because it was designed by Andrew Higgins and built in large numbers by Higgins Industries of Louisiana. The craft could carry thirty-six passengers. *National World War II Museum*

◀ Besides troops, the landing craft, vehicle, personnel (LCVP) could carry a single wheeled vehicle weighing up to 6,000 pounds, or 8,100 pounds of general cargo. Power came from a single gasoline or diesel engine. *National Archives*

▶ This photograph was taken onboard a landing craft, vehicle, personnel (LCVP) heading toward Omaha Beach on June 6, 1944. The LCVP was 36 feet 3 inches long and had a beam of 10 feet 10 inches. Armament consisted of two .30-caliber machine guns. *National World War II Museum*

◀ Field Marshal Erwin Rommel, the famed desert tactician, was appointed by Hitler as commander of Army Group B in January 1944. Under his command the German defenses along the French coast facing England were greatly improved. His appointment also proved a morale boost for the German defenders. *National World War II Museum*

▲ The DUKW seen here carrying a 105mm towed howitzer was popularly referred to by its nickname, "duck," and was a version of the standard American-built GMC 6x6 truck, converted to an amphibious vehicle. Rough seas took a heavy toll on DUKWs on June 6, 1944. *National Archives*

▲ Visible from an Allied plane flying low over the French invasion beaches are some of the beach obstacles installed by the German military to deter Allied landing craft from coming ashore. Many of these obstacles had mines attached. *National World War II Museum*

▶ A Rhino ferry operated by members of the U.S. Navy's construction battalions, known as Seabees, heads toward the French shore. The ferries consisted of steel pontoons lashed together to form a floating barge and were conceived and constructed by the Seabees. *National World War II Museum*

⬆ Some of the German defensive emplacements along the Allied invasion beach sites did not face out to sea, as seen in this photograph, but were designed to fire down the length of a beach in conjunction with other defensive positions to catch invading forces in a deadly crossfire. *National World War II Museum*

⬆ The German media referred to their defensive positions facing England by a number of names, which included the Atlantic Wall, Fortress Europe, and the Steel Coast. Guns such as the captured one pictured were capable of sinking ships and posed a serious threat to the Allied invasion fleet. *National World War II Museum*

⬆ German defensive positions along the French coast in the summer of 1944 ranged from a single machine gun to massive 14-inch guns, as seen here, capable of firing projectiles weighing almost a ton out to a range of up to twenty miles. *National Archives*

▲ One of the most deadly and feared German weapons of World War II was the series of 88mm guns (nicknamed the "88" by Allied soldiers). The version pictured was a towed antitank gun designated the PaK 43/41. It was the same gun mounted in the Tiger B heavy tank. *Michael Green*

◀ Among the numerous types of beach defensive fortifications encountered by the Allied troops that invaded France on June 6, 1944, were the turrets of obsolete tanks fitted on top of underground concrete bunkers. Although most were from captured French tanks, the turret pictured is German. *National World War II Museum*

▶ American soldiers examine a captured German 105mm artillery piece. The German designation was 10cm K18. The standard medium gun for the German army, it had a maximum range of 20,850 yards. The barrel was almost 18 feet long.
National Archives

◀ British general Sir Bernard L. Montgomery served under American general Dwight Eisenhower as the ground commander of the Allied assault on the Normandy beaches. Montgomery rose to fame as commander of Allied forces fighting the Germans in North Africa in 1942–43. *National World War II Museum*

▶ On display at a U.S. Army base is this collection of German antitank and antipersonnel mines and grenades used to educate American soldiers about what they would encounter on the ground in France. The Germans emplaced hundreds of thousands of mines to deter an invasion of France. *National Archives*

▶ The standard infantry rifle for the U.S. Army in World War II was the M1 Garand. Fully loaded, the M1 held eight rounds secured in a metal clip that was loaded as a single unit into the top of the weapon's receiver. The empty clip ejected with the last empty cartridge. *National Archives*

▲ The famous Browning automatic rifle (BAR) used by the U.S. Army in World War II was a twenty-pound gas-operated weapon with a twenty-round detachable box magazine that inserted into the bottom of the weapon's receiver. It could fire in semiautomatic or full-automatic mode. *U.S. Army*

▲ A prototype of the American Martin B-26 Marauder medium bomber in flight. This seven-seat aircraft was powered by two 2,000-horsepower radial piston engines, which allowed it to fly at a speed of up to 317 miles per hour at 14,500 feet. Maximum bomb load was 5,200 pounds. *National Archives*

▲ An American soldier poses with the standard German military bolt-action rifle of World War II referred to as the Karabine 98k, which weighed 8.6 pounds and fired a 7.92mm round. It had an internal five-round box magazine. *National Archives*

▶ Pictured flying over the Normandy beaches is a U.S. Army Air Forces B-17 heavy four-engine bomber, which had a crew of ten and a service ceiling of 35,600 feet. The aircraft could carry a bomb load of 6,000 pounds up to 2,000 miles. *National World War II Museum*

▲ The American Lockheed P-38 Lightning was a single-seat fighter that could also operate as a fighter-bomber. It was decided that its hard-to-mistake outline, due to its unusual twin-boom layout, meant it was unlikely to be shot at by those in the invasion fleet on June 6, 1944, as it flew air cover. *National Archives*

▶ Sitting on an airfield is a Republic single-seat P-47 Thunderbolt fighter, which also performed in the ground attack role with great success. Power for the aircraft came from a 2,300-

horsepower radial piston engine, which gave it a top speed of 428 miles per hour. *National Archives*

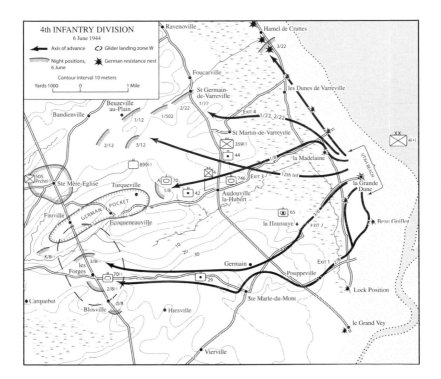

Map One:
⬆ This map shows the territory occupied by Hitler's Third Reich on
June 6, 1944, with an arrow pointing to the location of the Allied
seaborne invasion of Normandy, in northwestern France. The Red
Army had almost completely pushed the German military out of the
Soviet Union by this time, and half of the Italian boot had been freed
by the armies of the advancing western Allies.

Murmansk

NORWAY

SWEDEN

FINLAND

Leningrad

North
Sea

ESTONIA

Baltic Sea

LATVIA

Moscow

EIRE

DENMARK

LITHUANIA

Smolensk

U.S.S.R.

GREAT
BRITAIN

NETHERLANDS

GERMANY

POLAND

BELG.

ATLANTIC
OCEAN

FRANCE

CZECHOSLOVAKIA

SWITZ.

AUSTRIA

HUNGARY

Odessa

PORTUGAL

SPAIN

ITALY

YUGOSLAVIA

ROMANIA

Black
Sea

Rome

BULGARIA

ALBANIA

SPANISH MOROCCO

Mediterranean Sea

GREECE

TURKEY

MOROCCO

ALGERIA

TUNISIA

Map Two:
▲ A detailed map showing the progress of the U.S. Army's 4th Infantry
Division, which landed on Utah Beach on June 6, 1944. Marked on the
map are the night positions on June 6 of the various units that made
up the American division as well as the location of the main German
resistance that first day of the invasion.

Donald E. Irwin (U.S. Navy)

A variety of naval vessels landed American troops of the 1st and 29th Infantry divisions on Omaha Beach. The largest vessel was the LST. Donald Irwin describes the ordeal of getting his LST onto Omaha Beach.

ON JUNE 2 OR 3, MY LCT was loaded with sixty-five U.S. troops, most of them from the U.S. Army, 29th Infantry Division, plus an assortment of bulldozers and jeeps and trailers that belonged to some ordnance and engineering outfits.

Then my executive officer, Ens. George Pilmore, and I and the army officer aboard went ashore to be briefed. We were told by a navy four-striper captain where we were going. He said not to worry; Omaha Beach was going to be heavily bombed by hundreds of bombers and shelled for one hour, right up to H hour at 6:30 a.m., by our battleships and cruisers. He said we were throwing everything at the beach but the kitchen sink, and that too. There wouldn't be enough Germans left to give us a fight. It was impressed upon us that we must get our troops off the boats immediately as soon as we hit the beach. Not to do so could screw up the invasion, and we were to order them off at gunpoint, if necessary.

Our orders were to land our troops and equipment on the Dog Red sector of Omaha Beach at 7:30 a.m., one hour after H hour at 6:30 a.m. We were in the H+60 minutes assault wave.

We left Portland Harbor with the rest of our flotilla of LCTs the morning of June 4. As we entered the English Channel, it was extremely rough. After proceeding what I would say was halfway across the Channel toward the invasion beaches, we were suddenly given orders to turn around and return to port. They said the weather was much too bad.

We tied up again at a buoy in Portland Harbor to await further orders. We were now a sealed ship, and only the skippers of the ships were allowed ashore.

Then the new orders came. We were to leave at 3:30 a.m. on June 5 and proceed to Omaha Beach.

Outside of the sea being fairly rough and soldiers getting seasick, the trip across the English Channel was quite uneventful. As I recall, when dawn broke, the Normandy beach lay ahead, and not much was to be seen but haze and smoke, and ships were everywhere.

But then as we headed toward the Dog Red sector of Omaha Beach, abreast of four other LCTs to make our landing at 7:30 a.m., things began to happen. I and my executive officer, Ensign Pilmore, were on the conning tower. The crew was, of course, at battle stations. We were so heavily attired that even with life jackets I feared we would go straight to the bottom if the ship sank. I recall in addition to my life jacket and helmet I had on navy foul weather gear and, on top of that, impregnated clothing as a protection against poison gas that the Germans might use. In addition, I had my gas mask, a .45 pistol on my belt, and a pair of binoculars around my neck. As we headed toward the beach, the most earsplitting, deafening, horrendous sound I have ever heard or probably will ever hear took place. It was the guns of the battleship USS *Texas* firing over our heads and into the beach. As I glanced back over my shoulder, it looked as if the *Texas*'s giant 14-inch guns were pointed right at us, but of course they weren't. Their trajectory to reach their targets on the beach was so flat that it just looked that way. Then I recall thinking, as we stood on the conning tower and I directed U.S. LCT 614 toward the beach, how tranquil it seemed heading in. Only a few shells zipped by overhead. Perhaps the U.S. Navy officer who briefed us shortly before we left Portland Harbor, England, was right when he said, "There won't be any Germans left to bother you guys when you hit the beach."

But things did change, and how. As we approached the beach, when we were still quite a distance out, the sea seemed to get much rougher. There were five- to six-foot waves, and the current was getting much stronger as the tide was coming in real fast. I attempted to get close enough to the beach so I could drop my ramp and get the sixty-five troops and equipment ashore in relatively shallow water. I had already dropped my anchor to have help pulling away from the beach.

As I tried to get in close, I remember seeing the water starting to splash ahead, and I thought that the battleship firing behind us was firing short. But no such thing. The Germans had started to open up with 88mm guns and mortars.

We finally dropped the ramp to get our troops and equipment off, and then all hell did break loose. We came under intense fire, as did the LCTs to the right and left of us. Most of the fire seemed to be rifle, machine gun, and mortar fire. But I found I still couldn't get the soldiers and equipment off because the water was still too deep. We spent about an hour trying to get our landing craft closer to the beach. Then, as I recall, a couple of bulldozers were driven off our ramp in pretty deep water. They did reach the shore, only to be blasted by German gunners with phosphorus shells, which started them burning.

Then some of the soldiers, with a couple of the commissioned officers leading, took off from the ramp in water up to their armpits with rifles held high over their heads and headed for shore. Then a series of things happened, and I saw sights I'll never forget. Two of the soldiers got shot just as they stepped off the ramp. They were quickly pulled back onboard the ship. One was shot in the back, but it appeared to be a grazing wound and not serious. The other was shot in the stomach, a more serious wound. I recall a bullet just missing a rifle grenade on his belt. Had it hit the grenade, it would probably have blown him to bits.

The German shellfire grew so intense that I and a member of my crew stood behind the chart house for protection. I remember suddenly seeing him reel and start to fall, and blood was coming from beneath his eye. I caught him before he hit the deck, thinking, of course, that he was fatally wounded. He regained consciousness shortly, and after the flow of blood was stemmed he seemed to be in pretty good shape. Apparently a piece of shrapnel from a mortar round or an 88mm cannon had sliced him as neatly as a knife, and the impact caused him to lose consciousness. He refused to leave the ship and his crewmates and go aboard a hospital ship. The wound healed in time, and he fully recovered.

But now, with soldiers getting shot going off the ramp, I had a problem. The rest of the troops refused to leave, and I had orders that I should disembark these troops and equipment here and now. It had been stressed that failing to do so could jeopardize invasion plans, and an officer could be subject to court-martial. It was even suggested that orders were to be carried out at gunpoint if necessary. But I recall I could in no way force human beings to step off the ramp into almost certain wounding or death, because by now the situation had grown much worse. The shellfire had become even more intense, and the sea continued to get rougher. The pandemonium seemed to be everywhere, with lots of smoke and explosions. There were bodies floating in the water. It was evident that the invasion force at Omaha Beach was taking a bad beating.

Every once in a while ahead of us on the beach, we could see U.S. soldiers huddled at the base of a cliff. They weren't moving inland. The Germans were firing at them from the front, and the heavy tide was bringing the sea ever closer to them from behind. At this point, we ourselves had come under intense rifle and machine gun fire. Bullets were pinging and ricocheting off the boat. The men in my crew who were still at their battle stations and had been standing erect on our way to the beach were now flattened against the boat as if they were a part of it. I recall a couple of my crew yelling, "Skipper, let's get out of here." After an hour of trying to get my load of troops and vehicles off, believe me I was ready.

Finally, there was a reprieve. Orders came over the radio from our command ship to retract from the beach. The beach was described as being too hot from German gunfire, and our orders were to withdraw, go out into the English Channel, anchor, and await further orders. What welcome orders, but little did I know that my troubles were just beginning.

When I gave the command to raise and secure the ramp of the landing craft, I noticed what appeared to be a German mine bobbing in the water close to the end of the ramp, but the mine never quite made contact with the ramp. If it had, we never would have made it out of there.

With the ramp up and secured, we attempted to retract from the beach by winding in the anchor cable with our gasoline-engine-driven winch and backing down or reversing with the three screws or propellers on the stern of the landing craft.

At about this time, we rescued four or five sailors from drowning near our landing craft by pulling them out of the sea. They were completely fatigued and as blue from the cold water as any living human being I'd ever seen. The one thing I'll never forget is that they were so exhilarated and so very thankful at having their lives saved that they completely emptied their pockets and gave my crew everything they had in their possession, including their Colt .45 pistols. Come to find out, they had had their LCVP [landing craft, vehicle, personnel] boat blown out from under them by the Germans while they were trying to get some troops or equipment ashore. We found out later that they were from the USS *Carrol*, a navy attack transport anchored in the Channel.

As we continued to try to back away from the beach, we were suddenly stopped and found that we were hung up on a German underwater post type of obstacle. After some tense moments, we got free of the obstacle. But the process had rendered useless one of the outside screws or propellers of our LCT, so I had only two screws to operate with. We were indeed fortunate to get free from the German underwater beach obstacles, as I have since learned that, before our arrival, the demolition teams that were to land at low tide when the obstacles were exposed and blow them up had suffered 50 percent casualties and gotten very little of their assignments accomplished. They were to have blown sixteen lanes or paths, each fifty yards wide, so landing craft could get through the thickly spaced obstacles. However, only five lanes were cleared, adding to the great difficulty for landing craft attempting to get to the beach.

Another sight I'll never forget, and it might have been during the full hour that I tried to get close enough to the beach to get my troops off, was two soldiers nearby who were trying their best to survive. One man had his arms around one of the large wooden post obstacles that the Germans had driven into the beach. Hanging onto his waist was another American soldier. They were using the post as protection against the German rifle and machine gun fire that was coming at them from the beach. So accurate was this fire that the bullets were splintering the sides of the post. Adding to the perilous position of these two men was the incoming tide, which was raising the water ever higher on the post. Sooner or later, they would have no post left for protection. I often wondered if they survived.

Back to our attempt to withdraw from the beach and the most panic-stricken moments we had. Just as we had the anchor cable nearly all in, and the moment came when our large anchor should be coming into sight, the anchor wouldn't lift. It was hooked onto something, and our thoughts were: Here we were, sitting ducks for German 88mm cannon shellfire, and we could get entangled in more obstacles. Try as we might, we couldn't free the anchor. And then we tried one more way to free it. I gave the command, "All engines ahead full." This did cause the anchor to move. Soon, coming to the surface was a small landing craft that had been sunk by the Germans, and our anchor had hooked into it.

As we made a turn away from the beach with our two operable engines still ahead at full speed, the wrecked craft finally pulled free from our anchor. What a relief. We got the anchor pulled in and secured, and then headed into the English Channel, where we anchored and awaited further orders.

We still had most of our troops and equipment aboard. Finally, we got the orders around two that afternoon to proceed to the beach and attempt once more to get our troops and vehicles off. This time around, the German shelling and gunfire had been much reduced. We still had trouble getting in close enough to the beach so our troops could wade ashore and the waterproof vehicles could make it. In fact, many of the vehicles didn't. They simply drowned out in the water and stalled.

We never did get all of our troops and vehicles ashore. One U.S. sergeant I had aboard said he was sure he would lose his jeep and trailer in the water, so he chose to stay with his jeep and trailer until we beached again. But we didn't beach again on the American beaches. Not until we were at the British invasion area did he and his equipment get ashore over the beach. I often wondered how many weeks it took him to get back with his American outfit.

After our second landing attempt at Omaha Beach, with D-Day winding down and dusk coming on, my thought was where to anchor for the night, as ships of all sizes were everywhere. As I was thinking about a desirable anchor site, I saw fairly close by the huge, looming figure of one of our battleships. It was either the USS *Texas* or the USS *Arkansas*; both had assisted in the landing. You never know how tremendously huge a battleship is until you look up at it from fairly close by from an LCT.

Anyway, the thought entered my mind: what could offer more security than anchoring close to a battleship, and believe me, after what had happened in the preceding hours, we were looking for security. So, we anchored far enough away from the battleship so that when it swung on its anchor chain it wouldn't hit us, yet close enough to feel secure. It was just starting to get dark. We were all dead tired, having been in continuous operation some thirty-six hours since leaving Portland, England, plus the landing itself, which had left us all in a state of shock. I don't believe that any of us had any appetites then or probably for several days afterwards.

We had orders to proceed the next morning to the British D-Day invasion beaches that had the code names of Gold, Juno, and Sword and were around fifteen miles east of Omaha Beach. But now we just settled in for a good night's sleep. Suddenly there was a terrible explosion between our boat and the battleship. German aerial reconnaissance had spotted the battleship's anchoring place, and the German plane had passed overhead and dropped a bomb meant for the battleship. It missed the battleship but almost got us. We started the engine, raised anchor, and got out of there as fast as we could. We anchored by some smaller ships, and thereafter continued that practice. We learned an extremely valuable lesson. The enemy was after the larger ships, and we could be killed by just being an innocent bystander. The German plane, by the way, took several passes at the battleship, and the battleship, knowing it had been discovered for sure, opened fire and shot the plane down.

The next morning we proceeded as per our orders to the British Normandy invasion beaches. Only some forty-eight hours or so had elapsed, and we had experienced life-threatening action we would never forget.

Andrew A. Fellner (U.S. Army)

Unbeknownst to the American soldiers landing on Omaha Beach and those who commanded them, instead of one German division defending the beach, two divisions were in place. Andrew Fellner describes the intense resistance encountered on the landing.

ON THE MORNING OF JUNE 6, WE could hear the shelling, most of which was from our destroyers and battleships going toward the beach. Since we were belowdeck, it was difficult to tell how close we were to the beach. Without a doubt, there was true fear in us. Our LCI [landing craft, infantry] stopped and the first squad began debarking. In what seemed like a very short time, they came back belowdeck again. Most of the men were wet, and some had gone in the water and found it too deep. I'm not sure how many we lost from drowning.

Our boat used the winch to withdraw from the beach. Then we again went in. We began to debark and found the water over our heads. The tide was in, and it was a lateral tide. This made it very difficult to go toward the beach.

Equipment became wet with salt water. I remember trying to keep my head above the water, in the event of concussion from shells landing nearby.

Finally reaching the beach and gasping for air, we just fell flat on the sand. Confusion was extreme. We had been placed too far from our designated area. My weapon was effective, but it was one of the rare ones.

We crawled to the main ground and began digging. One foxhole began a community event, it seemed that this was the only way to survive. Three other men from my company and I were lying on the sand, and we noticed one stretcher with a wounded soldier. He had a stomach wound. There were many dead and wounded around us, and it seemed unusual that only one person was on a litter.

The shelling and mortar fire from the Germans were heavy, and we couldn't move. Also, rapid fire was heavy. I was lying on the sand when an officer came toward us. He was wearing a pistol, and I think he was a ranking officer.

He told us to take the stretcher to an LST [landing ship, tank] that was about fifty feet from shore. Since it seemed that none of the wounded was being removed, the request appeared to be fruitless, and that LST was quite far from shore to risk four men.

I believe we told him to go to hell. So, out comes his pistol, and he did threaten to use it. We picked up the litter and proceeded back in the water. As we neared the LST, the water was chin high for me. I was in the lead, and the man with me was about four to six inches shorter. So he was swallowing water. We managed to place the litter on the ramp of the LST, then started back. We couldn't have been more than thirty feet away when a shell struck the ramp. I'll never know whether the wounded man survived and how the men on the LST fared. To this day, I think the officer who had his pistol on us was General Cota of the 29th Division. May God bless him and the rest of them.

I noticed my watch had stopped, so time was lost. The salt water had affected my watch and ate the tripping mechanism on my lighter. A can of my K rations had a hole eaten through the metal. There were many dead and wounded at the time. I wondered how they could be identified. I saw torsos, no arms, no head, no legs. Some floated to the beaches bleached white from the salt water. Boats were being blown out of the water. A shell struck an LST, and it burned throughout the night. A battleship that was burning broadside came up to the beach. I remember at one time feeling a warm sensation going down my leg and thought that this was a case of fear. After reaching inside my trousers, I scratched my hand on a shell fragment. A second fragment hit me in the same area, but this one was hot, so I knew what it was.

During the day, we noticed that our boats were backing up. This brought concern that they were possibly giving up on this beach. Fortunately, this didn't happen. At one time during the day when the tide had receded and there appeared to be a long stretch of sand, men came off the assault boats. Some were carrying duffel bags. That seemed funny, but it wasn't. They were picked off like flies. Twenty men came off one boat, and I counted sixteen of them hit by rifle fire. Whoever was in charge must have thought we had gone inland and the beach was secured. We were screaming for them to take cover, but the noise made it impossible for them to hear.

Early in the day, we lost one of our men who had entered the service at a very young age. No name from me, please. Apparently, he had been consumed by uncontrollable fear and started running up and down the beach. A bullet killed him. I know that fear was with most of us, but after a while we accepted our lot. Show me an atheist, and I'll show you a person who hasn't seen sure death looking at him.

We began a slow entry on the mainland starting with units of the 29th Division. But getting to the high ground was difficult. Some prisoners were taken during the day, and that's when I got an Austrian rifle, which was very accurate. My M1 had become fouled with sand. We had to improvise.

My memory of this day becomes shorter and shorter, even though the day was a long one. I never could understand why the Germans didn't counterattack us early in the day. Had they, I wouldn't be making this tape. During the night, we were bombed and strafed by JU-88s, but, believe it or not, a guy named Dave and I were able to sleep a little bit that night.

Elmer Seed (U.S. Army)

The Germans had heavily fortified Omaha Beach in the months before the Allied invasion of Normandy. Elmer Seed describes some of the obstacles he had to deal with before being wounded on Omaha.

AT 1000 HOURS ON JUNE 6, OUR unit was aboard an LCI along with other men we didn't know. We were tossed about quite a lot because an LCI drives in about five feet of water and just sort of floats on the top. That's what I'm told about it, anyway.

But it didn't seem that way while we were in it. The sea was very, very rough. Most men were seasick and couldn't keep their food down. What we ate, I just don't remember, but I know we ate.

The ship was tossed about like a cork in a clothes washing machine. I was on deck most of the time, holding on for dear life. Before going up, I talked to different men, and each one had his own idea about what he would do once he got out, or if he got out, or if we made it, or whatever might happen. I told a friend of mine, "I'm so disgusted, this is my third invasion already, and it's like I'm playing baseball, three strikes and you're out." I wondered if I was going to make it, so I said, "I just wish they could take my right leg from the knee on down, just to send me home." It's a good thing the good Lord wasn't listening, because he didn't answer my prayers. He just gave me a scare, I guess, and that's where I was wounded, which I'll get to later.

I couldn't sleep, as my bunk was the one first up in the bow of the ship, and every time we went across a wave and came down, the chains would buckle up and snap with a great force, and you couldn't sleep, no matter how sleepy you were.

The sea was so rough that when we were on the crest of a wave, you could see thousands of ships in the convoy. But when we were down between the waves, you couldn't see any other ships.

Later, before dawn, we were all put down below, to keep down on casualties when the shelling started from the Germans. We landed about two hours later than we were supposed to. The beach was so crowded with men and equipment that other ships couldn't get in. The beach was heavily mined, and only a narrow lane had been opened up to the ridge to get away from the beach. There were so many mines on the beach that it looked like Macy's was having a two-for-one sale.

Finally, we were ordered up out of the bottom of the ship— out of the hull, rather—and had our rifles on ready fire and even had our safeties off just in case we didn't have time to do it later. I almost got sick when I first got up on deck to get to the gangplank. One of the soldiers had started to go down the gangplank when a shell must have hit nearby. There he stood, his body up against a rail and his head over the railing. From what I could see, the only thing that held him together was his spinal cord.

We all proceeded down the gangplank to get onto the beach while the tide was in, so the ship was able to get quite a ways in. There was no way to get up off the beach, though, because there was a lane up there that was crowded, and everything would just jam. A major came up and ordered us across a minefield that was marked plainly as can be that it was heavily mined. But he said he got orders from the G-2 that it was marked only to stall the assault.

The major, whoever he was, could have been in a different unit; there was no way to tell, crowded as it was. We started across the minefield as we were ordered. Then we saw two or three of the men who ran ahead of us. They were about fifty feet in and were blown up. We could see body parts fly. Every one of us tried to re-trace our steps to get back out.

As I was backing out, I made sure I had my rifle toward the major who had given us the orders to charge through this minefield. Where he disappeared to, I'm not sure. Maybe somebody had already shot him. Next thing we knew, their

88s were peppering the beach with their shells, which was really awesome. They had what looked like a pistol arrangement. It was on a base plate with eight tubes through it, and it looked like a bunch of stovepipes. But they single-shot the 88s and zeroed in and then all would fire at one time, just automatic. This was really very shocking.

The shells were coming in so heavily that I dove in a shell hole that had been there already. My body fell in, but not my right leg. And that's when I felt a hot sensation in my leg. A piece of shrapnel went through the back of my knee, up a little above the knee, and down through the calf and tore it open. Luckily it didn't hit any bones, but just tore up all the tissue. I was bleeding like a stuck pig, and I yelled for a medic. One of them did come over. I don't know how he managed to find me with all the other injured, but he did. He gave me a shot and patched me up the best he could. Then I and quite a few of us went over to the LCIs that were already beached. The tide had gone out, so the boats were on surface, and the back of them tapered at a 60-degree angle, which made a good place to be protected from the shells coming in. There were others under there with me; most of them had injuries and weren't able to run. Whenever the navy came in with supplies, they would take the wounded back to an LST [landing ship, tank] farther out that was set up as a hospital ship.

I was on their next trip. But the LCI was bouncing in the rough water, and I fell out of the boat. I was going down for the second or third time when one of the navy men noticed me and grabbed hold of me and pulled me aboard with the help of another sailor. I must have passed out for a while, because the next thing I knew, they were strapping me in a wire basket and hoisting me up the side of the LST hospital ship. It looked like the Empire State Building. That's how it must feel to bungee jumpers, bouncing back and forth. I was too excited to know what was really going on.

I was treated aboard the LST. I must have been dead tired and slept quite a bit, for the next thing I remember I was in a hospital in one of the most bombed-out cities in England. I was in the hospital for two months and in rehabilitation for two months.

Charles R. Sullivan (U.S. Navy)

One of the strangest vessels to cross the English Channel to land on Omaha Beach was the Rhino, a large self-propelled barge. Charles Sullivan recounts his experience on a Rhino on D-Day.

I WAS A MEMBER OF THE 111TH Naval Construction Battalion (Seabee), and we landed on D-Day at Omaha Beach. We started in with the first wave after the UDTs [underwater demolition teams] had cleared away some of the mines and obstacles.

We manned pontoon barges (Rhinos) that had off-loaded LSTs carrying men, tanks, trucks, artillery, and jeeps a mile or more off shore and brought them into the beach. Each Rhino could take the full load of an LST. The LSTs then could return to England for more troops and equipment. If the LST had gone into the beach, it would have had to wait until the next tide to return and been a sitting duck for German artillery.

We trained for months along the English and Welsh coasts till we could hook up to and unload an LST in less than thirty minutes. When fully loaded, we sat low in the water, only a few inches above the sea bottom, and from land we looked like a floating island. We were unsinkable. Each pontoon was a sealed unit thirty pontoons long and eight pontoons wide with two large outboard motors all bound together by steel beams and metal crossties. We needed only twelve to eighteen inches of water to float.

We had eighteen Rhinos, and each unloaded three or four LSTs on D-Day at Omaha Beach. I was a crew member on Rhino #1. We had trained in Britain and come across the Channel on LST 314, which was the ship we unloaded at H hour and returned to England, only to be sunk on her return trip. Most of the crew was lost. For most of D-Day we were under fire from German gun emplacements and machine guns. We did hit and explode a few mines, but our casualties were light considering all that was happening at Omaha Beach that day.

We continued to operate on Omaha Beach in the same manner till the Port of Cherbourg became operational.

Harold Baumgarten (U.S. Army)

There were three infantry battalions in each U.S. Army infantry regiment. Harold Baumgarten landed on Omaha Beach as part of the 1st Battalion of the 116th Infantry Regiment of the 29th Infantry Division.

We would hit Omaha Beach at Dog Green strip, near the seaside town of Vierville-sur-Mer. The 16th Infantry Regiment of the 1st Infantry Division was on our left, and we were supported by the 5th Ranger outfit on our right.

The British and Canadians were on the left side of the 1st Division. We were to land on what would be the west flank of Omaha Beach, with the British and Canadians on the east flank. We saw photos of the Germans preparing the defenses on the beach. In May 1944 our P-38 planes were diving over the beach taking photos.

We were to neutralize all enemy positions on our beach, then take Vierville-sur-Mer, France. We were then to move westward and relieve the Rangers at Maisy, France, where they were to destroy a radar station after climbing the cliffs at Pointe du Hoc. Then we were to try to take Isigny, about ten miles from Omaha Beach, all on the first day.

The main objective was to cut off the Cherbourg peninsula and isolate it so we could utilize the great seaport of Cherbourg for reinforcing and supplying our troops in France without German ground interference.

At Camp D-1, I was in with a new Company B boat team, which I had not trained with. I had to make friends fast, and it was a lonely time for me. I made friends with Robert Ditmar of Fairfield, Connecticut; Pfc. Clarius Riggs; Sergeant Barnes; Lieutenant Donaldson; and Pfc. Robert Garbet.

We left the marshalling area with full battle equipment, about a hundred pounds per man, and went in trucks to the huge seaport of Weymouth, England. That night of June 1, we boarded a liberty ship, given to the British by lend-lease, known as the *Empire Anvil* in my memory, although some of my buddies who landed said it was the *Empire Javelin*. [Editor's note: D-Day records show that the *Empire Anvil* carried Assault Group O-1, and *Empire Javelin* carried Assault Group O-2, so the writer could have been on either ship.] This ship would carry us across the Channel to Normandy. We had used this same vessel on a practice landing on Slapton Sands beach a month previous.

The harbor of Weymouth was crowded with ships of every size, shape, and description, most of them flying the Stars and Stripes, Old Glory. We had the old battleships *Arkansas, Nevada*, and *Texas* with us. The latter had the task of landing the Rangers at Maisy. We had cruisers, destroyers, dummy battleships, and even rocket-firing ships. The weather was nasty, and the invasion, which was known as Operation Overlord, was called off for June 4.

We practiced cruising around the harbor in our little British LCAs [landing craft, assault]. We practiced going up and down the rope ladders, as we did in the amphibious training school, with our heavy equipment. If you fell down, you would drown in that harbor. For the actual landing we were lowered from the ship after we were already in the LCAs.

However, on the evening of June 5, the harbor came alive. I could see one ship signaling to the other that this was it. The weather had cleared a little, and the invasion could be delayed no longer. We would hit the beach the next morning—at 6:30 a.m. on June 6, 1944, to be called D-Day.

That evening, Chaplain Kelley (from New Britain, Connecticut) held a mass service on the deck of the *Anvil* in which he requested God to safely see us through the landing.

At 4:30 a.m. we left the *Anvil* on British LCAs. It was pitch black and the Channel was rough. Before that, we had heard Eisenhower's speech on how the country was with us and so forth and it was to be a magnificent mission, and wished us

Godspeed and good luck. The huge bluish-black waves rose high over the sides of our little craft and batted the boat as well as us with unimaginable fury. It was as if the waves were trying to crush our assault boat and us in it. We were all soaking wet. I tried to keep my rifle dry by putting a plastic cover, actually a condom, over the barrel. I was now a rifleman and I was landing with an M1 rifle, not a BAR. I tried to get some sleep as we moved toward the beach about ten miles away. We could see a reddish glow on the horizon; it must have been coming from areas behind the beaches where the Air Corps was bombing.

Then the fury of the waves broke our front ramp and the boat began to fill with icy Channel water. The water reached my waist, and things looked black for us as our little boat began to sink. But Lieutenant Donaldson rammed his body against the inner door of the ship and said, "Well, what the hell are you waiting for? Take off your helmets and start bailing the water out."

The sky lightened, and an American cruiser, seeing our impending demise, signaled and asked if we wished to come aboard. But Lieutenant Donaldson, without hesitating, told the British sailor in charge of our boat to signal back "no." He said, "Our paratroopers are in there being cut to ribbons, and we've got to get in and rescue them."

All our equipment as well as ourselves were wet. Our TNT was floating around the boat. We were dead tired from working the hand pumps and bailing out water with our helmets. We were shivering from the cold. In fact, our feet were frozen blue.

Suddenly the sky was black with a steady stream of planes in formation, thousands of them. I saw the P 51 Mustang fighter planes for the first time that morning. In the distance, we could hear the bombs exploding, raining havoc and destruction upon the enemy. Reddish-orange flames reached skyward from enemy installations miles inland.

At about 7:00 a.m. I saw the beach with its huge seawall at the foot of a massive 150-foot bluff. We had made it. But then an 88mm shell landed right in the middle of the LCA beside us, and splinters of the boat, equipment, and bodies were thrown into the air. Lieutenant Donaldson cautioned us to get down. Bullets were passing through the thin wooden sides of our vessel. The ramp at the front of the boat was lowered, and the inner door was opened. In a British LCA we could get out only one at a time on the ramp, and a German machine gun trained on the ramp took a heavy toll of lives. Many of my thirty buddies went down as they left the LCA.

I got a bullet through the top of my helmet. Then, as I waded through the deep water, a bullet aimed at my heart hit the receiver of my M1 rifle, as I carried it at port arms, and embedded itself in my ammunition. I waded through the waist-deep water, watching many of my buddies fall alongside me. The water was being shot up all around me, and many a bullet ricocheted at me off the surface of the water. Clarius Riggs, who left the assault boat in front of me, went under, being shot to death.

As we reached the dry sand, I heard a hollow thud about eight to ten feet to my right and a little in front of me, and I saw Pvt. Robert Ditmar of Fairfield, Connecticut, hold his chest and heard him yell, "I'm hit, I'm hit!" I hit the ground and watched him as he continued to go forward about ten more yards. He tripped over a tank obstacle and, as he fell, his body made a complete turn and he lay sprawled on the damp sand with his head facing the Germans, his face looking skyward. He seemed to be suffering from shock and was yelling, "Mother, Mom . . . ," and kept rolling around on the sand. There were three or four others wounded and dying right near him. Sergeant Barnes got shot down right in front of me, and Sgt. "Pilgim" Robertson from my boat team had a gaping wound in the upper right corner of his forehead. He was walking crazily in the water, without his helmet. Then I saw him get down on his knees and start praying with his rosary beads. At this moment, the Germans cut him in half with their deadly crossfire, which was coming from pillboxes and what we thought was a reinforced building overlooking the beach. Later on I found out it was a pillbox built into the mountain on the right flank of the beach. This pillbox could fire sideways across the part of the beach where we landed, and snipers were also firing at us from vantage points in front of us, from dugouts, and from pillboxes in front of us. I saw the reflection from the helmet of one of the snipers and took aim. I later found out that I got a bull's-eye on him. It was the only time that my rifle fired. A bullet that later hit the rifle must have shattered the wood, and the rifle broke in half and I had to throw it away.

When I threw away the rifle, a private named Kafklas (Company A, 116th Infantry) picked up the pieces and crawled toward me to give it back to me, as if he thought I was quitting the fight, which I wasn't. He later died. He simply keeled over and stopped breathing.

Shells were continually landing all about me, in a definite pattern. When I raised my head to curse the Germans in the pillbox on our right flank who were shooting up the sand in front of me, one of the fragments from an 88mm shell that exploded about twenty yards in front of me hit me in my left cheek. It felt like I was hit with a baseball bat, only the results were much worse. My upper jaw was shattered and my left cheek was blown open. My upper lip was cut in half. The roof of my mouth was cut up, and teeth and gum tissue were lying all around in my mouth. Blood poured freely from the gaping wound. I washed my face in the cold, dirty Channel water, and managed somehow not to pass out. I got rid of most of my equipment. I was happy that I was not wearing the invasion jacket. I wore a regular army zippered field jacket, with a Star of David drawn on the back and "The Bronx, New York" written on it. Had I worn the invasion jacket, I probably would have drowned. In order to get my equipment off, I had to unbuckle the life preserver, which was under my arms and extending up near my neck. In trying to take it off, I accidentally squeezed the carbon dioxide capsules, and my life preserver pulled my arms up. I was out of the six inches of water that I was in, and made a perfect target. The same 88mm shell that sent a fragment into my face hit Pvt. Bedford Hoback, Company A, 116th Infantry, in the face, and he died. (He was one of the twenty-plus men of Company A from Bedford, Virginia—one of the "Boys from Bedford"—who died on D-Day. His brother, who also landed on D-Day, was missing in action.) I saw Sergeant Draper and Vargos and all of Company A dying in the water to my left. It was ultra sad for me because these men who had landed a little before me in Company A were friends I had trained with. The people I had landed with I didn't know.

The water was rising about an inch a minute as the tide was coming in, so I had to get moving or drown. I had to reach a fifteen-foot seawall, which appeared to be about two hundred yards in front of me. I crawled forward, trying to take cover behind bodies and water obstacles made of steel. I picked up another rifle along the way. The Germans were zeroing in on me, though, and a bullet went through the thick steel rails of the tripod-shaped obstacle that I was behind. I continued forward in a dead-man's float with each wave of the incoming tide.

Finally, I came to dry sand and had only another hundred yards or maybe less to go. As I started across the sand, crawling very fast, the Germans in the pillbox on the right flank were shooting up the sand all around me. I expected a bullet to rip through me at any moment. I was out of danger from the enemy on the left flank because of a bend in the wall that ran parallel to the beach, hence bent in the direction of the shoreline, and I reached the stone wall without further injury. I was now safe from the flat trajectory weapons of the enemy. All I had to fear now were enemy mines and artillery shells.

I looked back on the beach I had crossed and saw three of our battalion's twelve special tanks knocked out in the water, a dead man hanging out of the turret of one of them. Incidentally, one of these tanks fired his 75mm gun shells right into that pillbox on the right flank and could not knock them out.

At the wall, I met Dominick Surro, a boy from Georgia about my age, a rugged fellow from Company A, 116th. He looked at my face and said, "Stay here, I'm going to run down the beach and get help." He got killed later by a sniper.

I looked down at him being washed around by the incoming water. I saw the bodies of my buddies who had tried in vain to clear the beach. It looked like the beach was littered with the refuse of a wrecked ship instead of dead bodies of the once-proud, tough, and well-trained combat infantrymen of the 1st Battalion of the 116th Infantry.

There was no medical aid available at this time, and many men had bled to death. Many had fainted from the sight of blood that poured from superficial wounds and, as a result, they drowned. I ran down the wall to the left a hundred yards or so, giving a hand to many of the wounded who were trying to pull themselves against the wall. The wall, which was slanted upward at about a 50-degree angle, seemed to get lower the farther I ran to the left, or southeast. I finally came to the end of the wall, which was about six feet high. I saw a road leading up the side of the bluff to Vierville-sur-Mer. Another special tank was knocked out here. It blew up in the afternoon and burned. By special tank, I mean a Sherman tank, transformed into a boat by air cells and a rubber and canvas apron. It entered the water on its own power and, with the waterproof walls lowered, the big tank landed ready for action. This was a secret weapon that was credited for preserving at least 10,000 lives on D-Day in Normandy, but this was not true. They were easy targets and were knocked out by the enemy. I saw five knocked out—three on Dog Green beach and two at the Vierville-sur-Mer draw. The majority of the thirty or more tanks went down in the English Channel.

Lying face down in the sand in front of the Vierville-sur-Mer draw was our boat's walkie-talkie radioman and my best buddy, Pfc. Robert Garbet, of Newport News, Virginia.

He was dead, his back to the enemy, so he had probably been spun around by the force of a bullet. I met some of my buddies from Company A here, and they helped me up to the seawall. They were Gilbert Pittinger of New Jersey, a fellow named Kaufman, and a fellow named Zymczack. Some of them were wounded and were taking cover on the wall, which was made of cobblestones. Private First Class Harold Weber, Company A, from Springfield, Massachusetts, had his face shot off and was lying there, dying.

I understand that we were outnumbered in the invasion, because the Germans just happened to have an SS [Waffen] division on maneuvers in the area. Things looked pretty black and one sided until Brig. Gen. Norman D. Cota rallied us by capturing some men himself and running around the beach with a hand grenade and a pistol in his hand. He was accompanied by a major whose name I didn't know. They ran down the beach under fire and sent a call for reinforcements. The 1st Battalion was almost completely wiped out, and the 115th Regiment had trouble landing because the water was very rough in the Channel. It apparently landed later in the morning.

Later in the day, every man who could walk and fire a weapon charged up the hill toward the enemy. I got hit in my left foot while crawling by a mine.

I forgot to mention that on the beach itself, Tech. Sgt. Cecil Breeden dressed my face wound. He was one of the two aidmen in Company A. The other one was Thomas Mullins, of Worchester, Massachusetts, who was shot and killed. I did not know who the aidmen were in Company B; in fact, all I knew were the few men I mentioned before. While Technical

Sergeant Breeden was dressing my face wound with powder and cleaning me up and putting a bandage on my face, shells started to land all over, and I grabbed him by the shirt to pull him down. He hit my hand away and said, "You're injured now. When I get hurt, you can take care of me."

We went up into Vierville-sur-Mer and knocked out a pillbox with a forty-pound charge of TNT and sheer guts. German prisoners were being taken by the hundreds. If they moved the wrong way, they were shot, because we knew of treachery where they may have been reaching for a hand grenade or something to get us. I was continually being bandaged up by navy amphibious engineers, who were without their equipment.

At the end of June 6, we were in only about 880 yards, or a mile. After going into Vierville-sur-Mer, I noticed I was with some Company D men who had cleared the beach from the third company, and we were heading westward up the hill of the beach. That night in the moonlight, you could look down and see the bodies, which looked like piled-up driftwood floating in the water.

Even though I wore a waterproof Rima wristwatch, with automatic winding and a luminous dial, and I could see what time it was, the minutes seemed like hours, and there was no way to keep track of time. But I was fighting with the bandage on my face. When I was wounded in the left foot while crawling, I had tried to bandage it myself. I took the shoe off and saw a big hole in the dorsum of my left foot. When shells started to land, I ripped off the bandage and pulled the shoe back on, then dove for protection behind whatever cover I could find (a hedgerow).

Sergeant John Frazier of Company A (I think he's from Orange, Virginia) seemed to be shot in the back and was paralyzed and couldn't move. I later found out his legs were shattered. While I was leaning over him, a mortar shell landed and I was shot in the left side of the head through my helmet. I guess the helmet saved my life. Blood came streaming again over my left ear and down onto my face. I dragged Sergeant Frazier behind the wall we were to cover; he was still alive. This happened at about 10 a.m. on D-Day.

Along the way, I had taken another bullet through the face. As the evening progressed, I was starting to feel very weak from all the bleeding. I had not eaten since leaving the *Empire Javelin*, which was probably at nine or ten in the morning of the previous day, so I had not eaten for over twenty-four hours. I was not in any severe pain, though, because we were the first American troops that were ever allowed to carry our own morphine. We each carried a grain of morphine, in what looked like a small toothpaste tube, inside our paratroop first-aid kit, and all we had to do was shoot ourself under the skin and squeeze the tube. A small amount was enough to relieve the pain.

I noticed as it got dark that I became very trigger happy, and I started to fire at anything that moved in front of me. That night, some German planes flew over, and I could see the swastikas on the planes. The navy took them on, and I thought that some of them were knocked out, but I never read about that. But the navy tracer bullets fired at the airplanes made the sky look like the Fourth of July.

About 3:00 a.m. on June 7, I found myself lying near a road above the bluffs, south of Vierville-sur-Mer. I guess it would be the Grandcamp road. I got an ambulance to stop by firing at him, and two men came out and asked if I could sit up in the ambulance. I muttered something like, "Anything to get out of here," but I'm sure it was unintelligible because of the teeth and gum tissue still lying on my tongue. I put my arm around the neck of one of the two ambulance men and limped to the back of the vehicle. I sat down in the ambulance, and then fell back on the cold metal floor because of weakness and loss of blood. I don't think I passed out because I remember everything. My hands were already blue from loss of blood. I was driven to what I think was the town east of the beach, near St. Laurent sur Mer, because when they stopped I took note of where we were. They took me out and put me on a stretcher. I remember seeing a huge statue, although in retrospect I think it was a church near the beach, silhouetted in the darkness. I was then laid out on the sand in a stretcher amongst a line of stretchers containing some of my wounded buddies. I was suffering from shock and had the chills. I requested a blanket, and they gave me some more morphine and I went to sleep.

The next morning I saw the German prisoners marching by me. The 175th Infantry Regiment of the 29th apparently landed around that time, and German snipers opened up on the beach, including the area holding the wounded. I got shot in my right knee while I was on the stretcher. Aidmen were also wounded.

Finally at about 3 p.m. on June 7, I was taken off the beach and out to LST 291, U.S. Navy. There, a navy doctor took off my clothes, cleaned up my wounds, and gave me blood plasma and some kind of dextrose or glucose. By that time, I had not eaten for almost forty-eight hours.

Robert E. Walker (U.S. Army)

The disorder on Omaha Beach due to heavy German resistance caused the plans of all the various seaborne invading units to fall into disarray. Robert Walker's story describes the chaos he found on Omaha.

I DIDN'T LAND IN NORMANDY. I SWAM in. It's a long story and I'll have to give you some background about how I got there that day.

In early 1943 I was shipped to the ETO [European theater of operations] with a detachment of officers and noncoms to join the 29th Infantry Division, which was then in England. My first assignment in the division was S-2 (Intelligence staff officer) of the 1st Battalion, 116th Regiment. Here I soon learned that I was considered a standard second lieutenant infantry officer. My background as a law or German language specialist was nice, but not too important.

During the many, many practice landing exercises in which I had participated in 1943 and 1944, I had been in various kinds of boats—LCVPs [landing craft, vehicle, personnel], LCTs [landing craft, tank], ducks, and once even on the invasion flagship USS *Ancon*. There was only one type of landing craft I had not been on, and that was an LCI, which means landing craft, infantry. Wouldn't you know, for the invasion I was assigned to LCI #91. I was also designated the billeting officer. There were few 116th Regiment people on the boat with me. We constituted an alternate regimental staff, a possible substitute for the regular staff, if needed.

I knew that the ship's capacity was about 180 combat-loaded infantrymen, but my roster showed we had

200 people. Besides being overcrowded, we had various kinds of special equipment, like large rolls of telephone wire, lots of Bangalore torpedoes, satchel charges, grapnels, flame throwers, and much more. Despite the crowded conditions, I heard no grumbling or complaints. Maybe the soldiers felt it wouldn't be so bad because it was going to be a short trip.

Everyone crowded in the bunks, and the surplus stayed on the gangways and ladders and on deck. It was quiet during the night on June 4—probably because all of the poker games, crap games, religious services, and letter writing had already been taken care of.

The skipper on LCI 91 was a Coast Guard lieutenant from Boston. He told me he had entered the Coast Guard expecting he would spend the war guarding the Atlantic coast near his home. Instead, he said, he was now on his third amphibious invasion, after North Africa and Sicily.

After we were all onboard, word came that the invasion had been changed from June 5 to June 6. We also heard, along with every kind of rumor imaginable, that in the United States it had already been broadcast that the invasion had begun. There was surprisingly little reaction among the troops, as if everyone was already numb to the situation. Or maybe it was just because they were good soldiers. For myself, I wasn't exactly panicky, but I did feel that, if the report were true, all chance of tactical surprise was lost because of the premature announcement.

We unloaded the boat. Then we loaded again as before, and finally on the night of June 5 the ships began crossing the Channel. H hour was set for 6:30 a.m., and LCI 91 was to make its approach to Omaha Beach, Dog Red, at H+45 minutes. Again the night was quiet. Some slept, including me. Breakfast was set for 4:00 a.m. Most everyone was lined up for chow by 3:30 a.m. The ocean was very rough and choppy.

It was also very dark outside. I had expected to hear bombardment and firing, but I heard and saw nothing. Breakfast was scrambled eggs, sausages, bread, and jam, all from a new type of field ration, the 10-in-1 box, intended to provide a full meal for ten people in the field. It had never been issued to us during our training.

We all had K rations in our packs. We had them in the pockets of our impregnated wool uniforms. The breakfast on the boat seemed greasy, but most of us ate it and enjoyed it.

In numerous briefings back in England, we had been familiarized with the looks of the invasion beaches by means of pictures, maps, drawings, aerial photographs, sand table layouts, and three-dimensional rubber models. We had been cautioned, however, that the beach might not look that way on D-Day morning due to the intensive aerial bombardment that had been planned. It was to begin with heavy bombers at midnight. These were B-17s dropping blockbusters from midnight till 3:00 a.m. Then medium bombers would traverse the beaches from 3 till 5 a.m. After that there would be wave after wave of fighter-bombers, which would bomb anything that moved and anything missed by the heavy and medium bombers. They would also make strafing runs. At the beach exits, Vierville-sur-Mer on the right and Colleville on the left, we were told not to expect any house or church steeples still standing, and of course there were to be no buildings or houses left standing on the beaches. "Don't expect to see green grass back of the beach," they said. "The bombing will rip it up and leave only brown earth." The Air Corps bombardment of the beaches and beach exits was also to be supplemented by naval guns from the invasion fleet prior to H hour.

Aboard the LCI, dawn came at 5:30 a.m. or thereabouts. I looked toward the shore, and my heart took a nosedive. I couldn't believe how peaceful, how untouched, and how tranquil the scene was. The terrain was green. All buildings and houses were intact. The church steeples were proudly and defiantly standing in place. "Where," I yelled to no one in particular, "is the damned Air Corps?" Looking skyward I saw not one plane, enemy or friendly, in the sky. Later I did see a flight of four P-47s over us, identified by their new markings of broad black and white stripes on the undersides of the wings. But they were not bombing and strafing. That was the only group of planes I saw before landing on the beach. Of course, it was nice not to have any enemy in the sky, but it was most disheartening to realize that in a few more minutes our troops would have to cross the beach, which apparently was untouched by any bombardment.

The minutes flew by. Everything was quiet. No firing could be heard and I could see no evidence of artillery fire. Our LCI was about a thousand yards offshore when we saw the first troop-loaded LCVPs moving in over the white-capped waves. I could see the obstacles that the Germans had planted in the water, the pilings with the mines on them, and the things called tetrahedrons, or element C, which were crisscrossed I-beams. The invasion plan had called for advance parties of Seabees, engineers, and demolition teams to blow these obstacles before the troops landed at 6:30 a.m. None were blown and no Seabees could be seen.

At 6:30 a.m. or shortly thereafter, we could see the LCVPs of the first wave head for the shore. I was on deck watching to the right toward Dog Red. I was still unable to hear any sounds of battle, but when the boats approached the obstacles and when the ramps went down, it appeared that something was terribly wrong out there. The landing craft were milling around, and there were no troops rushing across the beach. Now we could hear and see gunfire. I was supposed to land on Omaha Dog Red, but our landing craft was far to the left. It was in line with Dog White.

Between 6:30 a.m. and the time our LCI made its landing run may have been about an hour. But it seemed like ten minutes. The front deck was crowded. We were beginning to get small-arms fire. I could hear some bullets hit the sides of the boat. Our LCI had a pair of movable ramps alongside the bow that would be lowered when the troops were to land. I was supposed to go down the ramp on the starboard side.

As our boats moved into the lines of underwater obstacles, it got caught on one of the pilings that was slanted downward into the water toward the boat. The boat slid up on the piling and there was an explosion. It tore the starboard landing ramp completely off the boat and hurled it high into the air before it landed in the sea about twenty yards away. The LCI began to back off. Seeing that I could not get off on the starboard side, I headed over to the port ramp. It was entirely engulfed in flames.

We began to have casualties from small-arms fire on the front deck.

As I backed away from the flames on the port side, I heard

a blast and saw that a man wearing a flame thrower had been hit and his fuel tank was on fire. Several men standing nearby had burns. One man had a water blister on his face that seemed to be six inches across. The man with the flame thrower was screaming in agony. He went over to the starboard side and dived into the sea. I could see that even the soles of his boots were on fire.

Just then the captain of the ship came running to the front deck, waving his arms and yelling, "Everybody over the side." I climbed over the port rail and dropped into the sea, my hobnailed combat boots scratching on the side of the boat.

I had no qualms about being in the water. Our practice landings had us in the English Channel many times. I was wearing a Mae West life preserver, which would inflate with a CO2 cartridge. Besides that I had another life preserver. It was simply a rubberized bag meant to carry a new type of gas mask that was issued just before the invasion. When the opening was rolled up and fastened, it enclosed air, which gave a measure of buoyancy. It was worn on the chest, which would help keep its wearer right-side-up in the water. In addition, I was well oriented on what the ocean bottom was like. I knew that approximately a hundred yards offshore was a sandbar in about five feet of water at this time of morning, which would allow me to touch down and catch my breath if I needed to. My uniform was a wool shirt and wool pants that were heavily impregnated with a smelly chemical compound for protection against a possible gas attack. I wore heavy socks, combat boots, and a light field jacket. Along with my steel helmet I carried a carbine and a rifle belt pack with ammunition. On my back was strapped a canvas musette bag, which had maps, papers, pens, pencils, toilet articles, and a couple of K ration boxes.

Once overboard, I quickly discovered that my head was not staying above water. Despite the two life preservers, the choppy waves were going over the top of my head. Although I swallowed some seawater, I knew I could swim well enough to keep afloat, so I headed for shore. It was not easy to swim fully clothed with a loaded rifle and equipment, but I managed to do it and also look around a bit. There were others around me swimming, dying, and dead. Explosions were going off to my left, and in the air I saw a cluster of mortar rounds coming in. I could see their tail fins before they hit the water, where they exploded. The nearest was about forty yards away. I wondered if the fragments were traveling laterally over the water toward me. As far as I could tell, they were not. I had also once heard there was danger in the water from an explosion for a swimmer who was treading water rather than floating on the surface. At the next big nearby explosion, I tensed to see if there was any compression that might cause me harm. There wasn't.

About fifty yards away, several mortar shells hit around a swimmer. One of the shells landed directly on him and suddenly he was gone.

I wasn't thinking of anything except getting on shore and joining my unit. Even though it looked like chaos on the beach, I didn't want to be in the water any longer than necessary. I was also getting very tired from my swimming effort and was gasping for breath. I knew I had to reach that sandbar and get a bit of rest. Carefully judging the distance, I swam a bit more and decided to try standing up. Miracle of miracles! I found I was standing on the bottom with my head out of the water. What a relief!

In the next instant, however, the rough waves swept me off the sandbar and again into water over my head. I felt too exhausted to swim the rest of the distance, so I decided I'd have to give up some of my burdens. First I dropped my rifle. Next came my helmet and then the harness with the musette bag. With that much gone, I was able to swim the next hundred yards or so and touch bottom. Here I was on Omaha Beach. Instead of being a fierce, well-trained, fighting infantry warrior, I was an exhausted, almost helpless, unarmed survivor of a shipwreck.

Things were not going well on the beach, but I knew that was where I wanted to be. There was no place to hide in the water. The shore and the water were littered with bodies and all kinds of damaged equipment, such as boats, vehicles, tanks, trailers, and lots of junk.

There was firing from above the beach. The only firing I saw by the assault troops was by a tank destroyer, about ten yards from the edge of the water, firing its cannon into the cliffs above the beach. I saw it start to move laterally along the beach and noted it was about to roll over a dead body. Then I saw it turn and go around the body.

I kept coming into shore and out of the water. It's hard to imagine how naked you feel without a steel helmet. When I reached waist-deep water, I got on my knees and crawled the rest of the way. I was on Dog White beach. Near the water I saw the body of Captain Zappacosta, a company commander from our 1st Battalion. I later learned he had been killed immediately after the ramp of his LCVP went down, while it was coming in to Omaha Dog Red.

I wanted to run across Dog White beach to the shelter of the seawall, but I was too tired to run. Although there was rifle fire coming in, it didn't seem to be coming close to me, so I kept walking as fast as I could. Dead bodies were all around me. There were also some casualties with horrible wounds.

On my way to the seawall, I kept looking around for a helmet and a gun. Nothing like that was in sight. I continued on to the seawall and saw dozens of soldiers, mostly wounded, at its base. Their wounds were ghastly.

I was still looking for a gun and a helmet and went at least a hundred yards each way along the seawall to find a weapon. I saw a few guns and helmets, but they were in the hands of wounded soldiers and I didn't think I should take anything away from them.

Rumors were flying along the seawall. One rumor had it that there was a simultaneous landing in southern France. Another rumor had it that there had been another Allied crossing at the Calais area.

Still unarmed, I went all the way to the end of the seawall on the right and across a road that paralleled the seawall on the other side. There were several signs reading "ACHTUNG MINEN." Beyond the road was a wide ditch and a low area, somewhat swampy. The high grasses and reeds gave good cover. About fifteen yards inland from the road, I came across a lieutenant from one of the Ranger battalions. He had a radio and said he was in contact with one of the battleships offshore. I asked him if he could find out from the ship anything about how the attack was going on other parts of the beach. He relayed the question and received a quick answer, "Situation normal." The lieutenant also said he had radio contact with someone in the 2nd Battalion of the 116th, near Colleville sur Mer. He relayed a fire order from the battalion to the battleship. After the first round came in, the 2nd Battalion radioed, "Cease firing. Mission accomplished." We thought it was strange since there had been no request to fire for effect.

A couple of days later I saw Lt. Bob Hargrove, who was the 2nd Battalion S-2 (he was awarded a Distinguished Service Cross for his actions on D-Day). I mentioned the fire order and he told me he himself had radioed it. Then I asked why he ordered a cease-fire after only one round. He said it was because the first round came right on top of him and his men and he wanted no more naval gunfire on his position.

The Ranger lieutenant was from the Ranger battalion assigned to assault Pointe du Hoc, but he had been mistakenly landed on Omaha Dog Red. He said he had heard on his radio that the unit he was assigned to had touched down at Pointe du Hoc.

I then left the Ranger lieutenant and continued up the steep side of the ridge above the beach. About a third of the way up, I saw the body of a soldier of the 1st Division whose M1 rifle and helmet, with 1st Division markings, were by him. I relieved him of these items plus his ammunition belt, then continued on.

At this point I could not see anyone from the 116th and realized that I was alone and completely on my own. I decided to continue up to the ridge to see what I could see up there and to possibly find a road that led to the right, where I knew the 116th was supposed to attack.

I passed many dead bodies, all face down, facing forward as if they had been hit while charging straight up to the top of the ridge. Although I heard small-arms fire to the right and left, it was not near me so I continued upward. There were folds in the ground offering good cover, so I didn't think I was exposed most of the time.

I lost all track of time for the rest of the day. My waterproof wristwatch had given up in the English Channel, so I threw it away. I assumed it was around noon when I left the beach and probably late in the afternoon when I made it to the top of the ridge. About halfway to the top, I rested awhile in a small gully. After a while, I heard someone nearby who was groaning and calling for help. He was about fifteen to twenty feet away. Cautiously I went over to investigate and saw that it was a German soldier, gravely wounded in his groin. He had already been treated by a medical aidman. A bandage was loosely fixed over the wound, and it had been sprinkled with sulfa powder. He was gasping, *"Wasser, wasser,"* German for water. I assumed he had been given a sulfa pill, which causes great thirst. In German I told the man I had no water with me and didn't know where to get any. He then said there was a spring, he called it "ein born," about fifty feet away. I didn't believe him, but I made my way over to the area he indicated. Incredibly, there was a spring, a sort of waterhole with apparently clear water in it. I filled my helmet and brought it to him. After drinking thirstily, he thanked me profusely. I left him some water in his canteen cup. Later on his groans became weaker and he soon died.

I felt I had to keep going to the top to see if I could find regimental headquarters. It was beginning to get dark when I reached the top of the ridge. All I could see over the ridge was a lot of plowed ground extending at least a mile inland. There was no evidence that soldiers had crossed the plowed ground, and I could see no troops. To the left I also saw nothing but plowed ground. About a mile to the right front were some trees and farmhouses, and I heard rifle and machine gun fire there. But I felt it would be foolish to try to cross the plowed fields.

I felt lost, but I knew that the 116th Regiment was to go through Vierville-sur-Mer and then turn right toward the area where the Rangers were to land at Pointe du Hoc. I knew I would have to make my way along the ridge toward Vierville-sur-Mer to contact the 116th.

As it was getting dark, I decided to stay put for the night, then head for Vierville-sur-Mer in the morning. That night I was joined by a lieutenant from Headquarters Company of the 116th; he agreed we should stay there the night. The firing was less after dark and we even slept a few hours.

Technically, since the day ended here, my story of D-Day should end here, but you may be interested in how and when I got back to my unit.

The next day the lieutenant with me set about exploring our surroundings and reporting back to me. We soon located a few groups of other stragglers, like ourselves, some from the 116th and some from other units. During the day, we discovered that the cliff-like ridge was covered with well-concealed foxholes and many semi-permanent bunkers. Those we saw were now empty, but we could see that the bunkers were practically unnoticeable from the front. Their firing openings were toward the flank so they could bring flanking crossfire to the beach as well as all the way up the slope of the ridge. Some had diagrams of fields of fire, and these were framed under glass and mounted on the walls beside the firing platforms.

The lieutenant with me contacted several groups of our soldiers and advised them to stay put and be on call to set out in the morning to find the 116th. During the day, we were contacted by some eight to ten GIs who had captured a German sergeant in one of the bunkers. They were on their way to take him to the beach when one of them saw me and said, "There's Captain Walker. Take this guy over to him and see what he can find out from him, talking German." I went over to the group and saw they had bayonets fixed and were standing in a circle around a man in a German uniform lying on the ground. Aside from the wounded and dead Germans I had seen, this was my first sight of a live enemy. The American soldiers looked like they would have been glad to kill him in an instant.

The German, lying on his back with hands clasped over his helmet, looked surprisingly calm. I asked him in German for his name, unit, and assignment. He spoke freely and even told me the location of his command post, where he had been directing artillery fire to the beaches. During a pause in the questioning, he stated, in German of course, "Do you know you're a landsman [countryman] of mine?" Intrigued, I asked him from what province he came. He replied, "You're from Bavaria, aren't you?" It was not news to me that most Germans could identify an accent and know what geographical area it came from. I also knew my ancestors spoke with somewhat of a Bavarian accent. So the German sergeant was right, in a way, but I didn't tell him so. What I said was, "I'll ask the questions, you just answer them." After I was through, I had the sergeant taken to the beach to be evacuated to England.

At daybreak of D+2, we formed a detachment column of forty-one men and set out to find the 116th. In Vierville-sur-Mer, we saw an MP [military policeman] from the 29th Division who directed us down the road toward Grandcamp. We found the 116th with remnants of the 1st Battalion, a few other fragmented units, a firing battery from the 116th Cannon Company, the intelligence and reconnaissance (I&R) platoon, and several Rangers. They were four miles down the road running west from Vierville-sur-Mer. I had not once fired my M1 rifle up to that time.

Along the several miles we marched, we were fired on a few times by snipers. I was told several times that the German snipers were in trees and their favorite targets were officers, who could be identified by their shiny insignia. At one point, we were told that General Gerhardt, commanding general of the 29th Division, had just come by and saw a man eating an orange and throwing the peelings on the ground. The general stopped his jeep and profanely lectured the man, making him pick up every peeling. He also warned against throwing empty cans from K rations on the road. Not only were we not to litter the countryside, but the tuna can type of K ration container could make deep circular cuts in vehicle tires. It was clear that the general was going around jacking up discipline and getting things more normal, if there is such a thing in combat.

Back at the 116th, I resumed the duties of assistant S-3 and everyone seemed glad to see me. They thought I hadn't been able to make it across the beach. I was glad to get a new 29th Division helmet, a new rifle, and some C rations.

Roy Arnn (U.S. Army)

The soldiers who came ashore on Omaha Beach on June 6, 1944, had rehearsed their jobs in training over and over until they became second nature to them. Roy Arnn found out that his training did little to prepare him for what he encountered in combat.

WE HAD A FEW ACCIDENTS AND FATALITIES during training. As we practiced making hand grenades with quarter pound blocks of TNT, one of the fellows (Private Vest) was killed when the grenade blew up as he pulled the fuse lighter. I turned around just as he was being blown backwards. The lieutenant and I rushed over to him. We made a stretcher out of our rifles and took him to the hospital in a truck. His arm and leg were blown off and he was burned and had internal injuries. On the way to the hospital he kept asking me to put a blanket around his foot as it was cold. He died soon after we arrived at the hospital, so we went back to our tents. I was smoking at the time, but could no longer smoke or eat dinner as I kept smelling and tasting burned flesh from picking him up and putting him on the stretcher. I think I took about three showers that evening with GI soap before trying to eat again. I couldn't overcome the smell of burned flesh for about three days.

One day Lieutenant Ross, who now lives in Portland, Oregon, came to us and said things were happening and we would be leaving for the south coast of England for a final briefing and the invasion. I think we went to Portsmouth or Southampton.

After arriving in Portsmouth we were given briefings almost every day and told of our assignments. After being shown photos of the obstacles and being briefed on where we were to land on the beach in France, we were no longer allowed outside the fenced area, and there were guards about every fifty feet. We were assigned to boat crew #8 and were to land in the first wave on Omaha Beach with the 1st Infantry Division. The Ranger battalion was to land and climb the cliffs to our right.

Our boat crew's job was to make gaps through the obstacles at low tide so that the second wave could make it through as the tide came in. The 1st Division was to attack the German positions. My assignment, as sergeant with three other men, was to clear the area of mines and booby traps in a gap from the obstacles inland. I think it was about fifty yards from the obstacles to the tide high-water mark.

We knew that it was getting close to invasion time as we were loaded on an LCT [landing craft, tank] about a week before the invasion. While onboard and waiting, the fellows in my squad wanted to grow goatees and mustaches, and I told them to go ahead. They said we all had to or none, so I agreed. The day before we left port, June 4, Captain Howard told me to have everyone shave their beards off. I told him that I had checked beards with the gas masks on and they did not interfere, in case we got gassed by the Germans. He said to shave them off anyway, and I refused. He said that he would court-martial me, and I told him to go ahead as none of us might be alive tomorrow anyway.

All the ships moved out on June 4, and during the night we returned to port because the weather was so bad. We did take off the next night, June 5, so we could hit the beach at daybreak on June 6.

Somewhere in the English Channel we had to transfer from the LCT to our LCMs [landing craft, mechanized assault boat], which we had towed behind us. We each had a pack of plastic explosives (about five pounds each) that we carried on our chests and backs. These could be used to blow up the obstacles on the beach. I also had a mine detector, my rifle, a coil of rope with a triple hook on it, and a couple of rolls of tape that would be used to mark the gap or lane from the obstacles inland. The rope would be used to trip any booby-trap wires, et cetera, by throwing it ahead of me and then dragging it back.

We were all pretty seasick after getting into the assault boat because of the rough water, and we were using the puke bags that we had around our necks. As the assault boat neared the beach, machine gun fire hit around the front of the boat, and some of the seasickness left.

When the ramp went down, we started for the obstacles. I was one of the last ones off the boat, as we had to put a rubber raft filled with plastic explosives into the water so it could be taken to the beach. We waded in about two feet of water to reach the beach.

As I went through the obstacles, I disposed of the plastic explosives that were on my back and chest. I then hit the ground as a machine gun in a house to our left pinned us down. I was trying to get the mine detector out of the box, but couldn't as the lid was jammed. There was no place to hide in the open, and people in the house kept firing. As I got my rifle up to my shoulder to shoot, a tank came up out of the water. The gunner put a shell into the house. About the same time, a sniper shot at me. The bullet kicked sand in my face and passed under my left armpit, which caused me to flatten out. At the same time a shell from a German 88 artillery piece exploded near my feet. Had I not been flattened out, the shrapnel from the artillery shell would have probably killed me. Instead the shrapnel hit my right shoulder and leg. The explosion and concussion seemed to push me into the ground and knocked the breath out of me. The force of the explosion blew my helmet off and cut the corner of my left eye. I soon lost sight in my eye because blood was running into it. I turned to look behind me and tried to yell to Corporal Lee to get a medic. He looked at me with astonishment and started screaming for the medic, as though he himself were hit.

Max Norris was the medic, and as he tried to get the rifle from my shoulder; it hurt something awful. I found out later that the scapula and clavicle were broken besides the deep wounds in my shoulder and leg. He took my first-aid kit and gave me a shot of morphine, also some sulfa drugs, then bandaged my shoulder and leg. I must have been one of the first ones hit, as calls for medics started coming from all over.

As I lay there wondering just how badly I had been hit, the tidewater started to go around me from the incoming tide. I tried to get up and run or crawl to the high-water mark, but I couldn't get my leg to work. I fell back down a couple of times. The Germans were firing everything they could, and Lieutenant Ross told me to stay down and he would come out to get me. He crawled out to me and I put my head on his butt and grabbed his leg. He crawled and dragged me to the high-water mark, where I stayed for most of the morning. As he left, he was wounded in the leg.

Later that day some of the fellows in my unit (I can't remember their names) tried to get me on a stretcher and onto one of the small assault boats returning to one of the larger ships at anchor. They took me down near the water to wait for an assault boat. About that time the Germans started hitting the beach with artillery, so the fellows picked me up in the stretcher and started back to the high-water mark. As the shells came near, they dropped me to hit the ground, and one of the shells hit so close that it blew me out of the stretcher. A small piece of shrapnel hit me in the little finger on my left hand. The fellows loaded me back on the stretcher and left me at the high-water mark, as they had other work to do.

I prayed to God before we hit the beach that morning and also after I was hit and a few times more while lying in the sand and rocks unable to move about. Things on the beach did not look good. One soldier near me was crying and asking for his parents. Other wounded soldiers were nearby, as were a couple of dead bodies that the tide had washed in. Sometime that afternoon some fellows picked me up and moved me to an aid station. While lying on the stretcher I guess I went into shock and started to shake. One fellow sat on me to keep me from bouncing off the stretcher. Soon after that Max Norris (our medic) took me back to the water and got me on an assault boat back to an LST [landing ship, tank].

At a reunion in Denver many years later, Max (who had become a doctor) told me that every time I breathed, bubbles would come from the wound in my shoulder as if my lung might be punctured, but it wasn't.

I felt safer on the LST as the doctors had cut my clothes off and attended to my wounds. I found out then how big the holes were in my shoulder and leg. The clothing we wore consisted of two sets of pants, with one treated in case of contact with some sort of gas and the other with a map made of a very thin material sown into the seat of the pants in case we were captured. These helped stop the bleeding in my thigh because a piece of my pants, about six inches square, had been jammed into the wound. I soon found out that the LST we were on had not unloaded, and it made a run for the beach that evening with more shelling.

As soon as the LST had unloaded its supplies, we started back to England. Most of the wounded were on stretchers on the side of the tank deck. While I was about half asleep, Captain Howard (the officer who was going to court-martial me) stopped to ask me how I was doing. He had his arm in a sling. He pointed out Lieutenant Ross sitting on a stretcher across the tank deck. The captain never said anything about a court-martial. I believe we arrived back in England on the afternoon of June 7 or 8.

Alan Anderson (U.S. Army)

Plans for the taking of Omaha Beach had anticipated that the infantrymen in the first assault wave would clear the beachhead for the follow-on units. Alan Anderson, who was in an antiaircraft unit, found out that the plans had not unfolded as anticipated.

I WAS DRAFTED INTO THE ARMY FROM my teaching position at Emmons, Minnesota, and I reported for active duty at Fort Sheridan, Illinois, on January 6, 1943.

From Fort Sheridan I was sent to Camp Stewart in Georgia, and we trained there for approximately six months. I was assigned to the 467th Antiaircraft Artillery Automatic Weapons Battalion. After our basic training, we were sent to California by train. We trained in the Mojave Desert at Camp Ibis Coxcomb and several other camps in the Mojave area. After approximately one year of training in the United States, we returned to the East Coast and departed from Fort Dix for England.

We traveled in a troop carrier, which was a converted World War I English cruiser, and I recall it could make only about fourteen knots. We took the northern route across the Atlantic in the extreme January cold. It was thought at the time that this would confuse the German submarines, as they would not anticipate that troops would be carried on that northern route during the rough and cold winter weather.

It didn't exactly work that way, though. A convoy ahead of us by a few days was hit by several submarines, and many ships were sunk. I recall seeing the bodies of any number of sailors and soldiers floating in the water. Our convoy was quite small, consisting of about five ships with one destroyer escort, and we were harassed by a sub. I think the sub was sunk by the destroyer that was accompanying us, as there was some debris indicating that it had sunk the submarine.

We arrived in the United Kingdom at Liverpool after a crossing of about ten days. The first few days of June were spent in an intensive review of aerial photographs and where we were to take up our positions after the landing. We had been advised that we were to land on the French coast on Omaha Beach. The initial landing was to take place at 6 a.m., and our unit was destined to be put on the beach at 8 a.m. I recall one event from the first days in June when we were all called into a tent and some colonel from public relations got up and made an impassioned and patriotic speech about what a privilege it was for us to have this opportunity to be in this eventful invasion that would change the history of the world. At the end of his speech he made the remarkable announcement that he couldn't go with us. My buddy Arkie Markum poked me and said, "Well, he can have my place if he really wants to go!"

He also said that the army was prepared to accept 100 percent casualties for the first twenty-four hours. It's really strange that the human mind doesn't seem able to comprehend that an assignment like that might not apply to you and you could very well be lost in a suicide mission, which was possible as far as the contemplated invasion of the French coast.

On June 2 or 3, we made a dry run with our vehicles to Weymouth, where we practiced loading our equipment on the LCVs [landing craft, vehicle] and were told how our equipment would be dispersed and what the loading order would be.

My crew was made up of what we called a section of the battery. We were called by code name Yellow Four, and section four was made up of two half-tracks, one with four .50-caliber machine guns on a mobile mount half-track and the other with two .50 calibers and a 37mm gun mount on the half-track.

As the sergeant, I was in charge. The rest of the men on the 37mm were Cpl. William "Bill" Brown, Cpl. George Davis, Pfc. Winifred Mowser, and Marvin Lowes. The technician fifth grade driving the half-track was John Howard. The other crew was made up of Cpl. Ray Isaacson and T. F. Bill Beverstorf, who was driving the half-track; the other members were Pfc. Ralph Slyman and Pfc. Bill Benton. We loaded on the LCVs at about 5 p.m. on June 4. We were wearing fatigues that were impregnated with chemicals for defense against a gas attack.

After dark on June 4, the various craft in our particular assault unit pulled out into the English Channel and traveled east for approximately six to seven hours. About midnight we turned around. I believe the maneuver was a feint that the invasion was going to be at Calais rather than on the Normandy beach. At about 1 a.m. on June 5, we turned around and started back. Then the word came that we were not going to make the invasion because the weather was too bad and we would not be able to complete the operation. We maneuvered about for a while in the Channel, and then headed back toward Weymouth. During this time, we were all very ill. When the U.S. sailors on the landing craft had given us paper bags, we wanted to know what they were for, and they said, "You'll find out." And of course we did, because these flat-bottomed boats were very rough in the weather conditions of the Channel, where the winds were quite strong and the waves were high. We all became violently seasick due to the rocking motion of the landing craft. The bags came in very handy.

There was little conversation during all of this time on the Channel. Most of us were thinking about our assignments, because it was the only way we could maintain our sanity. If we thought of the possibilities of what lay ahead, it would be more than our minds could really take.

I remember a conversation I had with Private First Class Mowser in which I relayed my fears of my competence as a sergeant leading men into battle for the first time and whether I was actually equal to the task, and I remember very vividly his response to me, "Well, Sergeant, the only way this war is ever going to end—we're going to have to cross the Channel and we're going to have to end it. It's obvious this is the only route as far as I'm concerned, and the quicker we get at it, I suppose the better off everyone will be. I want you to know that of all the men I've trained with here in this organization, I would rather go with you into combat than anyone I know." I treasure that remark, and it helped me at a time of great doubts about the ensuing operation and how I would carry out my responsibilities.

Most of the men were busy writing letters home. Some were reading, some were quite religious and were reading their New Testament scriptures that had been given out to us.

At about 5 p.m. on June 5, we turned around and again headed out into the English Channel, because the word had come that we would try to land on the morning of June 6. It was an extremely foggy night. It was raining intermittently and it was cold and we were very, very miserable because we had no heat and we were in the exposed area in the LCV. And of course there could be no light of any kind, because everything was in blackout.

I remember thinking at the time what this really meant to me, and all I could think about was that I was twenty-five years old and still single and a college graduate, and whether this was to be all of my life and what was it really for. I was thinking about the meaning of democracy and that sort of thing, but it doesn't have any meaning to a man in a situation like the one I was in. The only thing that meant anything to me was the thought that as long as I was there rather than some of my relatives, especially my two brothers, maybe we could get this mess over with before any more of the family had to be dragged into this situation. Few men are very patriotic when they're faced with these suicide missions.

At about 2 a.m. on June 6, we turned suddenly and headed toward shore. The boat speeded up and it became obvious that we were moving toward our destination. Then, as the first rays of the sun began to appear, I saw all of the ships. As far as I could see, the water was full of boats of every type and description, and everything seemed to be traveling in an established order. It was obvious that the navy was in very good control of this situation. There was also a large number of planes crossing overhead, and I could hear the assault on the Normandy coast. By this time, of course, as daylight came, we could see the flashes and the bursting of bombs. We had been listening to a lot of that all night long, as all types of aircraft were passing overhead. We could hear the bombing coming from inland, and also hear the droning of the slower planes that were carrying the paratroopers inland for their landings.

The shelling of the coast began in earnest just about daylight. The battleship *Texas* and some cruisers were firing at the shore. Then at about 6 a.m. I could see the LCIs [landing craft, infantry] start approaching the shore, and it

191

seemed that initially they were landing without too much difficulty. But then, shortly after the initial wave was onshore, the counterfire began in earnest. Some of the larger vessels were unloading men farther out in the Channel, and I could see that machine guns were ripping into the ramps and the men were tumbling just like corncobs off a conveyer belt and were being machine-gunned down and dropping dead into the water. The German machine gunners were firing directly at them from the pillboxes on the beach.

We were due to land at about 8 a.m., and the navy or coast guard unit in charge of putting us onshore started to maneuver into position to put us on land. As we headed in toward shore, we came under intensive machine gun and artillery fire. We milled around a bit, because it was obvious that there were no vehicles surviving on the beach. Some amphibious tanks had landed and were promptly destroyed, and the few ducks and other craft that were on Omaha Beach were burning and disabled. All had been unable to land a defensive line on the beach to get on the higher ground.

As we watched the slaughter around us, we thought perhaps we could help neutralize some of the German fire. We had one gun in a position where we could train it on one of the pillboxes ahead of us, so we unleashed the 37mm and the .50 calibers, then turned the gun turret around so we could get some fire on the gun emplacements on the shore. As we did that, an 88 shell came through the side of the boat and exploded directly underneath a half-track. One of the men from the third gun section had already climbed into the gun turret and was going to start firing. His name was Everett C. Martin and he took the full blast of that exploding shell, and it blew him off the track and onto the floor of the LCV. He was badly wounded. Staff Sergeant Micsell, myself, and a medic whose name I don't recall picked him up and put him on a blanket. The medic was with the 467th Platoon, of which I was a member.

A nearby small naval vessel—a rescue hospital craft—came by, and we lifted Martin over the side, then the navy men got a hold of the blanket and we managed to transfer him to this rescue vessel. The blanket was soaked in blood and I thought he had practically no chance of survival. I heard afterwards that he did live, but he had 206 pieces of shrapnel removed from his body from that shell burst.

The naval officer in charge of the landing was up on the bridge, and after we had gotten Martin onto the navy craft, I went up there. The officer was standing on the bridge and there was a flag alongside his head. About that time a barrage of machine gun fire came along and cut that flag off. When the officer realized how close he had come to being killed, he looked bewildered—the kind of look that sometimes comes on men's faces when they're first under fire.

When we got in pretty close to shore, I saw a man in the water who was part of the crew removing underwater obstacles. He was badly wounded, and he was raising his hand for someone to help him. As we were going to his rescue, we were trying to find a rope or something we could throw over to him. But then the officer received orders for us to put back out to sea because the beach was obviously not secure. I remember with horror this poor man as he lay in the water raising his hand and waving to us, then sliding back under the water. Obviously he drowned. The water was tinted red with the blood that was flowing from his wounds.

We then pulled back offshore approximately a quarter of a mile or so, and circled around awaiting further orders. I noticed that some of the additional infantry units were landing farther off to our left and attempting to get on shore there.

Then for approximately two hours, everything was relatively quiet. Onshore and offshore, it seemed that there was a lull in the fighting. Then, at about noon, I noticed that several of the bigger naval craft, notably the *Texas* and a cruiser, had moved in relatively close—I suppose within two or three miles of shore—and were firing against the concrete gun emplacements along the beach, trying to neutralize them. This went on for quite some time, and we could see the burst of these heavier shells, some 14-inchers from the battleship, that were crashing into the gun emplacements and concrete bunkers.

Then at about 2 p.m. we again got orders to land. The feeling was that the infantry that had gotten onshore and some of the paratroopers had probably neutralized some of the gun positions along the coast, so it would be possible to get the vehicles safely onshore. So we put in to shore. Things were relatively quiet until we put the ramps down and some of our vehicles started going ashore. I was one of the first units to unload, and my second half track was at the beginning of the ramp that was closest to the exit where the ramp opened up. When that ramp was lowered, the half-track drove safely through the water. We were in approximately five feet of water, but the motor was waterproof and we had a breather tube out through the cab.

The half-track, under the supervision of Cpl. Ray Isaacson, made it safely to shore. I had given them directions to take the exit where a hole had been blown in the wall and there was a track through there onto the upper beach. And the driver did that. He just took off through the water and he turned and went right straight through and around, and up onto the beach, and on up the hill, with little problem.

When it came time for my half-track to be unloaded, we realized that the landing craft had shifted somewhat in the water. When we started into the water, we hit an antitank ditch that had been dug by the Germans ahead of time, and the vehicle submerged. I remember looking over at my driver, John Howard, and seeing the water fill the cab and engulf his head so that he was underwater. I was urging him at all costs not to take his foot off the foot pedal because we would lose our momentum. However, my urgings did no good, because we went down deeper and deeper into the hole, and finally the motor stopped as the water went over the top of the breathing pipe, which was protruding approximately a foot above the top of the cab on the half-track.

John Howard and I had to wait inside the cab for the water to fill it completely because the pressure prevented us from opening the doors. I stood up on the seat. There was a three-quarter opening in the tarpaulin that covered the top of the cab. This was a button-down arrangement, and there was room enough so that one could stand up there. As I stood up, somehow or other my life belt, which we were all wearing, became inflated, and I got caught while trying to push myself through the opening. I almost drowned. I was unable to unbutton the buttons on that cover, and I tore some of the skin off my side, but with extreme difficulty I managed to extricate myself and get out of the cab and stand on top of it. After the water filled the cab, John got through the door on his side. But when both of us were on top of the cab, we came under withering machine gun fire. The men in the back of the half-track were just barely holding on as they were treading water. The vehicle was listing to one side, and it was obvious we couldn't stay there, so I gave them the word: "Over the side! Let's head for shore!"

So we started to swim for it to try to reach shore. The problem was that we had helmets on, and bandoleers, and we were carrying rifles, individual weapons, and bayonets, et cetera, which made us top heavy and flipped us over in the water so that our feet were up and our head was down. We had to abandon our weapons and our helmet and everything else so we could get upright in the water, and then swim for it.

The undertow was absolutely terrible, and it was very difficult to make any progress. I must have floundered in the water for at least four or five minutes before I managed to make it to shore. Some of the other men had less luck than I did, and they drifted farther away and didn't make it to shore for about ten minutes. And when they did, they were way down the beach from where we had initially gone into the water.

I finally got onshore, and then I went back to just above where my vehicle had hit the antitank ditch. I figured that perhaps I could get back into the cab and retrieve my gun, some ammunition and hand grenades and Bangalore torpedoes and other things that we had for occasions when we had to function as engineers or fight as infantry.

Meanwhile I dug into the sand about thirty feet or so from the exit. We were coming under tremendous mortar fire and machine gun fire. By this time the Germans had zeroed in on this exit route, which was the only route I knew off Omaha Beach. Anyone in that vicinity who tried to go out through this exit was just committing suicide. Mortars were coming in. There was rifle fire, machine gun fire, and everything imaginable directed on that exit. Every time somebody tried to make it through the exit, they were killed.

One man near me was told by an officer (whom I later learned was General Roosevelt) that we had to get off the beach. The man near me stood up and tried to go forward, but he was shot right between the eyes. He fell not more than five feet from me.

Several other men who came up were killed in a similar manner. I decided then that it was best to dig in and stay put for the time being, because there was no place to go and I had no weapons or tools. I then proceeded to dig into the sand with my hands, and I found a helmet, which I used to dig deeper. I was able to build a mound of sand so we had some cover. Several other men joined me and we built ourselves a little parapet. The machine gun was firing at us and into that sand, and a couple of shells came through the sand. One of them fell on the back of my hand. It was burning hot, I suppose from spinning through and penetrating that layer of sand before it reached the inside. It was one of those quirks that defy explanation. I remember looking at it and thinking how odd that was. Then I heard a bunch of mortar shells go over, and I saw seven men running along the beach, and all of a sudden they just disappeared. They were there and then they were gone. It was a long time before I could comprehend that they had been blown to bits right in front of my eyes.

At about this time, Cpl. William K. Brown (we called him Bill) came crawling down the beach and alongside where I was and said, "What are we going to do, Sergeant?" I said, "Well, maybe we can hook onto this burning half-track here and use it to retrieve ours." We thought that maybe when the tide went down we could reach the winch on our track, use the burnt-out vehicle as an anchor to winch our track out of the antitank ditch, and get it up where we could use it. It wasn't a very practical idea, but what do you do when you're in that type of situation?

I turned on my left side to talk to Corporal Brown, and just then a shell landed right beyond him and wounded him badly in both legs. A couple of other fellows and myself managed to get him over to a small shelter on the right of the area where we were, where the wounded were being assembled and picked up and transported to a naval hospital ship. I never saw Corporal Brown again, although I did learn from the company that he had recovered from his wounds and in fact had rejoined another outfit before the end of the war.

As I think back on it, if he hadn't been where he was, I would have received the full charge of that exploding shell probably in my stomach and chest, and chances are I wouldn't have been around to tell this tale.

An abandoned half-track and a duck [amphibious truck] were standing just beyond where I was. I recall the duck, because it had landed earlier and the driver had been killed. He was beginning to turn black in the afternoon sunlight.

About that time, there came a tremendous barrage of shellfire, and it hit the ammunition in this half-track and the ammunition started exploding. It was flying up above our heads and blowing up from our equipment. With their artillery and mortar fire, the Germans methodically blew up every one of the vehicles that had been incapacitated in one way or another along the beach. This made the experience more harrying all the time because of the exploding ammunition and the number of wounded.

Maybe ten or fifteen minutes later, I heard a shell burst not more than five or six feet from me. It hit the bank where we had dug into the sand. I heard some fellow ask about his buddy, and one of our fellows, Luther Winkler, said, "He's dead. His whole head is blown away." I went over to see how Winkler was, and his face looked like raw hamburger. He had been cut and the skin of his face was shredded. I don't know how he ever survived that shell burst. We then had to get him out of there. I found a medic to help me, and we moved Winkler over to the same area where Corporal Brown was on the shore. For some miraculous reason or other, that area was not hit, and those men were eventually picked up. I saw them leave with the navy craft that had landed; it took them out to the hospital ship, so two of our men, and others whom I also saw there, all managed to get off the beach.

Around this time, the navy started firing against the pillboxes in our area. And these big 12- or 16-inch shells that were coming in were landing not more than thirty or forty yards in front of us. They were blasting away at these pillboxes, which were not yet neutralized. It created such a vacuum around those shells that they practically pulled you right out of the hole. I remember being just lifted up when some of these shells went over us, and kind of slammed back down in the ground after the shell had gone by and exploded. It was an awful experience, and the concussion was beyond belief. We were showered with debris and sand, and smoke was everywhere. This continued for a considerable period of time. We could hardly hear or see anything else. I was deaf for about three days afterwards.

In any event, we were unable to move off the beach. How we survived there, I will never know, but at about nine-thirty that night, the firing quit. I surmised that the flashes from the mortars and artillery were becoming obvious to the naval gunners in the Channel and they were bringing firepower to bear on them, because they were beginning to fire some inland.

Finally the firing let up enough for us to pick up. About eighteen or nineteen of us were in that area, and we had two guns. I managed to get an M1 rifle and clean that up and find some ammunition. Then we went up the hill off of Omaha Beach toward the village of Vierville-sur-Mer, which was just above us.

I remember coming up to the first pillbox, which had been knocked out earlier and was being used as a hospital or aid station. A lot of wounded men were there, and as I went around a corner, some man came running toward me, holding his intestines in his hands. He had been hit by shrapnel, and he was hollering, "Help me! Help me!" His intestines were kind of hanging and running out through his fingers. The next thing I knew he fell, probably dead, within maybe five or ten feet of the aid station.

It was now beginning to get dark, but we continued on up the hill, which lay just above the exit. I saw a ditch off to the left-hand side and found four or five soldiers there. They were Rangers. I said to them, "Where is the front line?" One of them said, "This is the front line. There are Germans on the other side over there and across south of there on the other corner, and they've got machine guns, so stay down because there's heavy fire at times from those weapons."

We joined them in this ditch, and a couple of our men dug in for the night alongside what looked like a pile of wood that was covered up. When morning came and we could see what was going on, the men realized that they had dug in right next to a pile of 88 shells.

I had not really slept for two nights and all of a day, and I was absolutely overtaken by fatigue. My clothes were still wet, and the chemical-impregnated material used against the possibility of being gassed smelled to high heaven. It was hardly bearable. I had a chocolate bar from my C rations, and I managed to eat a bite or two of that, and I had picked up a canteen, so I had a little water and managed to take a drink. My lips were parched, and I could hardly close my mouth because it was full of sand and other debris from the artillery pounding we had taken on the beach.

I was worried about the whereabouts of my other crew, and in fact all of my crew. None of my own men were with me, and I felt responsible. But the Rangers' advice to us was to stay put. Because of the fluid condition of the area we were in, it was not yet secure in any way. In fact, the battle was still raging for possession of the hillside where we were digging in. Periodic gunfire was coming from two corners—that is, German machine gun fire was crisscrossing back and forth across the area, and we fired back in return. Finally one of the Rangers said, "Well, Sergeant, why don't you catch a little nap here. I'll stay awake for a couple hours and then I'll wake you and then maybe I can get a little sleep."

So I lay down. A burst of machine gun fire came in at an angle pretty close to my head, but I just moved over a little bit and thought, "Well, he can't get me here," and fell sound asleep. I was totally exhausted. The Ranger woke me at about one in the morning—I suppose this would be on June 7—and then he lay down and I took over. We stayed put until daylight, at which time I told him that I absolutely had to get up to see what had happened to my other gun crew.

I took off across the hillside toward the small red barn where I had told the driver to take the other half-track. As I started up there, I came under fire from one of the other machine guns, and I ran zigzag as fast as I could. I rounded a curve and saw that I was just below the red barn. Out of it came a German soldier, and he ran toward me. I remember thinking as I ran, "Well, how am I going to deal with this?" But someone who must have been in the crew that flushed him out of the barn appeared around the corner and shot him. He fell maybe five or six feet from me.

I found my crew behind the barn. They had driven the half-track there and had taken some shellfire. The gun—that is, the quad .50-caliber mount—had been neutralized and was out of action. I was hoping it would have been available to us. I also learned that Cpl. Ray Isaacson had been wounded. He was shot in the knee and was having considerable pain and would have to be evacuated. An infantry aidman took

Corporal Isaacson down to the pillbox aid station below the hill, and from there he was evacuated.

Just about that time, we came under a tremendous amount of fire. The Germans had launched a counterattack in the orchard to our right. A machine gun of the 29th Division was just to my right, and the gunner had been shot and killed. I heard the shot that hit him, and I went up through the hedgerow because I thought I knew where the shot had come from. Just as I pushed my head through the hedgerow, a branch let go and hit me in the face and I spun around. Just then a shot was fired and it clipped my jacket. I'm sure if that branch hadn't hit me, I would have been drilled dead center. The shot revealed the whereabouts of the sniper who was firing. An infantrymen on the right fired and hit him, and he was dangling from the tree. I have a notion he might have been tied in that tree.

There was a lot of fire all around us, and a number of men came back out of the orchard. A sergeant from the infantry started yelling, "Men, I'm going to stop right here. I'm not going back on that beach. I spent all day yesterday there. I may get killed, but if I get killed, it's going to be here, not down there." So they all stopped and strung up a defense line and started firing back.

This went on for some time. We were engaged in a cross-fire with maybe fifty or so Germans. Next, I heard some firing coming from the left. A viaduct ran down toward Vierville-sur-Mer, and apparently some of our guys had worked their way down there and gotten behind the Germans who were pushing up through this orchard, and they brought them under merciless fire. A number of them were hit, and about eighteen surrendered and came up out of the orchard with their hands over their heads. That was our first major break.

Things were relatively quiet after that. We just held our positions. At around noon I went over to where I could look down on the beach, and I saw two columns coming en masse up the hill. I heard afterwards that it was the 2nd Infantry, and I believe the 30th, that were then coming ashore without any particular trouble whatsoever. That was the first time I felt that the situation was in hand and that at least the invasion had succeeded.

In a short time, a couple of other members of our platoon came around, and there started to be some mobility in the area. I then was advised that earlier that morning, my gunner, Winifred Mowser, had been shot to death by a sniper.

Earl Asker (U.S. Army)

Firepower for the infantrymen landing on Omaha Beach was to have come from a large number of amphibious Sherman tanks. Unfortunately, most of them sank. Earl Asker was in command of three nonamphibious Sherman tanks that did land successfully on Omaha.

AT THE LAST PART OF OCTOBER 1943, the 741st Tank Battalion was boarding a boat for England. Approximately 2,000 men were onboard this ship. It was an uneventful trip, with just a few alerts that German U-boats were probably in the vicinity. After landing in England, we moved to the town of Swindon in the middle of the night to avoid being observed by enemy planes.

We got settled in Barton Stacey Camp. Through November, December, and January, we maneuvered around England, getting a little practice in movement and becoming accustomed to the European type of roads. It was disappointing to be training during the Christmas vacation and New Year's, but that probably kept us out of trouble. Then suddenly two companies, A and B of the 741st Tank Battalion, were sent into a secret maneuver area and none of the rest of us knew a thing about what we were doing. Company C, Headquarters, and Service Company were left out in the open and kept Barton Stacey Camp intact.

I remember standing in the field some time in the first part of May, and the sky was filled with planes. Another lieutenant was standing alongside me, and I said, "Well, it looks like we're going to take off pretty soon." And he said, "Oh, no, we'll never go into the invasion." And I said, "What do you think those airplanes are doing up there? Maneuvering around for the fun of it?"

Around May 15 we started moving to the staging area and went aboard an LST [landing ship, tank] on June 4. That night, we moved out and I went to bed and slept like a rock. I thought it was rather peculiar that nobody woke me at four the next morning. When I woke up, the sun was shining, and I got dressed and went out, and sure enough I couldn't see the coast, so I knew something was wrong or had been changed, and sure enough we did not make the invasion. We were back in England.

So another day went by, and on the night of June 5 I couldn't sleep a wink, so a friend and I played cards all night. This time we were awakened at dawn and started to move things onto a raft. As platoon leader, I was ready for the invasion with three "land" tanks. The two companies that were away on a secret mission were educated in the use of a floating tank. It was an ordinary tank with canvas that was inflated so it was able to support the thirty-ton tank in the water. Two propellers moved the tank into shore. When it got there, the canvas was removed and the vehicle started to maneuver as an ordinary tank. That type of tank was a failure in the choppy seas. Only about five or six inches were between the top of the boat-like affair and the water, and most of those tanks went under by flooding. Matter of fact, our tank battalion, which started off with roughly seventy tanks, had by the next day only three. Those were the three that I was commanding.

Each component of that invasion had a part to play and knew exactly when to get in. Omaha Blue, where we went, wasn't easily accessible during the fighting, so we started to line up at Omaha Red to support the infantry. They couldn't make much headway on the beach at six in the morning, so the raft that I was on just sat and waited. We had a ringside seat. I remember landing craft going sky high as they hit land mines, and the artillery firing going out into the water, and huge warships that were pounding shells into the cliff behind the beach, attempting to knock out an observer that seemed able to get artillery shells close to the boats that were in there doing the offensive artillery work.

Well, our outfit sat on the raft waiting and waiting, and finally we got called in. It was dark when we landed, and I went across the beach and started up to the top of the cliff. By then the infantry and other components of the army were able to establish a base on top near Coté sur Mer. I started to line up with the battalion commander, the colonel, and the other officers. I imagine that of the total of around five hundred men, there was something like seventy-four men who we could muster together, in three tanks. So for several days we sat around waiting to see whether the entire battalion would be given up and we would be farmed out to other fighting components. But finally our colonel was able to talk enough and we started to build up our tank supply. I acted as liaison officer in the beginning, and we didn't see a great deal of action. I stayed around Headquarters Company of the 16th Infantry Regiment, 1st Division.

There were small incidents that occurred at this time. One was that Company C was able to surprise some German soldiers on bicycles, and there was a small fracas. And I was assigned to A Company as platoon leader.

We started to move in toward St. Lo, and I was assigned by the colonel to support a company of infantrymen. I later found out that we were to attack close in with artillery. I met the company commander on an assignment during the morning of June 17, and I asked him if we couldn't possibly reconnoiter the area in which we were to make the attack. He was very depressed and he didn't want to go on this reconnaissance, but he showed me on a map where they intended to go. The initial approach had run into 88 artillery fire, and they wanted us to go up and see if we could knock it out.

I had five tanks, and when we started to move out, all the artillery started to open fire on us. We made it about half a mile in through the fields. Each field was surrounded by hedgerows, and we had to carefully guard ourselves against snipers. Our tank commander held his head out of the tank for about ten seconds and then ducked down. We never closed the top of our tanks because seeing was impossible through the periscope, and I was a little upset because artillery fire was beginning to move in on us. All of a sudden I noticed five shells hit in front of our tank. Then everything went brown and I went out like a light. Never felt a thing, and woke up in England in between two white sheets.

Raymond F. Bednar (U.S. Navy)

Until the Allies could seize suitable French ports, the bulk of men and material would have to come across the invasion beaches such as Omaha. Raymond Bednar describes his role in that job during and after D-Day.

Omaha Beach was our destination, and when we got there, God that was a sight. These large battleships— cruisers—were two to five miles out running parallel to the beach, with the big 16-inch guns and 8-inch guns just blasting off. The destroyer escorts would go into the beach and then back down and shoot their guns. They had rocket ships and LCIs [landing craft, infantry], and everything that had a gun was shooting. The Germans were up there on the beach with the 88s, and they were shooting too. By the time we arrived, the navy and some of the advance troops had knocked out a lot of the pillboxes.

But it was one hell of a mess. Ships that hit mines— LCVPs [landing craft, vehicle, personnel], LCMs [landing craft, mechanized], LCIs, LCTs [landing craft, tank], and LSTs [landing ship, tank]—were broached. There were only about two openings on the beach that you could actually take troops in when we arrived.

The seas were high. Some lieutenant from the beach patrol told us to take this big thirty by thirty pontoon that they were going to use as a dock. It got loose from one of the LSTs and was just floating around. They were afraid that one of the ships would run into it. There we were with 50-foot LCM, and he told us to take it out to sea. The men I was with said they'd been at Anzio, Salerno, and Sicily and they knew what the hell was going on. They just said, "OK, Lieutenant," and as soon as he went, the coxswain just pulled the boat away. I said, "Where are you going?" He said, "Hell, we can't play with that, Mr. Bednar. We'll get killed. That's why he came after us. No one else wants to touch it. Just let it go. Those guys can avoid it." We did; we couldn't handle it.

I remember our first task. We went up to this transport, and the infantry started coming down with their guns and full packs and other equipment. I was standing there on the back of this LCM, just observing them. Some of them were crying, some of them were cursing their officers, some of them were seasick and vomiting on one another. I don't know how many of them we put in the boat before we headed for the beach. Others were following. There were only a couple of places to get in, and we had to wait our turn. I made a mistake by looking in the water. American GIs with their heads off, their arms off, their feet off had either been shot or had hit a mine or obstacles, and these large ships coming by were cutting them up. "My God," I said, "this is it." I guess for the next couple of days that's all Omaha Beach was: the dead and dying and the people coming in to replace them.

We still had our foul weather gear on. We still had our gas-impregnated clothing, gas mask, and life jackets. We looked like we were from Mars. But it was necessary. If people didn't wear that stuff and the boat hit a mine and they were thrown into the water, they were gone. But if you had this equipment, you had a pretty good chance of getting out alive. Someone could pick you out of the water. A lot of the fellas didn't want to bother with life jackets, and they didn't want to bother with this and that. They didn't do themselves any good.

Our job was to bring the troops in, and that's what we did. And we kept bringing them in. We didn't stop to eat. When we got hungry, we ate K rations. Sometimes we'd beg something off one of the ships we were working on—some hot coffee or some bread or sandwiches. We would just go from one ship to another to bring in the troops; we went wherever they would send us. There was always a man on the beach telling us where to go or someone out there telling us what to do. That's the story of my life—someone telling me what to do. This was it for the first day.

The second night I went ashore. There was firing everywhere and I can remember being huddled against this damn cliff with all these rocks near an aid station. I saw one fellow and I said, "Who are you?" He had a uniform on, but he didn't have any insignia. He turned out to be a newspaper reporter for the *Kansas City Star*. This was 1944; I don't know whether he is still alive or not. He didn't have to be there; he was there writing a story. The rest of us, we had to be there. I thought to myself, "What the hell kind of world is this? This guy is here and he doesn't have to be here and the rest of us wish to hell we were somewhere else."

I guess until the day I die, I will see American soldiers getting off these boats, single file, going up that hill on Omaha Beach. They had a path going up to the top of the hill and out of sight. It was just a sad, sad feeling. We started bringing the wounded back by boat the first few days. Then after about a week or so we started carrying the German prisoners to the transports.

We slept under boats and under trucks on the beach. We worked most of the time. We cooked some C rations underneath some of the old burned-out boats that were turned over on the beach. The army would drag them up there with their tanks and get them out of the way so they didn't clutter up the beach.

This went on for I don't know how long, about two weeks. Those first two weeks, we didn't think we were going to stay there. We were afraid that the Germans would come back and get us. We were scared to death that this was going to happen because the British on the left hadn't moved. Everyone was quite concerned as to when they were going to move. It was just one big mess. We kept bringing the troops in. The only place we could bring them in was Omaha Beach or Utah Beach or the British beaches. There were no piers. All the cargo had to be unloaded from the ship lying off the beach. I'll tell you one thing, when you talk about unloading ships, you've got to give credit to those army quartermaster corps. The soldiers were predominately Negro and they were in charge of the amphibious ducks. They put 155mm shells or 240mm shells and machine gun ammunition in big cargo nets and dropped them into the ducks. Often there was just too much in the sling and the duck would go so far and then just disappear in the waves. There were an awful lot of casualties with the quartermaster corps. Those men worked day and night, and what a job they did. I don't know whether their out-fits ever received any medals from the army, but they certainly earned them.

Richard P. Fahey (U.S. Army)

The U.S. Army had the most advanced field medical services of all the combatants in World War II. Richard Fahey recounts his bloody experiences on Omaha Beach.

AT 6:00 A.M. ON JUNE 6, WE climbed down the ropes thrown over the side of our ship and boarded landing craft that were sailing up and waiting below. We headed directly for the shore, but the Germans had placed wooden tripods loaded with explosives out in the water. Attempts to explode these things harmlessly were not very successful, and the tripods were like a fence, so close together as to make movement between them impossible for the landing craft. A few small sections had been blown open where the craft could penetrate single file up to the beach, but one craft was such an obvious target.

While waiting our turn, our craft came upon a bunch of American soldiers floating around helplessly in the water. They had been blown out of their craft. We fished them out of the water and, since they had nothing but the clothes on their back, we told them that we would transfer them onto some craft that were traveling back to the main ships and they would be taken back to England. To a man, they protested and insisted on going in. They had nothing, no guns, nothing! We each had a supply of six boxes of K rations, which was to last us for the first two days, so we each shared two boxes of our K rations with them, and these men came into the beach with us. When our turn came to enter the slot between the tripods that had been opened up, our craft headed full speed into the beach and we piled out.

There were virtually no army vehicles or jeeps on the beach, and the ones that had arrived were disabled and blown up by the Germans. There were many wounded and dead. I saw one man whose remains consisted only of a sheet of skin flattened on the sand. There was a circular place in the middle of the skin where the explosion had apparently occurred. The only parts of his body that remained were his hands, the calvarium [upper part] of his skull, and his feet.

I began to meet the friendly faces of the other soldiers whom I had been separated from for what seemed like such a long time. The Germans were honorable enough to respect the Red Cross bands on our arms and helmet, because the medics on the beach continued working within point-blank range of the Germans in the tunnel. There is always a bad apple in every crowd, though.

There was no way that any of us would go up that valley. The machine gun fire from the Germans was withering. So we wandered up and down the sand pulling the wounded to safety, or what was relative safety, behind disabled army vehicles, or sometimes into little foxholes that were dug out. I do not know who dug them. Maybe it was the Germans on watch duty.

I particularly remember meeting up with Sgt. Walter F. Braasch, Sgt. Warren L. Dieter, and Corporal Gardner. There were others, but these men stuck very close to me. About noon, some of the special trained men were going out in groups of three or four to the tripods in the water, wiring the tripods with explosives and running back ashore, shouting to warn everyone on the beach to get down while the tripod was blown. They would go out to the next tripod and do the same thing. Eventually, the impasse was opened up and it was possible to evacuate the wounded.

Sergeant Braasch came running to me at one point and told me that Col. Bernard E. Bullock, M.C., our commanding officer, had been wounded. He was a rugged Texan we all liked. I never saw him again. He was shot through the helmet and died.

Another one of our officers was lying dead on the beach, and one of my fellow soldiers induced me to place my hand into the gash in his back. A shell fragment had shattered his spine. He was a regular army officer and had been in Pearl Harbor at the time of the Japanese attack. He had come a long way to die.

I saw an LST [landing ship, tank] on the beach burning to a shell and was told that it carried a hundred men, some of whom were from our medical battalion. There was a great deal of confusion, and my timing of many events is not precise. I remember sitting down in the wide open spaces and opening my K rations only a few feet away from a German gun emplacement at the corner of the slope. I was in a state of battle shock and did not give a damn. While I sat there, staring in defiance, an army half-track with a large gun pulled up in front of that German gun emplacement and blew everything asunder. When night came and we could no longer see, I laid down in a slit trench, and Sergeant Braasch laid down in another nearby and we talked to each other all night long while some German up in the tunnel in the hill continuously kept bullets whistling past us. I can remember Sergeant Braasch sticking his helmet out of the edge of the trench and telling me, "Watch this," as he drew fire from that German up in the tunnel.

Turning inland [on June 7], we went up the valley to the site where our large pyramidal tents were, and even larger hospital tents were to be erected. I remember at one point running along the edge of a landing strip wire road. I tripped, and the heavy gauge wire on the edge went clean through my palm and stuck out the back of my hand. Before I could continue running, I had to close my eyes and pull my hand back to get the wire out. I treated it myself since, being a medical officer, I was the last court of appeal under such circumstances.

The large tent went up, and before many minutes had passed it was loaded with patients that the medics were carrying in from everywhere. There were American soldiers from the 1st Division and the 79th Division, but there were also British limeys, Canadians, Frenchmen, Germans, and women (including pregnant women, and even one woman in the process of delivery with a prolapsed umbilical cord hanging out). The company commander, who had better sense than I, had the latter woman taken by our ambulance to a nearby French hospital. Thank God. I might have tried to deliver her in that dirty tent.

I was in charge of the shock and wounded tent of the clearing company and was in the midst of all this morning's crowd, despairing because there was no blood available for transfusions, and all I could do was to run from one to the other starting intravenous solutions and stopping the bleeding. When I was complaining, one of the sergeants came up to me and said, "Don't worry, Captain. Take a look out there. There's all the blood you could ever use that the British have collected off their people and shipped over here by plane. The planes are landing on the airstrip over there, and they're coming in from England, bumper to bumper bringing supplies. They're pushing it out of the planes onto the ground and there's a pile of supplies a half mile long and six feet high all along that runway. They're unloading their cargo at one end of the wire strip and loading up with wounded before they take off at the other end of the strip. They're heading back off the runway going to England to return with another load of cargo. No worry, Captain. All we have to do is find it in that pile back there and bring it to you." No one had prepared me for this unbelievable service. The devotion to the cause was enough to bring tears to anybody's eyes.

I was satisfied and did not go to sleep for about seventy-two hours. I was young then and didn't mind. I did all I could. Most of the extremity wounds were placed by our medics into the planes that had unloaded supplies and were headed back to England. When soldiers had head wounds, we sent them back to England in planes that were instructed to bring them to a landing field near neurological surgical hospitals. These planes could fly the wounded back to any of these specialized centers in England. None was more than forty-five minutes away.

The patients we took care of were soldiers with abdominal and chest wounds who could not stand the trip back to

England. The army had sent in highly skilled surgeons in teams of four, and the surgery was done in the adjoining tent. My job was to prepare the wounded and try to bring them out of shock to ready them for the surgeons. Sometimes I assisted with the surgery when an assistant surgeon was exhausted. At other times, I would take a man with multiple wounds (before he went for abdominal surgery) into the next tent, where I had an X-ray machine and fluoroscope. Using local anesthesia, I would remove as many fragments in the extremities as were readily accessible using the fluoroscope. My company commander, Capt. Charles O. Butner, who had more sense than I had, came in one day and showed me the radiation burns he had on his fingers, and took my fluoroscope away from me. From then on, all I could use was the Picker X-ray machine and take roentgenograms. This slowed me down.

I remember a lieutenant who was hit on his steel helmet with a shrapnel fragment. The shrapnel knocked a large flap into the front of the steel helmet, bending it under his scalp in the frontal area of his head. He may have had a skull fracture hidden underneath, I do not know. Blood was streaming down his face. I sat him up on the edge of an army cot and took hold of the rim of the helmet and, by slowly wiggling it from side to side, managed to get it off his head. I dumped his dirt-filled hairy scalp flap out of the helmet. Then I cleaned the wound as best I could, and repaired the scalp with sutures and more sutures. As was the custom, I covered it with sulfanilamide powder. When I finished, he felt so good that he began shouting to let him go. "My men need me. I am going back out there, let me go," he said. I had to tell him that he was going back to England on the first plane leaving and that was final. He was a real nut—no, a real guy.

I met another soldier whom the medics carried in. He had the misfortune to step on a Bouncing Betty antipersonnel mine, which destroyed one foot and did a lot of scattered shrapnel damage. When the medics came to get him, he waved them away and instructed them to go find the mine removal crew. So the medics did what he told them and he calmly awaited their return. Meanwhile, he said he gave himself a shot with the morphine Syrette and took his eight sulfa tablets that he had been supplied.

4 | **RANGERS**

James W. Eikner (U.S. Army)

Located between the American invasion beaches of Omaha and Utah were prominent cliffs known as Pointe du Hoc, which sported a six-gun German artillery battery. James W. Eikner was part of the Ranger force sent to secure the cliffs.

I AM A VETERAN OF THE 2ND Ranger Battalion, which made history on June 6, 1944, the D-Day invasion of France. On the fortieth anniversary of D-Day, President Reagan addressed some Ranger veterans who made the historic and dangerous assault on the cliff-side enemy fortress at Pointe du Hoc. Indirectly through the media, he was speaking to the entire world. He told how these brave young men used rockets that trailed ropes and grapnel hooks, then scaled the vertical hundred-foot cliff to get at the enemy.

Due to the publicity given this event, most people associate the Rangers on D-Day with the assault at Pointe du Hoc, but the Ranger contribution to the success of D-Day was really much broader than just the Pointe du Hoc operation. Of course the operation there was one of the most unusual, one of the most daring, and one of the most dangerous in all of military history, and because of that it will always be the subject of books and movies.

During World War II there were six Ranger battalions. The 1st, 3rd, and 4th were organized overseas by Col. William O. Darby, who is really the father of the modern-day Ranger units. These Ranger units spearheaded the invasions into North Africa, Sicily, and Italy, and of course took part in many other hard-fought battles. The 2nd and 5th battalions, organized in the United States, spearheaded the invasion of D-Day into the German-held coast of France and then fought all across Europe in many hard fights thereafter. The 6th Battalion, also organized in the States, spearheaded the invasion into the Philippines, and there were other hard fights there.

The Ranger battalion was really a copy of the British commando with six rifle companies and one Headquarters Company. They had no specific way of operating, but the Rangers equipped and organized themselves and trained to meet whatever specific mission they were given. These units accepted only volunteers, and men were selected for their mental and physical stamina and their motivation to get the job done. Sometimes we were called suicide groups, but that wasn't true. We were simply spirited young people who took the view that if you were going to be a combat soldier, you may as well be the very best. Also we were anxious to get on with the war so as to bring things to a close and get home to our loved ones as soon as possible.

The training was exceedingly thorough, and we were made experts in all of the infantry weapons and tactics. When we went into battle, it wasn't all shaking of the knees and weeping and crying and so forth. We knew what we were getting into. We were volunteering for extra hazardous duty, confident that we could overcome any situation. Of course we were tense when under fire, but we were intent on getting the job done. We were actually looking forward to accomplishing our mission.

When General Bradley and his staff were making plans for D-Day, Operation Overlord, they were concerned about the large enemy gun installation atop the cliffs at Pointe du Hoc, which was equidistant between Omaha Beach and Utah Beach. The six 155mm guns there had a 25,000-yard range, and they could rain down much destruction on either of the beaches and reach far out into the sea to cause tremendous damage to naval craft out there. So this installation was seen as the most dangerous within the invasion area. Its early neutralization on D-Day morning was considered the primary objective for that day.

Toward the sea, the cliffs dropped about a hundred feet on average from vertical to near vertical with some overhang. Hardly anyone could conceive that the cliff side of the fortress would be assaulted from the sea. How could you do it? Back toward the land the usual defenses were set up—machine guns, antiaircraft weapons, minefields, barbed wire, large underground bunkers of reinforced concrete connected by underground tunnels—so it was a formidable position to attack from the land side. It would involve landing on the beach, and the closet beach suitable for landing was Omaha Beach, some five miles away. To try to land a unit there with the specific mission of taking Pointe du Hoc would have meant fighting through five miles of enemy territory while the big guns there brought destruction down on Omaha Beach. Some other way had to be found.

General Bradley had had happy experiences with the Rangers in North Africa and Sicily, and he often said that those boys were among the world's best soldiers and there was literally nothing they couldn't accomplish. Noting that there were two Ranger battalions in England at the time, the 2nd and the 5th, he called in the commanding officer of the 2nd Ranger Battalion, Lt. Col. James E. Rudder, a very talented man and a wonderful leader who was much loved by his Rangers. With sketches and aerial photographs, Colonel Rudder was made aware of the problem with Pointe du Hoc. Finally he said, "Well, sir, my Rangers can do the job." So the mission was turned over to him, and he was also given the 5th Ranger Battalion. The two battalions were out together with a Ranger force, and Colonel Rudder had overall command. The colonel went back and with his staff worked out a plan of attack on Pointe du Hoc. I was a member of Colonel Rudder's staff as communication officer and participated in those discussions.

Here is the plan that was presented to General Bradley and accepted. Three companies from 2nd Battalion (D, E, and F companies) would be specially equipped and trained to directly assault the cliff from the sea. Colonel Rudder would command that assault force, against the advice of General Bradley and his staff. They thought it was too dangerous for him to make the assault, and he should remain in an HQ, but he insisted that he would have to be there to make sure that the attack came off. We were thankful that he was there. I'm sure I would not be here today if he had not led us on the assault.

The assault had to succeed within a limited time frame because even after we landed and began our fight at Pointe du Hoc, if the big guns opened up say within thirty minutes or so, the air force would come in and bomb the area whether or not we were there. So if the assault was not successful within the time frame, a floating reserve would land at Omaha Beach.

This floating reserve was made up of the entire 5th Battalion and two companies of the 2nd Battalion. They would quickly pass through the lines of the 116th Infantry there, and then fight their way up to Pointe du Hoc, about five miles away. We expected that they would arrive there by noon on D-Day, but if things did go as well as we all hoped, then the reserve force would move in at Pointe du Hoc. Fighting together, we would quickly clean up the Pointe, then move west and fight on down to Grandcamp, which was the next objective.

One sixty-five-man unit from C Company of the 2nd Battalion probably had the most dangerous mission of all; they were assigned to land beneath the cliffs at Pointe De Lay Pierce. It was about halfway between Vierville-sur-Mer, which was right in the center of Omaha Beach, and Pointe du Hoc. The cliffs there were not quite as high or as steep as the ones at Pointe du Hoc, but the unit was to neutralize the large enemy defensive set up there that would be raining fire down on Omaha Beach. After that, they would fight on another two miles down Omaha Beach to Pointe du Hoc.

Prior to loading up on the converted Channel steamers, and while still in a marshalling area close by the port of embarkation, we were attacked by a small flight of enemy bombers. I can remember, when the eggs began to fall, rushing out of our tarpaper HQ and heading to a trench that I had expected to use, and low and behold it was already filled with GIs. So all I could do was flatten out on the ground and keep my fingers crossed. Thankfully everything came out all right.

Before we got on the boat; the whole 2nd Battalion came down with food poisoning—diarrhea and vomiting. We were all laid low and were concerned about whether we could go ahead with our mission. Some of us thought that perhaps this was an act of sabotage. We had been served wieners for the meal before we all got sick. I'm sure the contamination was from the wieners.

Neverthless we loaded up a little early, because General Eisenhower had originally established D-Day one day ahead of the time, but due to the rough weather he had postponed it for June 6. We actually postponed it after setting out for the coast of France and being called back.

While on the boats we were attacked by bombers again, the old German JU-88 dive-bomber, which is a slow, rumbling sort of craft that made a lot of noise. It was deadly, and I can remember hearing that thing dive down and once again having that uncomfortable feeling, "Well, here he comes." But there was no place to hide. You just had to cross your fingers and hope. Fortunately, the dive-bomber was shot down.

Finally, we were under way and headed toward the D-Day operation. We were all high spirited. There were a lot of poker games and a lot of storytelling, and everybody had a great time. Actually we got to bed a little late, probably too late, because we wouldn't be able to sleep again for three or four days. About three o'clock on D-Day morning we were aroused and went up and had a light breakfast. Our medical officer had ordered a light breakfast because the ocean was still quite rough, and he knew that if we ate too heavily, many of us would become seasick.

Following breakfast we were busy little beavers making sure that everyone had the right equipment and the boats or landing craft were being loaded up properly. Just before getting into the landing craft, Colonel Rudder and I decided to split up the small HQ group into two boats. They were British craft manned by British navy personnel. They were heavily loaded, and the route we were taking was such that the waves were headed right into us. Water began to leak in through the front ramp even though it was closed. Before too long we lost one entire boat with about twenty-six or twenty-seven people, plus one of the most gung-ho captains of the Rangers. Most of these men were picked up later and taken back to England. We got them back in about three weeks. We also lost a supply craft that went down with all six hands onboard. A second supply craft had to throw off about half of its load to stay afloat. In my own boat and many others, I discovered we had to rip up the floorboards and use our helmets to bail out the water. On top of that, some of the fellows were vomiting. You can imagine the situation while we were being shot at—bailing water with our helmets, dodging bullets, and vomiting all at the same time. Not much fun I can assure you.

Just about daybreak all hell broke out on the mainland, where, with the shelling from the big ships, it looked like a tremendous Fourth of July celebration. We were all standing up admiring it, really a sight to see. But then lo and behold, geysers of water began going up all around us. We thought we were being shelled, but we weren't. These were short rockets that were being fired toward the land from rocket boats behind us, and somebody had the wrong range. Once again there was a feeling of tenseness, but there you are and you can't go anywhere. The rocket ships were used in the European theater for the first time on D-Day, and they could fire hundreds of rockets simultaneously. It was a pretty thing to see, but somebody just had the wrong range. This was corrected, thank God.

Just as there was enough daylight to make out the headlands, things didn't look right to Colonel Rudder, who was in the lead craft of our little three-company flotilla that headed toward Pointe du Hoc. But we were some two to three miles east of Pointe du Hoc. Rudder convinced the British officer in charge of that craft that he was in error and made him flank right. Then we had to parallel the coastline for a couple of miles, which put us within small-arms range. I can remember when the first small arms hit our boat. It made a noise and somebody said, "What's that?" We looked up and there was a little round hole through one of the rope boxes. I said, "My God! These guys are playing for keeps." We had been standing up, except for those who were bailing water, so we all ducked down. The Germans were taking us under fire like shooting ducks in a tub, and it got worse as we came closer to the Pointe. At one time we were the target of 20mm guns firing incendiary, and we looked up and saw this big ball of fire coming at us. Fortunately my craft was not hit. One of our four DUKWs, an amphibious truck, was hit and several men were lost. We had London Fire Department hundred-foot fire ladders, and on top of these was a machine gun, so we could get over the cliff. Unfortunately none of these rigs was able to get in operating condition due to the roughness of the water. One got partway up the very narrow beach on Pointe du Hoc, but it was destroyed by a mine.

We landed at Pointe du Hoc some forty minutes late. We were out of our time frame, and Colonel Rudder sent the code message "Tilt," which told a floating reserve that it would land at Omaha Beach as soon as possible, pass through the lines of other forces there, then fight its way to Pointe du Hoc. Our small three-company task force had only 225 men initially, but we had already lost some of those due to the rough sea. We were on our own. We had some rocket-propelled grapnel hooks that trailed ladders made of ropes. We got into position a certain distance from shore so the angle was proper, and we fired two at a time. Some of the ropes didn't make it to the cliff top because the ropes had become wet and heavy. Some of the others pulled out, and the enemy cut some, but we did have enough to get the job done. Fortunately we had also brought along some portable rockets, so once we got on the beach we could fire up some of them.

We were under fire, of course, when we came in. The enemy had time enough to get out of the underground bunkers and shake his head, clear his brain, and take us under fire. Fortunately there was a small flotilla of destroyers in the vicinity, and also the old battleship *Texas*, which had participated in the shelling prior to our landing. [The battleships *Texas, Arkansas*, and *Nevada* all supported the D-Day landings, but for unknown reasons, most veterans of the landings seem to remember only the USS *Texas*.] Of course the air force bombed and the navy shelled Pointe du Hoc prior to our arriving, but things had been timed so that the shelling and bombing would let up just as we were touching down at 6:30 a.m. Well, we were forty minutes late, and we could see that the enemy was up and about.

I was the last one in from my boat. Most of us had something in the way of equipment to take off the boat. My responsibility was to take off a cloverleaf of mortar shells. These were fairly heavy 60mm mortar shells, and it would have been too bad if one of them had been hit while I was taking it off the boat. So I ran down the ramp and into water about up to my knees and headed on across what I thought was the beach. But I stepped into a shell hole that was covered with water. I went down over my head, and of course we were under fire. There was one machine gun especially on our left flank that was taking people under fire. Some of our people were getting hit, and I remember one young man who was hit three times on the landing craft and twice more on the beach. Believe it or not, that young man survived.

I laid down my cloverleaf of mortar shells under the cliff. There was a rope right in front of me, so I started up the cliff. Two or three guys were ahead of me, and the enemy was leaning over and shooting at us and throwing down hand grenades by the bushel basket full. A young guy above us, who was right at the edge of the cliff top, would reach over and fire, then duck down; fire and duck down; fire and duck. Finally he made it to the top. We called this guy Preacher because he was a dead shot with a rifle. Some of the fellas topside told me that the first thing he did when he got topside was to pull down his pants and relieve himself. The war had to stop for a while so Preacher could get organized.

Before we got to the top, about two-thirds of the way up, a tremendous explosion occurred just above us, and there was almost an argument between the colonel and me as to what it was. He thought it was a mine that the enemy had dangling over the cliff, but I was pretty sure it was a short shell from one of the naval craft. When it hit above us, it brought down tons of rock and dirt, and of course we all went back down the cliff. I caught on a little ledge where dirt had built up from debris, and I was covered up to my knees. The intense pressure on my legs was painful, and I think it caused some blood blisters.

The enemy was still up there shooting and throwing down grenades, and I got out my Tommy gun and took aim on one of the characters up there. But my gun wouldn't fire. So there I was in the grandest invasion in history with no weapon. I looked around and spied a youngster with a radio on his back down in a cave at water level beneath Pointe du Hoc. I scrambled down the cliff to him and said I had a number of priority messages to get out on his radio. One was written up in various publications. I sent the message, "Praise the Lord," a code phrase meaning that all the men were up the cliff. (In less than five minutes the first men had gotten up the cliff, and in less than thirty minutes all the essential people were up there.) I noticed that the man was wounded and in a lot of pain, so I opened his first-aid pack and gave him a shot of morphine, then painted a brown "M" on his forehead in iodine. This was so no one else would give him more morphine, which could have killed him.

Meanwhile a machine gun on the left flank was still raking the beach and was looking right down our throats.

I helped the other men in the cave stack up some rocks at the front of the cave to give them some protection from the enemy fire. Then I and my radioman went back along the beach again to locate the remainder of the HQ group. Along the way I ran into a commando colonel who had been working with us in our training and had come in with us on D-Day. He was walking up and down the beach, and I told him we were under fire and he could be hit. He said they can't hit you if you change your pace. I didn't think his philosophy was very sound, and sure enough about an hour later I saw him with a big bandage around his head. He had been wounded, although not severely.

I did locate my HQ group rather promptly. They were all set up in a large shell hole right on the edge of the cliff. This would be our HQ or command post until noon on the third day. This shell hole was open towards the sea and protected on the land side because the hole was made right against a very large bunker of reinforced concrete, so we felt snug in there while trying to get our radios in operation and get everything set up and going. The young Rangers who had scaled the cliff ahead of us had all been very carefully briefed and trained, and they knew their mission about knocking out the big guns and taking on the enemy in combat. They knew where everything was topside, despite the difficulty of finding their way through the shell holes and bomb holes.

But the big guns were not in place. Because of that, Cornelius Ryan said that perhaps the Ranger mission should not have taken place, thereby saving a lot of lives. As you will see, his conclusion wasn't really correct.

Once past the position where the guns were supposed to have been, our young Rangers continued to advance inland, fighting enemy on the way. One patrol led by a sergeant from D Company came upon the big guns about a mile inland. The enemy had moved them up there for better protection. (Prior to D-Day the air force had intermittently bombed the area, as well as other defenses on the coastline, but couldn't concentrate on Pointe du Hoc because that would have tipped off the enemy to the big push that would be made there.) While a buddy of his was standing guard, the sergeant sneaked into the big gun area where the guns were being camouflaged and put thermite grenades in the breach blocks to make them inoperable. There was a large enemy force within eyeball distance across the fields, as well as a large stockpile of shells ready to go, so if the Rangers had not been there, those guns would likely have been put into operation and brought much death and destruction down on our men, not only on Omaha but also on Utah Beach, which was within range. And because these guns could lob shells 25,000 yards, they could have caused much destruction at sea as well.

Francis W. Dawson (U.S. Army)

Of the two Ranger battalions assigned to take Pointe du Hoc, the majority of the men came in on Omaha Beach with orders to take the German position from the landward side. Francis Dawson's job was to link up with Rangers who came up the cliffs of Pointe du Hoc.

I WAS COMMISSIONED A SECOND LIEUTENANT, INFANTRY, United States Army Reserve, after attending military camp at Fort

231

Moultrie, South Carolina, in the 1930s. I entered active military duty on 9 January 1942 at Fort Benning, Georgia.

After completing Infantry School, basic course, I was assigned to Camp Roberts, California, then Camp Irwin, California, where I served as a test officer at the Desert Training Center. Then I was transferred to the 33rd Armored Regiment, 3rd Armored Division, which at the time was on maneuvers in the California desert. I was assigned as a tank platoon leader when the 3rd Armored deployed to Camp Pickett, Virginia; Indiantown Gap, Pennsylvania; and finally to England in 1943.

Around the third week of January 1944, I answered the call for volunteers for the 2nd and 5th Ranger battalions. We met with a cadre from the 2nd Ranger Infantry who interviewed us, asking why we wanted to be a Ranger. I imagine I gave him the right answer, for on 28 February the 33rd Armored Regiment received orders transferring two officers and fifteen enlisted men to the 5th Ranger Battalion. We boarded trucks to the railroad station, then boarded a train to Braunton, England, to the U.S. Army Assault Training Center. We were met by a cadre of the 2nd Ranger Battalion who were responsible for the training. For several weeks, they did their best to eliminate us, and the ones who survived were welcomed into the battalions as a Ranger.

Upon completing the course, the group with the 5th Rangers was trucked to the London railroad station, then boarded the train bound for Scotland. Upon reaching Glasgow, we were bussed to the dock. We boarded a ferry, and for a couple of hours we motored among the islands of northern Scotland to the island where the Rangers were taking training.

We were met on the dock by the battalion commander and his staff, who welcomed us to the 5th Ranger Battalion. That is the last I saw of him, as the battalion commander was relieved that day by Major Snyder.

We continued training in the hills of Scotland until the third day of April 1944. The battalions now moved back to southern England to the Assault Training Center for more training, including fire and movement, assaults on strongpoints, demolition, street fighting, and of course long marches and daily exercise. From 27 April 1944 to 5 May 1944, the battalion took part in amphibious maneuvers and training in every aspect expected to be encountered during the invasion.

On 6 May we moved to Swanage, England, where we had training in cliff scaling with ropes and steel ladders. On 17 May the battalion moved to Dorchester, England, then finally on 1 June to Weymouth Harbor, England. In these last several camps, we were in areas enclosed with barbed wire and with guards walking with live ammunition. No one came in or out who was not authorized.

On 1 June 1944, we were at Weymouth Harbor, where the battalion began loading on two ships: the HMS *Prince Leopold* and the HMS *Prince Baudouin*. D Company was on the *Prince Leopold*. We spent five days aboard this ship. It was very crowded and there was little space on deck for any type of exercise. Time was spent briefing and checking the platoon. Most of the time, the men just stayed in their assigned areas.

I shared a small compartment on the LCA [landing craft, assault] deck with Lt. Oscar Stowe, 1st Platoon leader of D Company. The compartment was located under an anti-aircraft gun position, which stayed active at all times and was very noisy with crew members walking around the gun. Time in my room was spent assembling my maps and marking targets on the map with numbers for called fire by the artillery and naval guns. And, finally, getting some sleep. The first day aboard ship I wanted to find out where my platoon was quartered and where my platoon LCA was located. We were being deck-loaded and we needed to know the route that my platoon would take getting to the LCA in the dark. I also made sure that my platoon sergeant, Jack Ronan, knew where I was bunked. I did not want to be left behind.

From 1 through 3 June, things were very routine. Check on the men, go to mess, get what exercise we could on deck in the space we had available. The night of 4 June, our ship moved out of the harbor, but later, to our surprise, we were back where we began. Rumors were flying that if the action didn't start soon, we would have to get off the ship and wait for better weather.

It was just another day aboard ship on 5 June, resting in my bunk and wondering what would happen next. We had a feeling that 6 June would be the day. Church services, which I think we all attended, were held on deck. There were no problems with equipment to keep up with. What I owned, I carried in a modified light infantry pack: two pairs of socks, a set of underwear, and some K rations. I carried a Thompson submachine gun, a .45-caliber pistol, a knife, and one ammo bag with submachine gun magazines, which I carried over my shoulder. Attached to my steel helmet was a quarter pound of TNT for use in digging a foxhole if needed. The blasting cap was securely wrapped and kept in my pocket. I wore impregnated wool pants and wool shirt. We wore jump boots and carried gas masks, as it was expected that the Germans would use gas. The gas masks were abandoned, though, shortly off the beach. I also carried one full canteen of water.

On the night of 5 June, we knew that tomorrow morning would be D-Day. It was around dusk that our ship started out of the harbor. I could see civilians in their homes as the ships moved through the narrow channel. When darkness began to fall, I again checked with my platoon to see that everyone was okay. Having only eighteen men, I really got to know them and what I expected from each one of them. I had a great platoon sergeant, Sergeant Ronan, and he kept me informed at all times. D Company was to be loaded on the port side, in two LCAs, one platoon in each. Company headquarters was divided among the two.

D Company 1st Sgt. Raymond M. Herlihy and several other Rangers from company headquarters were assigned to my LCA. I don't remember getting much sleep. At 3 a.m. I was up and dressed, and was heading to the ship's mess by 3:30 a.m. It was a sit-down breakfast. I must have had a good breakfast, because I did not eat again until late evening.

Around 4 a.m., Rangers were assembled on the deck near the assigned LCAs. A quick check of the platoon was made to be sure that everyone was there and had their equipment. This time, the LCAs had been lowered to the ship side, level with the deck, thus making it easy to load.

Over the PA [public address] system we heard a statement being read from General Eisenhower to "Soldiers and Sailors and Airmen of the Allied Expeditionary Force." Then came, "Rangers, disembark."

After having each been issued a life jacket, the ship was secured and we quickly stepped into the LCAs. I stood in front, beside the ramp. Beside me was First Sergeant Herlihy. After all the LCAs were loaded, we were lowered to the water. As we pulled away, the ship's captain over the PA system sounded: "Good hunting, Rangers!" As the LCAs began moving away from the ship and forming a single line, with about a hundred yards between boats, six-foot waves were causing the the boats to toss and bob. As the waves got rougher, water came into the boats, and the men started to bail, using their helmets. By this time, I was getting wet from the waves and the spray coming over the bow. For the next several hours, we looked ahead at the rear of the leading LCA. There was no communication among the boats. It was just like following the leader. I knew that if we did not go to Pointe du Hoc, we would have to go in on the beach.

Daylight broke. At times the lead LCA disappeared into the rolling seas, and waves broke over the boats. About five miles from the beach we began to circle, as in westerns as they circle the wagons, waiting for an Indian charge. I noticed that on our right, in the distance, a cruiser was controlling the assault boats that were hitting the beach. I could see the flag signals, and waited for the signal for us to make our run. In the meantime, I saw several large ships moving towards the beach. One fired a volley of rockets, and a destroyer that had cut across our front between us and the beach was firing at gun positions as it moved along.

Finally the signal came for us to move out. The LCAs formed a skirmish line parallel to the beach. I could not make out the shore due to the haze and smoke. I could see a building, but couldn't make out what type it was. As the LCA engines roared and we gathered speed, my eyes were still glued to the shoreline. Then I noticed the obstacles ahead: four posts set at an angle, with mines attached to the tops. We were just about upon them, and in the boat no one was talking. Every man was quiet. I imagine each had his own thoughts of what would happen when the ramp fell. One of the posts with the mine attached loomed just ahead.

The skipper made an abrupt turn to the left just as a tremendous wave hit the craft and lifted it over several obstacles. Then the craft beached itself. The ramp dropped and I was out and running for all I was worth. The water as I exited the boat was probably two feet deep. I could see my immediate destination—a seawall about a hundred yards ahead across the flat beach.

Five days on ship had taken their toll on my legs. After having just stood for several hours with the sea pounding, my legs would not move fast enough. But being the first out, I was a guide for the platoon to follow. We all ended up crowded behind the seawall. The men from the 29th Division were there, and we just had to push in for space. The wall was probably four feet high and made of wood. Being six foot four, I had to keep my head down. Our runner, Pfc. Robert Stein (who would be killed on Pointe du Hoc on 8 June by U.S. tank fire), was next to me behind the wall. I sent him to inform Lt.

George Miller, D Company commander, of our location. There was a lot of confusion, people there I did not know, some wounded, some in shock. Our platoon location on the beach was more to the left than the remainder of the company.

By that time, word had filtered down to me that it was time to move. With that, my two Bangalore torpedomen, Elwood Dorman and Ellis "Bill" Reed, shoved the explosives over the wall and under the triple barbed wire and pulled the fuses. Even behind the wall, with the shells exploding and a lot of machine gun fire sounding, tanks burning, and ships burning, one of the Bangalore torpedomen sounded off "Fire in the hole!" And as in training, everyone ducked, waiting for the explosive sound. Immediately I saw the situation, and with the help of 1st Sergeant Herlihy, who formed his hands as a cup in which I could place my boot, I was lifted over the wall, and on the double I went through the dust and on a path that the explosives had torn through the wire. I can still smell the powder as I ran along that path. As I was taught in Infantry School, when someone is shooting at you, you run, then hit the ground and start up again. This I did twice, and, realizing I was not hit, I continued.

The footpath led up the route I was to take near a fence of several strands of barbed wire. Signs reading "Attention: Mines" hung on the wire. This really put me on the alert as I started my climb. Now the smoke from fires on the hillside was blowing my way, but I was just ahead of the smoke. I could see the enemy positions beyond me, but so far they had not seen me.

I continued to the crest of the hill. There I found myself among Germans. The ones I did dispose of quickly caused the

238

others to decide to surrender. I was still alone, as I must have outdistanced my platoon in climbing, but I could not wait for them on the crest because I was receiving fire.

I kept moving along the crest in a bent-over position. Just over the crest toward the beach, I could see a machine gun position about seventy-five yards away with two men firing onto the beach. They did not see me, and I turned in the direction of my platoon. I wanted an automatic rifle, which had more firepower and range than my Thompson. I motioned for my BAR man to bring the automatic rifle, and Pfc. Harry Bolton came forward. In the meantime the machine gunner had spotted us, and before we could take him under fire, he turned the machine gun and killed my BAR man. I retrieved the BAR and opened fire on the Germans, killing them as they retreated, carrying the machine gun with them through some wire they had to cross.

By now, my platoon was on the move. So were others of the battalion who also had followed my movement up the bluff. Everyone was following the leader because the route crossed a mined area, and we had been trained to following a lead man's footsteps. Thus, it slowed the platoon's advance. From the top of the bluff I could see artillery shells hitting the beach. I watched as two large craft that were coming in to discharge the troops were hit and were burning.

Originally my platoon of D Company was supposed to be the rear guard of the battalion if we had to move and make a beach landing and move inland. Now we were leading the battalion. Since we were up front, we continued. We had no more enemy contact until we received some machine gun fire as soon as we got to the Vierville-sur-Mer road. We failed to eliminate this gun, which was moved back through the hedgerows as we attacked it. We withdrew and came back to the Vierville-sur-Mer road.

Our movement now was to outskirt the enemy around Vierville-sur-Mer and strike out toward Pointe du Hoc. But as night fell, we dug in and formed a perimeter for the beachhead south of Vierville-sur-Mer, reinforced by some elements of the 116th Infantry and other scattered remnants of other units. The only action my platoon had for the night of 6 June was several stray cows, which caused some alarm.

The next morning, 7 June, was attack time again. We advanced along the Vierville-sur-Mer road with two medium tanks in support of C and D companies, plus about 150 men of the 116th Infantry and about 80 men of the 2nd Ranger Battalion. For eight hours, we received heavy artillery bombardment. Again, we dug in for the night. On the morning of 8 June, C and D companies received orders to attack cross-country to Pointe du Hoc. We met no resistance, and contacted the 2nd Ranger Battalion on Pointe du Hoc. The battalion of the 116th Infantry and tanks of the 743rd Tank Battalion, who were attacking Pointe du Hoc from the southwest, caught the Rangers in their fire. My platoon received direct fire from U.S. tanks. This continued until they realized that we were American forces.

We then moved from Pointe du Hoc to Grandcamp, and the fighting lasted only a few more days before we were pulled out of combat to rest and recoup. General Bradley, accompanied by General Patton, paid a visit to the battalion two weeks later and awarded medals. I was awarded the Distinguished Service Cross.

Victor H. Fast (U.S. Army)

The Rangers who landed on Omaha Beach or climbed the cliffs of Pointe du Hoc on D-Day possessed a wide range of skills. Victor Fast recounts how his language skills helped out his unit on that fateful day.

I WAS A SERGEANT IN THE 5TH Ranger Battalion, which was spearheading the Omaha Dog White/Green amphibious landings in Normandy. I was Col. Max Schneider's interpreter (German) and therefore was in the LCA [landing craft, assault] with him. The first glimpse I had of the French shore was when he tapped me on the shoulder and said, "Hey, Vic, take a look at the beach and the cliffs."

I remember seeing smoke on the Omaha Beach hillside exactly where we were supposed to land. When Colonel Schneider saw the intense firepower of the German defenders' shells landing in our beachhead area, he ordered the British flotilla commander to land east of Omaha Dog Green. Colonel Schneider's presence of mind and shrewd strategy characterized a Ranger mind at work and an officer not afraid to make a decision. I'm convinced he saved a multitude of lives, maybe hundreds. I'm thankful to the good Lord for Colonel Schneider's presence.

I saw some of our LCAs overturn upon hitting underwater obstacles. Some hit element Cs, tetrahedrons, and hedgehogs with teller mines attached. Mortars, 88s, machine guns, and small-arms fire swept the beach as we approached. The naval bombardment had set the vegetation on fire. Colonel Schneider jumped into the Channel, and all the men in our LCA followed; we all swarmed to shore.

When I crawled up the beach to the seawall, I had an M1 rifle, two bandoliers of ammo, and several grenades. No helmet, no gas mask, no pack, because I had peeled all these off so I could swim. I immediately looked around for a helmet, a .45, et cetera. I found a helmet from a dead buddy, only to see that it was half full of a head. I quickly found another and wore it, as well as a .45 automatic, throughout the rest of the war.

We were lying behind the rock seawalls regrouping. General Cota walked up and then promptly hit the sand because of machine gun fire. He said to Colonel Schneider, "I'm expecting the Rangers to lead the way." We started inland through smoke, haze, and a field of Bouncing Bettys. When we captured some Germans, Colonel Schneider let me demonstrate my expertise. He told me to interview a number of the German soldiers. He didn't tell me who or what to ask; he just said to get whatever information I could. I used my common sense and picked the youngest (I was only twenty-one on June 4, 1944), most timid looking, lowest-ranking Kraut I could find. I took him away from the lieutenant and other captives and told him straightforward, "You are going to tell me what I want to know." First I told him that the war was over for him and to relax. I asked him if he had observed all the American and British bombers overhead earlier that morning, and he said, "Yes." Good. I wanted him to get in the "yes" mood. Then I told him I'd give him three choices when answering me. One, if you tell me nothing, nothing at all, you just keep your mouth shut, and I'll send you over to the Russians. Of course, I couldn't do anything of the sort. Second, if you give me information, such as location of minefields, number of your comrades in the immediate vicinity, et cetera, and you leave any doubt in my mind that you're telling the truth, I'll turn you over to my Jewish buddy here standing next to me, Herb Epstein, and he'll take you behind that bush over there. You get what I mean. Herb nodded, signifying to me that he understood. He had not shaved for a day, he was big and burly, and he had a .45 on his hip and a Ranger knife in his boot and an automatic Thompson machine gun. He looked mean enough to scare the living daylights out of anybody. Herb was Colonel Schneider's intelligence sergeant. He knew Yiddish, not German, but he understood some of my questioning and knew more about the operation invasion than our intelligence captain. Third, if you tell me what you know and convince me you are telling me the truth, I'll send you to America and you will have a good life until the war is won by the Allies and then you'll get to go home.

So he told me of the little mines (Bouncing Bettys) and about the fortifications on Pointe du Hoc. He told me there were no troops as such in Vierville-sur-Mer, but inland there were numerous elite panzer divisions, et cetera. I thanked him. I said tell me more. He added that the beaches and bank approaches were covered with a crossfire from 88s to mortars and machine guns. I said yes, I know, because we came through a barrage on the way up the slope.

We proceeded up the Vierville-sur-Mer draw and drew fire from the sides and sniper fire from the church steeple, so Colonel Schneider called for naval bombardment of the church. It was promptly demolished. A girl sniper was found in the church rubble. D-Day night Colonel Schneider set up battalion HQ in a chateau with courtyard in the front and the back. I dug a foxhole (slit trench) just outside the front door and stood guard while medics tended to the wounded inside. We hung GI blankets over the windows to hide the candlelight indoors. Jerry came over and bombed us that night, and Father Lacey bailed out of the prone position in my foxhole.

After receiving reports from his company commanders soon after dark, Colonel Schneider realized he was short of 60mm mortar shells. He called me in and briefly ordered me to go down to the beach, get all the ammo I could retrieve, and bring it to his CP. I started to ask him how I was going to accomplish this, but stopped short of the question and left the room. I crawled in my foxhole and performed some quick mental maneuvers. I was a sergeant and only an interpreter. I had no squad, platoon, or anyone to help me. I decided to use my country ingenuity and get a Frenchman with a horse and two-wheeled cart and go down the Vierville-sur-Mer draw and load the cart with the 60mm mortar shells from the backs of my own fallen Rangers and from the dead of the 116th Regiment. After many hand signs, et cetera, I got a Frenchman I had seen with a horse and cart to harness the horse and let me have the rig. I proceeded down the draw, took ammo from the fallen dead, and returned without mishap. The moon was in and out of clouds, but I clanged down the road and back and fulfilled the mission ordered by the colonel, never giving it a second thought. Mulling it over now, I think I did all right.

I also remember one of our HQ Rangers boasting that he was going to have sex with a French woman within eight hours after he hit the beaches. Sure as hell, Herb Epstein cracked a door when we were clearing Vierville-sur-Mer and he saw the knucklehead in the act.

At one point I came across a GI who had a gaping stomach wound. I lit a cigarette for him, shot him full of morphine, and left. I'm sure he bled to death in no time. Two very close buddies of mine died on D-Day: motor pool Sgt. Walter J. Zack (killed in action) and 1st Lt. Dee C. Anderson (a Mormon from Salt Lake City). Dee was a young, clean-cut kid and as reliable as the day is long. He caught a bullet in the side of the head while leading his platoon across an opening in a hedgerow. Walt was killed on the beach directing traffic. A direct hit from an 88 splattered him on the beach.

Prior to D-Day we trained in Scotland for the landings—climbing, scaling cliffs, and hiking. We went to Weymouth, England, to board the HMS *Prince Leopold* and HMS *Prince Baudouin*. I happened to be on the *Prince Baudouin* with some British commandos who had landed at Dieppe, Dunkirk, and Africa. They had seen action that we had not. We lay around onboard cleaning our weapons and playing pinochle; the commandos joined in but were sweating. None of us made any remarks about their sweating, but inside we knew (I think) what was going through their minds.

We went into battle with the best—elite, highly trained, mostly civilian soldiers—with the goal of toppling Hitler's Atlantic Wall and bringing the war to an end. We believed in God, in the USA and Britain, and what they stood for. With that as our buckler, we could not fail.

Donald L. Scribner (U.S. Army)

Many of the Rangers who landed on Omaha Beach saw their planned missions fall by the wayside due to the overwhelming firepower advantage enjoyed by the Germans. Donald Scribner spent most of his time helping wounded buddies.

ON THE NIGHT OF JUNE 5, WE were approached by our colonel, James Rudder, who was in charge of the 2nd Ranger Infantry Battalion, and a great man he was. He explained to us our mission and what we were to do. The mission of our C Company was to land at H hour with a combat team from the 116th Infantry Regiment of the 29th Infantry Division on Omaha Dog Green beach. Able Company of the 116th Regiment had the mission of capturing the village of Vierville-sur-Mer if they could do so without too much resistance. Then a small Ranger company would simply follow them through the town. If the enemy were too strong for A Company of the 116th, then G Company of the Rangers would scale the cliffs at Pointe De Raz La Percee, on the western flank of Dog Green beach. Charlie Company was to destroy enemy gun positions located on the point with assistance from tanks firing from the beach. Navy destroyers would provide a pre-assault bombardment and remain on call should any company need additional power during battle.

However, after all the plans were drawn up, none of them came true. I remember quite well the rough crossing of the English Channel. The waves were very high. We were about ten miles from shore when Colonel Rudder talked to us prior to loading up the LCAs [landing craft, assault]. "Boys, you are going on the beach as the first Rangers in this combat to set foot on French soil, but don't worry about being alone. When D, E, and F take care of Pointe du Hoc, we will come down and give you a hand with your objective. Good luck and may God be with you." This scenario also did not develop.

First section and second section left our transport, the *St. Charles*, by climbing down the rope ladders alongside the ship. We loaded into two LCAs commanded by British sailors, and God bless them. They were beautiful and wonderful fellows who died with high honors as far as I'm concerned.

We rendezvoused in the Channel with Company A of the 116th Regiment, then started toward the beach. My buddy Walter Gallen, in our LCA, was celebrating his third wedding anniversary and we were singing "Happy Anniversary" to him. And I overheard some of the fellows saying, "It's going to be a cinch. I don't think they know we're coming." How wrong they were.

We almost got to the beach when all hell broke loose. We were hit by artillery fire, mortars, machine guns, you name it. The LCA that I was on was hit three times. The first shell hit the very front and tore the ramp completely off. The young man who was sitting in the front never knew what hit him. I know that the LCA started filling up with lots of blood. It was just as red as anything could be. Then it was hit again, on the port side. I started to go over to the rear starboard side. When I looked back, I noticed a 60mm mortar lying on the bottom. The young man who was to carry that ashore was dead. Just as I reached down to get it, a shell took out the rear starboard side, which I'd been heading toward.

I was a radio operator and a sniper and I was carrying a 305 radio. I also had my rifle, grenades, extra ammunition, and a bedroll, all of it on my back. When I finally got out of the LCA, I started sinking in the Channel from all the weight I was carrying. I didn't think I would ever stop going down. Somehow I made it to shore, but I was so tired that I dropped three times as I ran across the beach. Each time I dropped, machine guns burst in front of me in the sand. Miraculously I missed getting machine gun slugs through my body.

I finally made it to the cliffs. Our real mission was to follow A Company of the 116th Regiment of the 29th Division up the beach. Their objective was to take Vierville-sur-Mer. However, that did not come true. The 116th Regiment was practically wiped out, so our only alternative was to climb the cliffs to the right of the beachhead.

I looked back as I started up the beach, and I saw Walter Gallen lying in the sand with his hand raised, asking for help. I started back for him with Fred Beetle, a young man from southern Indiana. I say "man" because, literally, that's what he was, all man. I left Fred with Walter and headed off to find some medication. On the way I saw Oliver Reed, a buddy of mine from Fort Wayne, Indiana, sitting tight against the cliffs, kind of rolled up in a knot. His face was swollen and he was shivering. I could tell that he had been hit. I put my hand on his shoulder and told him to take it easy, that I would get him some help. I made it across the open beach to the other side trying to find medication for Oliver and for Walter Gallen. As I ran across the beach, I saw a lot of 116th Regiment men lying there, blown to bits, bodies lying all over. I found some medication and brought it back. When I reached Walter, he was dead, and Fred was gone.

When we first hit the beaches, our first sergeant, Duke Gollis, from Maine or Connecticut, had about half his head blown away but he was still standing at the bottom of the cliff firing his weapon, hollering at the Krauts up above to come out and fight. I saw him get hit across the chest with three bursts of machine gun bullets. He was quite a man. All of them were good men who gave their lives that day, and I hope no one ever forgets it. I know I won't. I was one of the very lucky ones, and I'll always be grateful for that.

I made it to the top of the cliff without realizing that Ralph Goranson, my captain, had followed me all across the beach. He said he was going to follow me from now on. I told him about the radio, that I was unable to raise anyone and had no communications whatsoever. He told me to take it off, as it wasn't doing us any good.

We had a lot of sniper fire that day, an awful lot of it. Lieutenant Moody and some of his men had started toward a fortified house held by the Germans back a few yards on top of the cliffs. They were firing their machine guns from there and directing artillery fire. They took that fortified house, and in doing so Lieutenant Moody lost his life.

I saw another man who had taken the house, L. K. Stephens, bleeding from the head, and I ran out to him. He was standing on a knoll. I stood up there and put sulfa drugs into his wound, which was clear across the top of his head.

When we landed we had diamond-shaped patches on our helmets; they stood for Ranger battalion. Whoever the sniper was who shot him got a center hit inside the diamond. It creased his skull practically the full length of his head. It was about as deep as my finger, sideways. Not one time did I get fired at while I was out there. If I was, they missed me.

We went back to where Captain Goranson was, then I went back down the cliffs to see how my buddies were doing. I crossed that beach for the second time that day looking for more medication. All I could see were bodies, a lot of American soldiers who gave their lives that day.

I came back on top of the cliff. There was a lot of firing from our navy, but the dive-bombers didn't do much good. I saw one of the pillboxes take a direct shell hit, but all it did was cause a dent about six inches deep. Those Germans really knew how to build safe enforcement places.

I thought the day would never end. The original plans were that after D, E, and F companies took Pointe du Hoc, they would meet up with us and we would continue fighting inland. However, that didn't occur. Not on D-Day it didn't. When night came, the snipers were thick. I must have fired at least two hundred rounds of ammunition that day. I fired at anything and everything that moved.

A couple of comical things happened on D-Day. Before we started up the cliffs, the Germans were lying out over the tops, firing their weapons and throwing what they called potato mashers, which were their hand grenades. Well, one of them got a little mixed up, and when he wanted the grenades to come over, he'd holler out, "Here come some more mashed potatoes!" We got a kick out of his name for potato mashers.

Also on that day, our navy ships were firing rockets and heavy artillery. Due to the rough sea, and I mean rough sea, their accuracy wasn't too great. A lot of the rockets landed in the Channel as well as on the beach. One of the shells hit a cliff where we were, and a man named Lindsay got knocked down from the concussion of it. I think he fell off the cliff because he was staggering around and cussing the Krauts, saying that they stole his damn rifle and blaming a colonel from the 116th Regiment for stealing it. All the time his rifle was right on his shoulder. However, before the day ended, he snapped out of it and seemed to be all right.

5 | UTAH BEACH

Orval Wakefield (U.S. Navy)

One element of the U.S. Navy's contribution to the landing on Utah Beach was the employment of naval combat demolition units, the forerunner of the navy SEALs, to take out beach obstacles. Orval Wakefield details his part in that assignment.

A RECRUITER CAME AROUND AND ASKED FOR volunteers for NCDU [naval combat demolition unit]. He explained to those who showed up (about forty men) why they were needed. It seemed that some marines had been landed at an island surrounded by coral reef, and when the marines got on the coral and stepped off into deep water, some of them drowned. It was decided then that the navy would be responsible for all obstacles underwater and on the beach. The army, navy, or marines would be landed safely. He also explained that this duty was extremely hazardous, that they needed good swimmers who would get special training physically and mentally, and that these men would be expendable. We would be working with booby-trapped obstacles. The good thing was that we were not doing KP duty and could get out at the end of the war. Although about forty men were there, after the briefing there were only two of us.

Everything turned out to be true. We were trained by quarrymen, coal miners, and explosive experts, then sent to Fort Pierce, Florida, on March 1, 1944, and into NCDU #132. We had hard physical training and explosives training. Everything was very secret. We had a six-man unit: one officer, one chief petty officer, and four rated sailors in a naval combat demolition unit. Some of these six-men units had been sent to both the Pacific and Europe. Those in the Pacific finally formed into hundred-man teams and were commissioned as such and were called UDTs [underwater demolition teams]. My NCDU team was sent to England via plane from New York on April 15. Maybe eight teams were there already.

Just before D-Day we were aboard an amphibious ship. We thought we were going ashore on June 5 so we were already excited and didn't sleep. On June 6 at midnight, we were still standing around, wondering what it would be like ashore as we watched all of the explosives going off. It seemed everything was lit up. There were shells going in and bombers and it looked like the biggest Fourth of July anyone could make. I told my CPO [chief petty officer] that no one could survive that, and he said, "You can bet there will be someone waiting when we get there."

After we got off our amphibious ship and into our LCP [landing craft, personnel], there was just our eight-man team that had been expanded by two young seamen who had volunteered. They as well as two army engineers had been sent to England by mistake.

The navy was responsible for obstacle removal, and our team had the explosives. Our LCP went around with other LCPs in order to line up to make the first wave go ashore. The big guns from the battleships were booming, and it felt like it shook the boat, it was so loud. Eventually, we all got seasick. By the time we got to shore, though, we were not afraid anymore. We were just glad to get our feet on solid ground. I was desperate to reach land. I got off the boat and the water was up to my chin. I was only five foot six inches tall.

Our outfits were marine greens, boots, helmets, and paper-boy sacks that had explosives in front and back. The explosives were plastic and they had been put in navy socks. We had tied a line on each end so it could be used ashore.

When we got out of the boats and onto the beach, I found that my legs would hardly hold me up and I knew something was wrong. I thought I was a coward. I finally found that I was carrying two seabags full of water and explosives that probably weighed at least a hundred pounds. I used my knife to cut both bags and let the water out. I was able to get up on the beach, which was about 250 yards from the seawall.

All the obstacles on our part of the beach were like children's jacks, only they were made out of six-inch I-beams five feet high. I doubt if anything could have crawled over those. We had previously been told that we had to get rid of those obstacles by the time the fourth wave came in. While we were working on the obstacles, the incoming GIs were dodging around them. The explosives were tied to the obstacles by Prima cord, which is a quarter-inch-thick cord that is an explosive in itself. It is not a fuse, and if one man was hit by a tracer bullet our explosives would all instantly explode. We looked down the lines of obstacles and started working on them, having to keep chasing the GIs out from behind them.

Finally we got everything loaded and got the GIs out of the obstacles. I don't think anybody stopped to think about being in no-man's-land loaded down with high explosives and knowing that if anything hit you it would be a disaster to the whole unit.

We finally shouted "fire in the hole" and blew the charges. Then we went up to the seawall, where we found a slight trench alongside a German 88 gun enclosure. We got in the shallow trench, if you can call it that, and watched what was happening on the beach. We realized that when we first came in, there was nothing there but obstacles, then men running, turning, and dodging. All of a sudden it was like a beehive. Amtracs were able to come through the water and also on the land. Caterpillar earthmovers had pushed sand against the seawall and into the interior. It looked like an anthill.

We had been successful. I don't think anything could have gotten by those obstacles; they were too tremendously made. But when we got up to the seawall after we blew our obstacles, there was the problem of getting the GIs up and over the seawall so they could go inland. The officers would say "go," and finally one went, then a second, and then they all went over that wall like a bunch of ants.

During the morning one plane flew into our airspace, and of course all the ships at sea and on the ground shot at the plane. No planes were supposed to be in that space. As it turned out, it was one of our own planes. The pilot did get out by parachute. I hope he got to the ground safely. One time when we were watching all these men come inshore and all of the wheeled vehicles, everything seemed to be going so well when all of a sudden it seemed like a cloud started from the horizon over the ocean. It came towards us and by the time it got to us, it still extended clear back to the horizon.

Our planes with gliders were going to be turned loose inland. It was a sight that you would never see again. That many planes seemed like just a cloud in the sky.

It turned out to be a pretty good day for our team, NCDU #132. Our units at Utah Beach had thirty casualties that day and at Omaha Beach they had 70 percent casualties for that day. I guess we were lucky that we lost only two of eight men.

Grant G. Gullickson (U.S. Navy)

U.S. Navy destroyers played an important part in providing close-range fire support to the soldiers on Utah Beach. Grant Gullickson recounts the price that one destroyer paid for that job.

UPON ARRIVING IN NORFOLK, VIRGINIA, I WAS transferred to a new destroyer that had just been placed in commission in Charleston, South Carolina, the USS *Cory*, DD-463. I was a machinist's mate second class, and I was assigned to the after engine room. The USS *Cory* left the shipyard in early 1942, probably around March. We operated in the Atlantic Ocean from Panama up to north of the Arctic Circle and participated in numerous antisubmarine operations. On one of these operations the USS *Cory* sank a German sub, the U 801. We also participated in the battle of the landing in North Africa in 1942 and in a raid on Bodo, Norway, with a British fleet in 1943.

In April 1944 we departed Norfolk, Virginia, escorting an ammunition ship in company with the USS *Forrest* and USS *Hobson*. We arrived in England in the latter part of April 1944.

While in England, we operated in local ops and worked with the army on an operation called Slapton Sands, in northwestern England. On June 6 we were out in the Channel, having left England on June 4. We proceeded across the Channel and were assigned to lead the first wave of boats into Utah Beach. Meanwhile I had been promoted to chief machinist's mate and was in charge of the forward engine room on the USS *Cory*. Anyhow, we had dropped some depth charges on a submarine contact on the way across the Channel and had a nipple rupture on one of our feed pumps. I had spent the whole night with my fellow crew members repairing this broken nipple, because we knew that when the big thing happened the next morning, all power was going to be required.

Around midnight that night we were close to shore. We had a smoke watch on destroyers, to watch the stacks to make sure that we weren't leaving any smoke that we shouldn't. Around two in the morning, we received word from smoke watch, our pipeline of information of what was going on topside. He said that it looked like the whole world had lit up. I stuck my head out of the hatch and had a breath of fresh air and the whole world did look lit up. Thousands of bombers were dropping illumination flares, what we call pathfinders. The whole earth seemed to shake. I immediately dogged the hatch down. Our four boilers were dripping with sweat, and the turbines were hissing steam. Our job was to give the skipper whatever speed was ordered—from full speed ahead to emergency astern. Overhead the guns roared as they fired on German targets on the beach.

The ship would shudder as German shells hit the water near the ship, some of them hitting the ship topside. We had been there only a few minutes, but it seemed like an eternity. I imagine we fired about four hundred or five hundred rounds. All of a sudden, the ship literally jumped out of the water; the floor plates came loose, the lights went out, and steam filled the space. It was total darkness, with severely hot and choking steam everywhere. We figured that this was it, that our grave was to be the forward engine room on the *Cory*. Then there was another rumble from underneath the ship. But then everything became really quiet and the steam that had filled the space dissipated. The water reached the upper level, up to our waist, but the steam had stopped. We grappled to open the hatch and get out of the space. I found out later that the reason the steam dissipated was that the boilers in the forward fire room, the source of our steam, had ruptured. Undoubtedly, the fact that these boilers ruptured and all the steam went up the stack saved our lives. We evacuated through the hatch, and by the time we got up on deck, the main deck was awash. In the machine shop near the exit hatch from the forward engine room, the deck was ruptured clean across. It was obvious that the *Cory* was dead.

I noticed that my life belt and shirt were missing. We wore life belts in the engineering space instead of life jackets; they weren't quite so clumsy. They had been ripped from my body by shrapnel, but it hadn't drawn any blood. But I knew from training that I would need a life belt or some type of floating device because the Channel water was 54 degrees. Although I was a pretty good swimmer, I knew that I would need something to keep me afloat. My head and chest hurt, but there was no blood. I was okay. The thing now was to make sure that all the guys were out of the engine room and away from the ship, because the shore batteries continued to shoot at it. The shells were hitting near and some were hitting the ship as it lay dead in the water.

Chief Peterson, who was in charge of the damage control party, was topside working with his repairmen doing what he could to save the ship. I said, "Pete, do you have any idea where I can find a life belt?" He said, "Yeah, up in the chief's quarters. I saw it hanging on the bunk as I went through there a little bit ago." I went up to the chief's quarters and got the life belt, then went to the after engine room, where CMM Charlie Brewer was in charge. He stuck his head out of the hatch and said, "I got a full head of vacuum, but I can't go anywhere; the screws are out of the water."

At this time, word came out to abandon ship. We were still receiving heavy fire from the shore. So I abandoned ship on the starboard side about midships. We didn't jump off the ship; we literally floated off it because the ship was underwater.

As I got in the water, I saw a floater net, a lifesaving device on a ship that is cast into the water as the ship is sinking. Swimming with my life belt on, I managed to grab hold of the net. This particular net had mostly gunner's mates around it. One of the gunners was seriously wounded. He was told by a shipmate that all that could be done was to keep his head out of the water, which we did. Shells continued to burst in the water around us, and each time one would hit, it felt like someone was trying to force a sea bag up your rectum.

A couple of hours later, the whaleboat from the USS *Fitch* arrived and towed the floater net alongside the *Fitch*. By this time we were almost incapacitated due to the cold water. Our hands were so numb that we were unable to grasp and hold a line to pull us out of the water. The *Fitch* people reached over the side and some literally came down and dragged us out of the water and brought us aboard. They gave us coffee, heavily laced with alcohol that they had somehow or other appropriated. It was torpedo alcohol or water testing alcohol, but I was so cold I couldn't hold a cup. The chief gunner's mate aboard the *Fitch* held the cup for me. He said, "Buddy, it's great to see you. Everything is going to be all right." The *Fitch* was just unbelievable in their generosity. They opened their lockers to provide us with dry clothes and prepared food and gave us medical help. You name it, they gave it to us.

I started to check around on the *Fitch* to see who was there from the *Cory*. I was saddened to find that Charlie Brewer, the chief machinist's mate from the aft engine room, lay dead in a bunk. A piece of shrapnel had hit him in the back of the head. It was such a small piece that you could barely see it. But he didn't make it.

Later we were transferred to the USS *Barnett*, a troop transport that was loaded with the bodies of sailors, soldiers, airmen, and the wounded, plus survivors of sunken ships. Onboard this ship was the body of my good friend Chief Peterson, who had told me earlier where the life jacket was. Shrapnel from an exploding shell had cost him his life. Also on this ship was Chief Rouinsky, "Big Chief," of the forward fire room. He had steam burns over 99 percent of his body. We tended to him and he could talk a little, but the burns were too much. He passed away the next day. We were off loaded in England and in time were transferred back to the States.

Sam Grundfast (U.S. Navy)

Among the many obstacles the Germans placed off Utah Beach were large sea mines. Sam Grundfast tells of his misfortune when his landing ship, tank (LST) encountered one of these underwater explosive devices.

WE PROCEEDED FROM GRENOCK, SCOTLAND, TO PLYMOUTH, England, where LCT [landing craft, tank] crews were organized and assigned to various landing craft that were brought over to England in pieces and assembled in Cardiff, Wales. The LCTs would be used to carry tanks to the beach when the invasion began. These tanks had canopies and an outboard motor, so we could launch at sea and proceed to the beach. They would look like small boats and act as support fire for the incoming troops in subsequent waves of the invasion. This particular unit was to precede H hour by twenty minutes.

We trained in and about Cardiff, Wales, and the English Channel, practicing how to launch these tanks while 3,000 to 4,000 yards from the beach. After a month or two, we became quite proficient at it.

On or about June 1, all units were quarantined, and then we knew that the landing at Normandy (named Overlord) was beginning. We didn't know the name Overlord at that time; we learned that later. At that time, I was stationed at Queen Anne's Battery, which was just up the road from Plymouth, England. There were many buzz bomb attacks in that area at night, but fortunately none of our units was hit by any of them.

On or about June 4, we assembled and proceeded towards France according to orders. We were in the unit that preceded the first wave. The only thing in front of us was a picket boat showing us the way in because it had navigational equipment. However, the weather was so bad and the seas were so rough that we received a flag signal to put about and follow the picket boat back into Portsmouth Harbor. Imagine the confusion: four thousand or so landing craft jammed into that small harbor. You could almost walk across the harbor going from boat to boat.

Then, after considerable speculation as to what would transpire, we received orders at about 2 a.m. on June 6 to reassemble and proceed back to our stations and then to our assigned beach, which was Utah Beach, and follow the orders as laid down in the Overlord program.

Because our unit was the first wave, we were due to hit Utah Beach at approximately H hour minus twenty minutes. My unit, which consisted of six LCTs, was therefore first in line. The only thing in front of us was the picket boat, which looked like a small fishing craft.

We were proceeding towards the beach in a line formation, one boat behind the other. We proceeded in this column form, passing underneath the 8-inch guns of the USS *Augusta*, a cruiser. Also, how could you miss the air force sortie overhead, with wave after wave of fighters and bombers. It was just fantastic.

At approximately 3:45 a.m. I was relieved of duty by the other officer. This was now June 6, because I was on duty from midnight til 4:00 a.m.; he was supposed to take it from 4:00 to 8:00 a.m. I was supposed to go below and try to get some sleep along with the other men who had been relieved of their duties when the second group came on duty at 4:00

a.m. Of course, how could you rest with 8-inch guns popping off and such overflights? But I did go down below, and maybe I had a premonition of what would happen, because I put whatever money I had into my pocket along with a fountain pen that was a gift to me upon graduation.

At about 5:00 a.m., since I couldn't sleep, I went topside and just stood where the other officer was on duty with the signalman and watched what was going on.

At approximately 5:40 a.m., I'd say forty minutes from launch time, we were maybe 6,000 yards from the beach. The water was so rough that the waves were at least six feet high. We received orders by flag and Morse light to form a line abreast and proceed into the beach. We were ordered not to launch the tanks because they might be swamped and sink in the rough seas where the water was too deep for the draft of the tank. Since I had been in Boy Scouts for a number of years (I was an Eagle Scout), I could read these messages before the signalman told me what they said.

A signal was sent from the lead boat to form a line abreast from a column. The other officer didn't give the command for the ship to steer left and pull into a line abreast. He just seemed to freeze. The signalman looked at me, I looked at him, and I then took over the command of the boat. I gave the signal that we were obeying the order by dropping the flag, which indicated that we were going to move into a line abreast.

A few minutes thereafter, when we were almost a line abreast, we hit what I later learned was a mine, powerful enough to destroy a ship let alone a small boat. It literally, I found out later, blew us sky high. The other officer in the boat was killed. Everyone was killed except me and two of the navy personnel—the motor machinist, Richard Abernathy, and the signalman, whose name I can't recall. And the four tanks were lost.

I didn't hear the explosion that blew up my boat, but when I opened my eyes I was underwater. I looked up and saw the surface of water somewhere above my head. I vividly remember paddling as fast as I could to reach the surface, which I obviously did. Were it not for the Mae West life jackets that I had everybody wear and made them tie up tight, I don't think I would be here today. I recall swimming around not seeing too much, but hearing somebody yell, "Skipper, Skipper!" It was Abernathy on what remained of our overturned craft. He grabbed me as I floated in his vicinity, and he pulled me up by the Mae West life jacket collar and onto the overturned boat. The boat didn't sink because it was deep enough to be resting on the bottom and still protrude above the surface of the water.

A short time thereafter, I remember that an LCM [landing craft, mechanized] that was going to the beach stopped by us. They somehow got me onto the back of this LCM. Abernathy jumped onboard with me and the LCM then proceeded to the beach with what was then the first wave of army units to land. I remember the coxswain of the LCM proceeding to the beach, dropping his ramp, and watching the soldiers debark. As soon as the last one was off, he raised the ramp and headed back out to the English Channel and safely. However, I saw many bullets land around the back of that LCM. I guess it was a miracle that none of them hit the LCM or me or anyone else on the boat, and we did make it back out to safety. I don't remember docking to a destroyer, but I do remember being hauled up hand by hand, people passing me up a ladder onto the deck of the destroyer, and someone yelling, "Take him down below to sickbay!" I couldn't see very well. I had bloodshot eyes, I guess, because nothing was clear. However, when they put me in some officers' room, I remember them cutting the clothes off me and putting me on a leather couch, which was very cold, and covering me with a blanket until they could get me into surgery.

In the surgery clinic, the medics patched up my face, sewed my nose back in place, patched up my right leg, and then bandaged me up and brought me back down to the room I was first placed in.

The destroyer I was on, I don't remember the name of it, must have gone back to England and docked at some pier in Plymouth or Portsmouth. I remember being put in an ambulance. I awoke about a week later at the 182nd Army General Hospital in Vernon, England.

Clair R. Galdonik (U.S. Army)

Although the American seaborne landing at Utah Beach went off much more smoothly than that at Omaha Beach due to lighter German resistance, men still lost their lives, as detailed by Clair Galdonik of the 4th Infantry Division.

JUNE 1 CAME, AND WE KNEW THAT D-Day was very close. All passes to town were canceled. Letter writing was not permitted. I sorted through my personal belongings and got everything down to a bare minimum. All I kept was a razor, a piece of soap, a toothbrush, my rosary beads, and my prayer book. On

June 2, I tried to put my spiritual life in order by going to confession and Holy Communion.

The day dragged because of inactivity. That afternoon all noncoms and officers were assembled in a sealed-off compound. Here we were told what our D-Day mission would be. The 4th Infantry Division would assault Utah Beach at 0630 hours in waves of three hundred men each. We would follow up after they pushed inland and give infantry support where needed.

On June 3, I was issued new clothing. This was followed by a review and a discussion with squads and platoons in our battalion so as to minimize the mistakes we might make when attacking the Germans in hopes of keeping our casualty rate down. The food was getting better, with more choice servings of meats and desserts, but I seemed to have lost my desire to eat as heartily as before the final preparations for D-Day were announced to us. This was basically true for the other men also.

On June 4 we were early risers. After breakfast we embarked by truck for the pier at Dartmouth to board a small troopship. Then it seemed as though life had lost its real meaning. Few words were spoken among us. No joking or prankster stunts pulled. We felt closer to one another now than ever before, although we had been together for months. Only when our boat left and proceeded into the English Channel to join the convoy headed for Normandy were we told that D-Day would be tomorrow, June 5.

The sea was rough and the wind had a real bite to it. I stayed in seclusion in my bunk. All the preparation for this day was behind me now. I spent much time in prayer. I don't remember how late in the day it was when we were informed that D-Day had been pushed back another day, to June 6. It was a relief for some of us and a disappointment for others. The waiting for history to be made was most difficult. Being cooped up on a small ship made our wait more miserable. I, like many others, became seasick, and the stench of soldiers throwing up permeated the craft.

I guess I slept a little that night. Came the dawn on June 5, and the weather continued to be bad, with an overcast sky and strong winds. Our troopship bobbed up and down so much that I couldn't eat anything. As the morning passed, weather conditions were a bit better. I found a baseball, so my buddy John, from New York, and I started playing catch on the deck to break the tension. That soon ended because I made a bad throw and the ball was swallowed up by the English Channel.

It was announced over the PA system that D-Day would definitely be June 6. No turning back this time. What a restless and sleepless night for me. I was in most of my battle dress at 0001 hours on June 6. The night was filled with the drone of our aircraft moving across the Channel to bomb inland and the C-47s to drop paratroopers of the 82nd and 101st Airborne divisions. More C-47s came, filled with men and supplies to land inland and cut off the Germans from moving to the beaches once the boats started landing the men from the Channel.

From 0001 to 0004 hours I sat huddled by my bunk. I glanced over and saw another close buddy of mine carefully folding up a mosquito net. I walked over to him and asked what plans he had for that. "Nothing," he replied. "Throw it away, then, Tom," I replied. "No, Clair, I'm taking it with me." How glad I am to this day that he didn't discard it. The punch line comes later that night of June 6.

At about 0500 hours, all heck broke loose. The battleships and cruisers started throwing salvos of shells from their big guns on four or five pillboxes on the beach that we would be going in on. What a show! Immediately, it gave me some assurance that no Germans on the beach could survive this bombardment.

We went out on deck, and a couple of our squads huddled together to exchange stories of our home life. How we longed to be back home, what our plans for the future would be if we survived this horrible war. How will we react in battle? Would it be easy to kill German soldiers? And a lot more discussion revolving around our mission when we are committed in battle.

I loved those guys, and I believe their feelings toward me were the same. We knew that some of us would not live to see our loved ones again. We talked openly and freely and even shared a few laughs.

Now it was time to crawl into the rest of our battle gear. The Higgins boats were starting to come our way, and that meant it was time to move out. The scramble nets were thrown over the side, and as my name was called I started the descent into a Higgins boat. Do I remember my thoughts as I crawled down the rope, and how I felt? Oh, yes. "Please, God, give my parents the necessary strength to carry on if I become a casualty, and give me the strength and courage that I need to see me through the perils of this long day." For a fleeting second it brought to mind a favorite wartime song of mine, recorded by Sammy Kaye, entitled "Dear Mom." I remember a few of the words to this day:

> Dear Mom,
> The weather today was cloudy and damp.
> Your letter arrived but was missing a stamp.
> That's all for tonight, the bugle just blew.
> Tomorrow's a big day with plenty to do.
> I like it here, Mom, but I'm lonesome for you,
> for I love you, dear Mom.

Seeing and hearing all these strange sights before me almost put me in a state of hypnosis. Was all this for real, or was it merely a dream? I soon found out as I dropped to the bottom of the boat that it was no dream. We were packed in, thirty tight, because of all of our extra equipment, and every piece was vital to us. Each loaded boat followed the others in line in a circle around the ship that we had debarked from, until all the troops were unloaded and ready to start inland toward Utah Beach.

Our wave was still behind the big warships firing. As we passed by them, I put my cold and wet hands over my ears to help deafen the sound of the terrific explosions as the big guns fired round after round at the shore installations. The big waves in the Channel bounced our craft like a bobber, and water splashed into our boat. A heavy mist was falling, so visibility was far from good. Each soldier was issued a vomit bag, but this time I didn't have to use it, probably because now I was wound up so tightly. There was no conversation now. Each soldier was making peace with himself as we got ever closer to the beach.

When we caught sight of it, I could see the exploding shells churning up the beach sand. We must have been five miles out and the time was about 0900 hours when the sky started to brighten. My feet were already soaking wet. My gun was still wrapped in plastic to keep the mechanism dry. I ripped off the plastic just before the ramp went down.

Then I saw hundreds of C-47s towing gliders filled with Airborne reinforcements. What a magnificent sight! They would repel a counterattack by the Germans to break through and throw us back into the sea. Fighter planes of our air force were circling overhead, bombing and strafing enemy positions while medium and heavy bombers were plastering targets farther inland. This was a morale factor and even brought some cheers and laughter to our sullen faces.

With the beach in sight more clearly now, I didn't like what I could see. The clouds of black smoke rising meant that the German artillery on the beach area was heavy. Because of many beach obstacles, our boat could not move in close to shore. As it came up on 1000 hours, the ramp went down. Then something dreadful happened. A boy in my squad started crying and yelling that he could not leave the boat and begged to be left on the craft. I had to make a quick decision, for the beach area was no place to hang around. I inflated my life jacket and grabbed his arm and pulled him into the water with me. I needed help, so another soldier came to my aid and grabbed his other arm. We inflated his life jacket and got him going. But the crying had not stopped. I felt so sorry for him, but it did make me forget my own fear as we headed for the beach. A shell came in close and we had to duck in the murky water with just our heads showing and rifles held high over our heads. As I moved closer to shore, another whining shell came in. Again I went down trying to escape the flying shrapnel and trying to watch my buddy, who had now stopped crying and was facing up, trying to get onshore safely. After a third shell, I was so exhausted, being weighed down, that I lost my fear of becoming a casualty on the beach.

I remember cursing the Germans, then telling someone close by, "I'm going for dry land and I won't stop until I get there." This was indeed an unsafe act by me. Fortunately, I got ashore, as did my buddy whose emotions had gotten the best of him. It made me feel good that we got him safely on the beach.

Something I feared more than German artillery was the danger of stepping on a land mine. There were so many of them that we had just one little area to work our way through that had been cleared of mines. So far so good, but enemy shelling had taken its toll on the beach area. Tanks and trucks were gutted and burning, but only a few dead Americans were there. It shook me up. Just a short while ago, they were among the living. I moved away from the beach area just as fast as my legs would move. I was only twenty-five years old then, but I had a difficult time getting going with the extra weight of dirty salt water that was now soaking my clothes. I discarded my life preserver and hastened the men behind me to get moving inland to escape the heavy shelling of the beach area. We could not fan out much after we got about 300 yards inland because the low-lying areas had been flooded by the Germans. I recall only one causeway leading from the beach, so we had to march single file until we moved out of this area.

Since the 4th Division was the spearhead, we encountered no German soldiers yet, but that would soon change. I cannot say how long it took us to get a little elbow room, or what time of day it was getting to be. Now we began to get intermittent artillery fire, and we wasted no time hitting the ground. We moved rapidly inland but were limited for space because the areas off the road were posted with signs in German reading "Mines." We were in a most precarious position. If German artillery had spotted us or if the German Luftwaffe had gotten through, we would not have made it.

I lost all track of time even though we continued to move inland. We still had not lost a man. The only Germans we saw thus far were the good ones, all of them dead. I saw the lifeless bodies of some 4th Division men. It was a dreadful feeling seeing this loss of life of our comrades, but later I was able to adjust to it. The invasion was going well, so I thought, because the 82nd and 101st Airborne had pretty well sealed off the German reinforcements heading for the beach.

We moved into position just behind the front lines as it started getting dark. My dear buddy, Tom, with the mosquito net, and I dug a foxhole and sat back-to-back in it. There would be no sleeping tonight, just a long wait for tomorrow, when our company or regiment would get its baptism of fire from mortars, artillery, and small-arms fire. We already knew the danger from artillery fire. I could have hugged Tom for bringing his mosquito net. The mosquitoes were vicious as we sat huddled in our foxhole, so we made good use of his net. I shivered the night through, but having someone next to me made it a bit warmer. Tom would make the supreme sacrifice to help liberate France. He was gunned down about a week later. It was a terrific loss to me.

I was not to have any sleep or rest this night. We had plenty of men standing guard duty so we felt pretty well locked in, but this soon changed. We had to make one more move to advance and keep abreast of the 4th Infantry Division, for their objective this night was to link up with the 82nd and 101st Airborne. This happened just before midnight, a very happy occasion to say the least; now we dug in again to await the dawn of D+1. I had no desire for food and threw away the can of cheese and dog biscuits, but I forced down a chocolate bar. Where the name "dogface" originated referring to an infantry soldier, I do not know. However, it was most fitting to me because I ate plenty of dirt my first day in Normandy.

Thus ended D-Day and my first day of combat, so far from home and separated from my loved ones. Shivering and soaking wet in a foxhole, and wondering what tomorrow would be like. I did not feel that I would lack courage for all the dangers that would confront me and the rest of the men. I put my fate into God's hands.

John L. Ahearn (U.S. Army)

The navy was much more successful in getting tanks onto Utah Beach than onto Omaha Beach. It was these tanks that helped to spearhead the 4th Infantry Division invasion, as described by John Ahearn.

IN APRIL 1944, MY MEDIUM TANK COMPANY participated in the training exercise Tiger at Slapton Sands. During that time we also demonstrated the efficacy of some rocket launchers that had been welded on the back of our tanks. A cockamamie idea, as it turned out, for they were totally ineffective and quickly removed.

Subsequently, however, my company, which consisted of seventeen tanks, was increased to twenty-five. There were dozer blades on those eight additional tanks. The blades were meant to assist with the seawalls, but more particularly in the hedgerow country. Because this was a last-minute decision, we had to tear apart our existing company organization and get sixteen additional personnel, two for each dozer tank, from the engineers. I had to reassign all the men in my company who had any experience with tanks. Former drivers became tank commanders. Gunners were made drivers, et cetera. The driver and the tank commander were the most important individuals, so it required a complete revamping.

A difficult thing occurred for me a few days, maybe a week, before the invasion. I had to go to a medical tent area to check up on one of my best drivers. I suspected that he was trying to avoid the invasion, because he didn't appear that sick. I just insisted that he be released and that he come with us. This was not an easy thing to do because he was otherwise a fine soldier.

In the weeks before the invasion, I was very busy supervising all this activity in my company. I was constantly under the surveillance of the battalion commander and his staff, because by this time we were the only combat company at Camp Upton.

Companies A and B had been fitted with the dual-drive tanks, the so-called DD tanks, and they were in other parts of the United Kingdom, getting ready for their particular show.

The battalion was assigned to the 8th Infantry Regiment of the 4th Division under the command of Col. James van Fleet. I recall one particular meeting, perhaps a week before the invasion, where he had gathered all of the officers who were going to participate, and had talked in broad terms about what our mission was going to be. I recall particularly that he used a lot of football metaphors.

It was also about this time that I was told I should meet with the British naval officer of the LCTs [landing craft, tank] that we were going to embark on, and was told to report to him, or rather meet with him, to plan our part of the invasion. The planning consisted of determining for each of the LCTs the three tanks that would go on that particular craft. Each LCT would carry one dozer blade tank and two normally equipped tanks. We also planned where we would be in the invasion: we were scheduled to arrive at the beach at H+15 minutes. The scheme of things was that A and B companies, with the DD tanks, would arrive at H hour with the assaulting elements of the 8th Infantry Division and would proceed immediately inland as fast as they could and accompany the infantrymen. C Company was to support Companies A and B and also take care of lateral defenses on the beach.

On June 4, C Company proceeded to the pier near Dartmouth, where all twenty-four tanks were loaded onto the eight LCTs. That evening we set sail for the invasion. But sometime during the night, the whole armada returned to the ports of England because of the heavy seas.

On the evening of June 5, we set out again. I visited the deck frequently, talked to the British officers, and chatted with my own men. Because of revamping my crews, I had new tank commanders. One of them was a boy named Owen Gavigan, who was only nineteen at the time and had just joined the battalion a few months before. However, he was very bright, and I felt that he had the capability of becoming a good tank commander.

That night I knew I wouldn't be able to sleep, but I wanted to get as much rest as possible, so I returned to my cot belowdeck and began reading a book that I had wanted to read for some time, *A Tree Grows in Brooklyn*. I particularly wanted to read it because it was about Williamsburg, an area of Brooklyn with which I had some familiarity. I managed to finish the book.

Around three or four in the morning, I again went up on deck. It was inky black, and several times I heard the commander of our boat yelling by megaphone to some of the control boats, trying to determine our position. Then we proceeded to get ready to mount our tanks, see that everybody was there, and all that. Everybody was ready to go.

About half past five or so, we heard the tremendous roar of the bombers going overhead to hit the beaches. Then to the south we saw the big flashes of light and heard the thunder of the guns of the battleships as they opened up, and then we saw fighters in the sky. It was a tremendous sight. As dawn broke, we got a clearer picture of where everybody was, and it became evident that there had been some problem with the DD tanks and that we were not going to come in at H+ 15 minutes but would arrive behind our tanks. We would indeed be the first tanks on the beach, or alongside some of the Company B tanks. My tanks did not have the DD flotation gear, but they had been weatherized and we were able to get into five or six feet of water because we had these flue-like objects (I don't recall the name) over the engines, and everything else was sealed. The British boats brought us in on the beach just as far as they could, and we got off in five or six feet of water. As it turned out, Owen Gavigan, because his tank was in front, was the first tank to land on Utah Beach, and mine was the second. We proceeded onto the beach, but it became evident that we were on the wrong stretch of beach. It was also evident to me that not all of my tanks had gotten in. As it developed, about six of the tanks had to return to England because of boat difficulties. I had to decide what to do. I saw Gen. Teddy Roosevelt on the beach, and got out of my tank and reported to him, and told him who I was and what my mission was. He told me to spread out toward the flanks until we could find an exit from the beach, and to take care and get inland as fast as we could, and to be generally supportive. I then directed Lieutenant Yeoman, who was my second in command, to take half of the tanks and proceed north, and I would proceed to the south.

At this time I was leading seven tanks. Of the original twenty-four, six had returned to England. Four of the dozer tanks, under the scheme of things, had reverted to the control of the engineers, so I divided the remaining fourteen between Lieutenant Yeoman and myself. We proceeded southward, trying to find an opening off the beach, and subsequently did find an opening, I don't know how many yards down the beach. However, at this opening was a small tank-like object that I had never been informed about and had never seen in the operations in Africa or Sicily. Although I was concerned, my mission was to get in as rapidly as possible, so we proceeded through. As it turned out, nothing happened. Later on, I read that a number of these so-called "Little Goliaths" [small radio-controlled tracked vehicles filled with explosives] had been controlled from one of the German strongpoints, and apparently the controls to these had been severed during the bombing. Lucky for us, as it turned out.

When we got inside the seawall, we again proceeded laterally between the seawall and the road, where we saw a number of infantrymen from the 2nd Battalion of the 8th Division who were proceeding northward. As we looked southward, it became evident that there was another German strongpoint, and although we saw no activity there, I had our tanks fire some shells into it. With this, a number of what turned out to be "impressed" soldiers, who were not really of German nationality, came out with their hands in the air and began running towards us. I dismounted from the tank to take them as prisoners, and as I began to approach them, they began yelling *"Achtung Minen"* and gesturing me to stay still. With this, I gestured for them to move toward the road, and the tanks moved toward the road, and we delivered these thirty or so prisoners to the infantry. Then we again proceeded southward until we came across a country road leading to the town of Pouppeville. At this juncture, I told one of my junior officers, Lieutenant Tighe, who was commanding the platoon with which I had associated myself, to proceed inland, and I, along with a couple of other tanks, would continue down this rather narrow road, across the dunes and across the hedgerows, to see if there were any further strongpoints that we might assault.

Shortly after this, as my tank proceeded down this small lane, it hit a land mine. The front left bogie was blown off, and we were immobilized. I radioed this information to Lieutenant Tighe, then proceeded on foot down the lane and across several hedgerows to see if there was anything we might take a look at.

I heard cries for help and, looking toward the beach, saw three figures who I surmised were injured paratroopers. I immediately returned to the tank and got the rather large first-aid kit that we carried, then I came back, proceeding behind the hedgerow that separated them from the hedgerow to the north. When I saw a break in the hedgerow, I proceeded to cross it to get as close to them as possible. While I was standing there contemplating my next move, a personnel mine went off under me. The explosion threw me into the bank of the hedgerows, and I was unconscious for a while. Subsequently I awakened and began yelling, and two of my crew, Sergeant Zampiello and Corporal Beard, came out to take a look. It was hard to find me, because I had rolled up against the embankment. I cautioned them not to come over, because of the presence of mines. My crewmates went back to the tank and got a long rope, threw it to me, and dragged me out from the hedgerow. My memory is fuzzy as to how I got back to the field hospital, which thankfully had arrived four to five hours after the invasion. I do know that I was on stretchers and in jeeps, had been transferred from one group to another, and subsequently arrived at the hospital. I later learned from our battalion maintenance officer, who wrote to me in the hospital, that they had discovered some 15,000 mines in that vicinity. So the odds were not very good that I would be unharmed.

During that night, it was decided that I would need surgery. As it turned out, because I had been wearing heavy paratroop boots, both feet were still on, but terribly mangled. Before the surgery, I was given about six bottles of plasma and was visited by the chaplain. Then in the early evening, in this makeshift tent with white sheets used as walls, I was operated on. I later found from notes that the decision was made to amputate one foot because the medics felt that I could not withstand both operations. So one foot was amputated, and I was prepared for transport the next day to England.

William R. Winters (U.S. Army)

Part of the reason that Utah Beach was less contested than Omaha Beach was the fact that strong sea currents had pushed the landing craft over a mile from the intended landing area, which was more heavily defended. William Winters happily recounts this lack of enemy resistance.

ON THE NIGHT OF JUNE 2, 1944, we moved to the docks at Plymouth and boarded a troop transport. Soon afterwards we were issued impregnated combat fatigues, underwear, and socks. The high command apparently thought the Germans might use gas on us, hence the impregnated clothing. We sailed early in the evening of June 5, and at approximately 2:00 a.m. all of the officers aboard had dinner with the ship's officers in the wardroom. After dinner we were briefed some more and told to put on our impregnated clothing at 2:30 a.m. At approximately 3:00 a.m. we would be loading into our landing craft.

At 3:00 a.m. we were topside and going down the cargo nets into our LCVPs [landing craft, vehicle, personnel]. After loading we started circling in several groups of ten in the English Channel. The water was rough. At the appropriate time we started our run toward the beaches, making our arrival at H hour, which was 6:30 a.m. The sky was starting to lighten. The landing craft scraped bottom and dropped the ramp, and we got off into the water. It was approximately up to our armpits at first, and we walked on in towards the beach.

Very little enemy fire was getting to the beach, although an occasional artillery round came in and we could hear some machine gun fire. When we hit the beach, I was very close to being seasick, and I was glad to have my feet on solid ground. I was thinking about the effect that this landing would have, what all the training and discipline were about, why I had become an officer, and that we had a job to do—so let's go do it.

We then moved up to a seawall and sprawled there temporarily. I took my .45 out of the holster, unwrapped it (we had wrapped our .45s in waterproof material), and fired it into the ground to make sure it worked. We then went over the seawall and started advancing inland. Within a short distance we ran into a lot of land mines, and several of our men stepped on them. From that point on we advanced very slowly and walked very gingerly. About half an hour after we had landed, two tanks landed and moved up to where we were. We advised them of the land mines, so they advanced in front of us and we followed in their track marks until we got out of the mined area.

Up to this point there was very little enemy fire, although an occasional artillery shell came in and there was sporadic machine gun and rifle fire. At approximately 9:30 a.m. my radio operator told me I had a call from Lieutenant Hurst, who was the executive officer of Battery C, and he wanted to talk to me.

I got on the radio and said, "Hi, Jim, glad you got in. How're things going?"

"We're in position, but we did have sad news coming in," he said. "Our B Battery [which was about one and a half miles off the beach] hit a marine mine and all fifty-nine officers and men, as well as our four self-propelled 105mm artillery guns and some jeeps, were lost." He then said, "How are you doing?"

"Fine, although I don't have much to do with artillery to fire up to this point and am pretty much tagging along with the infantry and keeping my head down."

"Well," he said, "get me a fire mission so I can see if these big babies still work."

I told him that I would do what I could and get back to him as soon as possible.

It wasn't much later that we suddenly ran into a lot of machine gun and rifle fire. I got on the radio and said, "Fire mission, coordinates such and such, fire number one only, for adjustment." Very shortly they gave me, "On the way," and I picked up the round and radioed back, "One hundred over, one hundred left." They gave me another, "On the way," and the round was in the target area, so I said, "Fire for effect." They gave me all four guns, and we ended up shooting three volleys before I said, "Cease fire, mission accomplished."

We started advancing and I fired four or five more missions. At about 4:30 p.m. we reached our objective, which was St. Mere-Dumont, where we relieved elements of the 101st Airborne. At approximately 5:00 p.m. planes started coming over; they were towing gliders. When the gliders were cut loose, they would land but were unable to stop in time and would run into a hedgerow, at which time the front end of the glider seemed to explode and equipment and men came out of the front. These gliders were made from plywood, and Normandy is certainly hedgerow country with every field almost completely covered on all sides by hedgerows.

We were then ordered to move out towards Ste. Meré Eglise. Our casualties had been light until this point, but on the way towards Ste. Meré Eglise we ran into hotly contested action, finally getting to the outskirts of Ste. Meré Eglise about an hour later. We arrived at the last hedgerow looking into Ste. Meré Eglise and stopped at that point. A lot of machine gun and rifle fire were coming in, and shortly some artillery on our right flank started coming in rather close to us. I knew this was our own artillery and immediately took a yellow smoke grenade from my pistol belt, pulled the pin, and threw the grenade. Yellow smoke came up, which meant friendly. Shortly after, the firing ceased.

Our paratroopers were in Ste. Meré Eglise, and I was afraid to fire any missions because we did not want to injure any of our own men. But I did select three areas where I knew I would not hit any of our men and fired one round in each of these areas. This was merely to let the Germans know we were very close and had artillery. At dark we settled down behind the hedgerows, and for the first time had a chance to relax. We ate some K rations, which were really our first meal that day. None of us slept much that night, and at daybreak we were ordered to move into Ste. Meré Eglise.

This we did rather rapidly with no opposition, and it appeared that the Germans had pulled out during the night. There were some sad sights in Ste. Meré Eglise. One paratrooper was hanging from a church steeple; the Germans had machine-gunned him. Another was hanging from a tree; he had also been machine-gunned. And there were several dead on the streets. After about an hour we were ordered to move out and head towards Cherbourg.

6 | AIR SUPPORT

Roger V. Lovelace (U.S. Army Air Corps)

The Allies had complete air superiority over the D-Day landing beaches. Roger V. Lovelace describes the awe-inspiring view of the Normandy invasion from his B-26 medium bomber.

WE WERE FLYING OUT OF GREAT DUNMOLE at the time of D-Day. I was perhaps at the level of about sixty missions or more by that time. Originally we had been told we would fly only about thirty missions, maybe thirty-five, and then we'd get to go home. When that time came, they suggested maybe fifty would be the appropriate number. But when crews started getting their fiftieth mission behind them, we were told that we couldn't go home now because we were getting too close to the big push and they couldn't spare any crews for rotation to the States. So by the time I completed my tour, I had personally been on seventy-six bombing missions over Europe from our base in England.

On D-Day, June 6, 1944, I was flying as a radio operator gunner, which meant I flew in the top turret of a B-26. I rarely had occasion to use radio equipment because during wartime we usually observed radio silence, so I was primarily there as a gunner.

We made landfall well south of the beachhead area. I don't remember exactly what beachhead we were assigned to, or even whether we were looking down at American or British troops. We could see gun flashes and shell bursts everywhere. The big guns of the battleships were firing broadside. Their fire was directed at some target well inland and out of sight.

We could see gunfire lacing across the water—I assume these were tracers—seemingly in almost every direction. I don't know what altitude we were maintaining at that part of the flight, but there were big orange balls looping into shore that appeared to come up almost to our altitude. Not far inland, our group turned north, then soon turned back towards the beaches. We broke up into flights of six, then dropped closer and closer down towards our scheduled bombing altitude. Then we went into trails, which means one aircraft behind the other, and were on our own.

As we approached the beachhead, all of the action came into view again. One of the best views anyone could get of the invasion of Normandy had to be the one we were looking at. Eisenhower himself had no place to stand where he could see the view that I was privy to see. I could see people, tanks, and trucks running every which way on the ground. By now the first wave was just a couple hundred yards offshore and zig-zagging towards the beach. A Douglas A-20 was flying right down on the water, parallel to the shore, and laying a smoke screen between the shore and the first assault. Suddenly, the A-20 just disintegrated into a ball of fire.

We were now running right down the shoreline looking for a target. We were drawing a lot of fire, not the usual 88mm but smaller rapid-fire stuff. I have this frozen image of a machine gunner with the guns set up by a barn. He was firing at us. For a second I could look right down the barrel of that gun. A waist gunner or a tail gunner could return fire, but up in the top turret I felt helpless. I couldn't bring my guns below horizontal; therefore, I couldn't fire on anything.

The bombardier shouted on the intercom, "Bombs away!" We turned away from the shoreline, gained altitude again, and flew over part of the invasion fleet. We even drew a few rounds of friendly fire from someone down there who couldn't identify us. They missed.

I looked down on that panorama again. Never in history had such an invasion force been assembled, and it will surely never happen again. I feel mighty privileged to have been there and seen that spectacle. I'll never forget it.

We flew a second mission that same day in the afternoon, our targets a little farther inland, and two more the day after the invasion. But after that, it was the same day-to-day war, and the invasion of France was part of the past. There was still a war left to win.

Robert Javis (U.S. Army Air Corps)

The 388th Bombardment Group flew their missions in B-17 four-engine bombers during D-Day. Robert Javis talks about his impressions of that important day and what he saw.

On June 5, 1944, in the early evening, we were alerted to engage in an early morning take-off. This was our twenty-second mission. By midnight the base was in motion. Everybody was moving. We went to breakfast, which consisted of the usual fresh eggs and bacon, toast, coffee, and milk. Next was the briefing. When the curtain was let up, we saw the route and knew that this was it, the big one. Besides that, across the top of the map in bold letters was "D-Day Invasion of Normandy."

We took off at 0227 hours in zero visibility fog up to approximately 8,000 to 10,000 feet. The tail gunners were each given an amber lens flash gun to keep from running into one another. It must have worked because we never heard of any midair collisions. Upon formation, which was very difficult since the buncher system was out and also because of the fog, we took a zigzag course to the Netherlands, back to England to Belgium, back to England to the Dunkirk area, back to England, then pow! the Normandy beach. We hit on Sword Beach, which was where the British and Canadians landed. The zigzag formation was to fool the Germans, or try to fool them as to where we were heading, and at the same time allow the ships to move the troops into landing position. Over the English Channel we had almost solid overcast, which meant bombing by PFF [preformed fragmentation]. Our instructions were to man the guns at all times but not to test-fire, as was our usual practice, because of the numbers concentrated on that day. We were told not to fire at anything that was not firing at us. Needless to say, it was a very tense situation.

The 388th led the whole Eighth Air Force on D-Day. Bombs were away on coastal gun installations at 0656 from 15,050 feet. We were told later that it was a "shack," which meant no more gun installation. We dropped 2,000-pound blockbusters—bombs filled with nothing but black powder, which created tremendous explosions. We found out a few days later that the German soldiers at the gun installations, which were concrete three to four feet thick, were all dead from the impact, with brains and blood coming out of their eyes and ears and the top of their heads. About fifteen to twenty minutes outside, two rockets were fired much to the east of us. They were very ineffective. Passing by Nantes, France, we took a lot of antiaircraft fire around a bridge.

On the next day, June 7, we took out the bridge, which was on the main supply road from southern France. We landed at 1043 hours, were off to debriefing, then to chow, then to shower, and finally to rest as it was now 1600. The next morning we would be heading out again.

R. L. Delashaw (U.S. Army Air Corps)

German submarines were perceived as a threat to the Allied D-Day invasion fleet. Antisubmarine patrol aircraft were used to protect the ships. R. L. Delashaw's job was to protect the antisubmarine patrol planes from German fighters.

I RECEIVED A CALL FROM OUR HEADQUARTERS to report to the air commodore at a British base about seventy to eighty miles north of us. I don't recall specifically the names or the unit designations of the RAF [Royal Air Force] unit we were to work with during D-Day. But we were to be under his operational control for a period of time.

I flew up to the base and was met by the group captain who commanded the Spitfire organization located on the

291

base. We reported to the air commodore, who then briefed us on our mission for D-Day. Briefly, our mission was to fly cover for the antisubmarine patrols that were to keep the Channel free of German submarines during our cross-Channel operations and subsequently to resupply and reinforce operations. This was necessary because intelligence said that there were seven hundred-plus German fighters and night fighters on the Brest peninsula, and they posed a real threat to the big, slow-moving aircraft that performed the antisubmarine warfare [ASW] role. This was of great concern to those who were planning the cross-Channel operation. Therefore, my complete P-47 group and the RAF Spitfire group plus the British night fighter organizations that took over our duties at night were to protect the ASW aircraft. Our duties were to provide medium cover at 12,000 to 14,000 feet, and the British Spitfires were to provide high cover at around 25,000 to 26,000 feet in daylight hours. This meant, of course, that we had to be on the line before dawn and stay until after dark, which involved leaving Christchurch base about an hour before dawn and getting back about an hour after sunset.

Our little base was not necessarily the best equipped for night and weather-type operations, and I have often wondered why we were chosen as the organization to perform this chore. I suspect that we were the fighter organization that was the farthest west, or at least the U.S. Air Force fighter organization that was the farthest west; hence, we were closest to the patrol line.

Anyhow, after the commodore briefed me and the group captain and I had talked, they advised me that I was then "bigoted," which meant no more flying missions until after the D-Day operation had been completed, and I would be advised when it was felt that I could again participate in combat operations. I was also given a top-secret copy of the air force portion of the plan. Upon return to Christchurch, there was little I could do with it other than carry it around or put it in my sleeping bag, as I had no facilities for the care of top-secret documents. And since no one but me was supposed to know about that mission until it was actually implemented, I could not very well do much about passing it on to my exec or operations officer.

I had a difficult time explaining why it was necessary to get out our field lighting kits and put the lights down the runway. A field lighting kit provides only one light for every few hundred feet on the left side only, but it does have lights to mark the end of the runway. The little hoods that go over these lights were directional, so you could see them only when you were lined up with the runway. Anyhow, I got the lights installed, and acquired the necessary maps and so forth with which to brief the pilots. When we were told to implement plans, I briefed the pilots on our mission. I'll never forget how disappointed most of them were, and some were outspokenly vociferous in their attitude that they did not want to do this mission. They wanted to participate in the actual combat that they visualized was going on down on the beach. Most of them had visions of flying over the beach and right down the little line and seeing people shooting at one another and hammering one another. This, of course, was not at all possible. In later activities we were intimately connected with the people on the ground, but usually it was with mechanized forces or large unit activities.

Our D-Day activity involved keeping eight aircraft on the line that started off at the entrance to the Channel and ran some hundred miles into the Bay of Biscay, then back and forth. One of the bright spots was that we were under British radar control, and they were able to place us on the patrol line and separate us so that one flight was going east and one flight was going west. We essentially covered the area so fighters were available within about five minutes of any spot on the whole line. I could not personally go on the early missions. In fact, I was not relieved of my bigoted status for a week, after which I did get out and fly on the mission two or three times. But I spent most of the actual day of June 6 going over the plans and preparations that were being made for us to move across the Channel at some future date. Our advanced echelons and their equipment were being readied, even then, for us to make the move. We flew the patrol line for something like ten days to two weeks. After about the first week, I began to tell my higher headquarters that it wasn't necessary to have us out there, that we could do more somewhere else, because even our intelligence had perceived that those seven hundred German fighters had disappeared from the Brest peninsula.

We were relieved of our patrol duties, then began to participate in the overall activities of our army and its movement into France and subsequently into Germany.

Al H. Cory (U.S. Army Air Corps)

Despite the valiant efforts of the Allied bombers to support the D-Day landing effort, they did little to suppress the German fortifications on the beaches. Al Cory describes the heart-pumping missions he flew on D-Day.

I WAITED FOR MORE MEN TO SHOW up. I first met our pilot, Lou Jarrett, from the Bronx, New York. I also met our radioman, our turret gunner, and our engineer. We were to have no copilot for a while on the B-26 Marauder. I took over that job until one became available. (I was fortunate in having flying experience, both in the PT-17 and the AT-11.) However, the B-26 would prove to be the toughest and hardest of the air force planes to fly, although we would eventually praise her for her strength and dependability. This plane, with its high-tailed fins, cigar-shaped body, and small nose and wings, was known as the "flying prostitute" because she had "no visible means of support!" Those big 2,000-horsepower engines sitting out there on each wing kept her up in the air, kept her alive. We did a lot of night flying, with me acting as copilot, watching the instruments and compass. I flew the ship on several missions during daylight, and I think I got pretty good at that.

We finally got a young copilot, 2nd Lt. Gwylym (William) Hughes. He was born in Wales and lived in Utica, New York. He turned out to be one hell of a pilot, very steady, with nerves of steel.

The night before the invasion of Normandy, I pedaled my bike around the base, out to where the hard stands were and our ships were parked. I saw a bunch of guys on top of the ships; they had white and black paint and were painting stripes around the wings and around the fuselage. I asked why, and the crew chief said, "I don't know, but they have to be ready by tomorrow morning." I beat it back to the hut where we all lived and told the guys what I saw. We all thought something real big was coming up. A day or so earlier, I had been in London, on leave to go to Torquay, England. I had about fifty-five missions in, and they were giving me a long-awaited rest. While I was waiting for the train, walking down the ramp at the station, two MPs stopped me and one of them said, "Lieutenant, may I see your orders, please?" As I showed them to him, he got out a list and said, "Are you with the 387th Bomb Group?" I answered affirmatively, and he said, "Well, you're to report back to base immediately." I beat it back, and it was that night that I saw the crews painting the stripes on all the planes on the base. The next day was June 6, 1944, the day of the invasion.

We sat there in the briefing room with our maps, which we had picked up earlier. The colonel came in momentarily. He was the type of CO who wouldn't ask his men to go on a hot mission alone. He would, on most flights, lead the way. I flew with him on several missions, and we were both wounded on the same day. A command pilot, he always had his hat cocked back on his head and a short, stubby cigar in his mouth. He said, "Hey, guys, good morning, good morning, good morning! Well, here we are. This is it!" What did he mean? "This is the big day we've been waiting for. It's what we all came here for." He hadn't said a word yet about a mission, but finally he said, "We're going to France at six [a.m.] as air support for the Allied forces invading the Normandy coast of Europe. This is to be the invasion." That's when the quiet erupted into a big roar. "Oh boy," everybody yelled. We were all pretty excited. The tactical officers got up and pulled down the charts and maps, and we took a grease pencil and marked our plastic-covered maps with a red line. No bombs were to fall on this side of that line. This side of the line would be all Allied troops, and beyond that line would be enemy territory. The bombing line was supposed to have been coordinated between the air forces and the ground forces.

That morning of June 6, at eleven o'clock high in front of us, I could see the battleships and cruisers a little ways back lobbing blasting shells, big shells, 16-inchers. They were shooting back at the coastal guns that were shooting at them. You could see the shells coming across through the air from Normandy and the 16-inch shells going back from the cruisers. The water was just full of boats like bunches of ants crawling around down there. I imagined all those young men huddled in the landing barges, all of them doubtless scared to death. I could see what they were heading into, and I prayed for all those brave young men about to come face to face with death. I knew how they felt. I just thought about that, and thought, "Man, I'm up here looking down at this tuff and they're out there waiting to get on that beach."

As we kept going farther and farther, I looked through my bombsight and checked it and the map again, and we were coming closer to a cloud layer. I told our pilot that the cloud layer was covering all of the target area. I couldn't see a thing below that. "We have go down lower," I said. "I can't see the target! I can't bomb. I can't identify that bomb line on the ground! The cloud's too low." We finally agreed that we'd all go down. The other flights followed us. We made a slow descent; I guess they finally realized what our situation was. We were all on radio silence, so we couldn't talk to one another.

We kept going down, kept going down. When we were sitting at 3,000 feet, I said, "That's not low enough; we've got to break through this darn layer." When we finally got down to where I could see, we were at 1,250 feet. That doesn't sound too good, but it was. I could see what they were doing, but my bombsight wouldn't be any good. I would have to change the intervalometer, and just drop my bombs one or two at a time, using my judgment. I had done this one time with a torpedo, and I knew how my bombs would fall on a split pattern. At least they would make foxholes for the guys who would be combing that beach.

Just when we got down that low, I looked around again and I could see the guys jumping off the barges into the surf and getting onto the beach. Not only that, I saw guys who fell and were floating in the surf, face down in the water. I could see the tracer bullets coming from the bunkers on the cliffs, right in front of it. They had machine guns buried in those cliffs somewhere, and they were spraying that beach. That's the way it looked, anyway. We'd see jeeps going off the end of these landing barges and into the water and sink right there. They had all these troops right behind them, and they just jumped in the water and sank, too, and the guys who got out, really I don't know how they got out of that surf. It must have been well over their head when they dropped because they went down, and not all of them came up.

Once they got on the beach, they crawled on their hands and knees, and I saw several of them lying face down on the sand. They were dead. I knew the ones in the water who were floating around were dead. I saw tanks coming off the landing barges, rolling down and heading right up the beach, toward the cliffs. They couldn't turn either way. They had to go straight ahead. I could imagine the guys who had fallen down on the beach who were wounded who couldn't move.

They couldn't move and the tankers couldn't turn. So what's next? I guess you can imagine what I'm going to say about the tankers that kept going and the guys who couldn't move who were wounded. The tankers kept going and *squish!* There were hundreds of American boys who were squashed by our tracks, by our own tank tracks trying to get a beachhead. I have that statement verified right here in Greensboro. I know a man who was a tank driver during the day on the same beach we were on, and he told me that. I said, "Hell, it's true. I was sitting out there looking at that. We couldn't move that tank. We had strict orders to just to move forward and don't go left or right unless we were called in. I heard the bodies burst open when we ran over them. It's awful, but that's the truth. You won't read it in any papers, either. That's what happened. A lot of those guys were buried up there, right in that sand, you know."

We finally got around to where I could see where my bombs were going to drop, so I set my intervalometer so that every two seconds a bomb would release. I also had a manual trip switch, so I'd drop a couple using my foot as the aiming point, because I couldn't use the bombsight. I know I was making good foxholes for some of those guys coming ashore. At least they had someplace to jump in. I could see Germans on the far side running away from the front, and a couple of trucks were being picked off by the U.S. fighters down below. They'd come in low, strafe, and machine-gun the trucks.

I told our pilot to break off and head west. Take a right-hand turn and zigzag with hard, fast movements, heading west, which we did, and all the flight followed. We were going along nice and easy, and I looked down at all that was going on down there. We finally got to the west coast of Normandy. We were coming around the big peninsula. It looked like a real old castle with a moat around it, really pretty. I noticed some little flickers of light on the ground. Those flickers, I soon found out, were 88mm flak guns—*wham*—exploding by our ship. Here they come! They were coming up fast. I figured, let's get out of here! I yelled, "Bank off to the left, keep going down, give it some speed, and let's get the hell out of here! They're bracketing us!"

About that time, something hit the plane—*whump,* like that. I could hear the little rat-tat-tat on the body of the plane—the bursting shells. I also felt something burst through the nose cone. That's when I felt that someone had slapped me in the chest with a sledgehammer. I thought for sure I was gone right there. My chest did not exactly hurt, but it was sore. Putting my hand inside my jacket, it felt kind of wet. I pulled it out—my fingers and hand were covered with blood. It wasn't coming from my chest; it was coming from the little finger on my right hand. A big slice was cut off the end. A piece of flak or glass had come through the side and ripped that finger. I wiped my hand off and reached down inside my jacket again, as I still felt that something had hit me. I reached down into the pocket of my second jacket, where I carried a little memo-address book and fountain pen, and felt something hard. Removing the notebook, I found a small jagged flak fragment stuck in the cover. One side was yellow; all other sides were jagged. It was a piece of shell casing that the memo book had helped stop!

We headed back toward the Channel and avoided that last bunch of flak guns; we got away from those and hightailed it back to England. The Channel was still rough, whitecaps still breaking, and a lot of boats were still milling around and heading toward the beaches. I don't know how many guys went in that day, but I'd say maybe ten thousand plus. We set course to our base, settled down, and landed without incident.

Everybody—all the ground crews, et cetera—was standing along the runways and hard stands, waiting for planes to come down. We taxied back to the hard stands, turned around, shut off the engines, and jumped out of the plane. The Red Cross gals were waiting with hot coffee and doughnuts. It felt good just to get back on the ground. The armorers came back to reload the ships with more bombs—500 pounders (tank-busters), I think.

In about a half hour or so we took off again, back to the same area, only we went farther down beyond our grease pencil line, into the St. Lo area. We were informed that there might be a concentration of German panzer tanks in the woods at St. Lo. The woods showed up perfectly. I identified the target and salvoed the bomb load right then as we were getting heavy flak. It was pitiful. You couldn't raise your head and look straight ahead because one of these blue lines might be coming right toward your face. Tracer shells from 40mm guns or something like that were coming right at us! You'd hear them hitting the ship and exploding, just smashing up and hitting the ship, like they were punching a hole. The crew sounded real worried. No matter where you looked, somebody was shooting at you. We could see German soldiers on the beach. We could identify them as German because they were nearer the bunkers than the Americans were. The beach was strewn with dead bodies. I'm telling you, it was really a bloody mess. There must have been three or four thousand bodies lying around on that beach. I could see only one beachhead. I don't know about the others, but this beach was really covered with dead bodies. What looked like a brown stain on the beach was blood turned brown where these men lay.

I had my sight fixed on that patch of woods. I used my bombsight now that we were higher. That was a whole load on that bunch of trees; down it went! Whatever was in those woods wasn't coming out of there—on wheels anyway, as far as I could see—because the other crews had the same target. We left, satisfied with what we accomplished.

William E. Satterwhite (U.S. Army Air Corps)

Among the many types of aircraft that provided air cover for the Allied invasion fleet on D-Day was the twin-engine P-38 Lightning fighter. William Satterwhite recounts what he saw from the cockpit of his plane.

Upon our arrival in southern England, we found that we were to be equipped with P-38 twin-engine fighters. We had been trained in single-engine aircraft. None of us had ever flown a twin-engine plane. But after ten hours orienting ourselves with the unfamiliar equipment, we went into combat in cross-Channel operations preparing for the invasion.

We were engaged in the interdiction of communications and transportation facilities and in strafing airdromes. Also, because of our long-range capability, we escorted some of the Eighth Air Force bombers in their deep strikes inside Germany. This took place until June 4, when we were briefed for the landing that was to have been on June 5.

The landings at Normandy were delayed for twenty-four hours due to the inclement weather conditions. About two or three in the morning of June 6, our group scrambled for the beachheads. We arrived over the landing sites as the pre-landing bombardment from the ships was taking place.

Due to the peculiar configuration of the P-38, our group was assigned to the lowest altitude, to reassure the troops on the surface that we were friendly aircraft. Additionally, as history has recorded, all aircraft participating in the invasion of France had three white and three black stripes, called invasion stripes, to further identify them as friendly to the Allied forces.

The 367th patrolled over the fleet to ensure that no enemy aircraft would attack the landing forces or the supporting ships off the coast. We were controlled by the beach master or his representative, whose call sign that day was Sweepstakes Charlie. As we covered the people on the surface, we could observe the operations until we were called in for a supportive strike somewhere on or behind the beaches.

Paratroopers and glider-borne troops had been inserted sometime shortly after midnight on D-Day. Our patrol continued throughout the landing of the first forces. Naval gunfire continued to cover the landing, and German resistance appeared from our point of observation to be devastating. Landing craft were being capsized, some were exploding, and the contents, including men and equipment, were being spilled into the surf in great numbers. The entire spectacle was awesome. Perhaps the greatest display of gunfire that history has recorded was in progress throughout the early morning hours of D-Day.

Our departures from covering the fleet and landings were dictated by Sweepstakes Charlie. The controller would assign targets where aircraft intervention might be of assistance, as in strafing.

There was much evidence of the dead and wounded in the way of bodies on the sandy beaches or floating in the surf. The surf was stained with fuel and oil and the blood of the wounded. Equipment bobbed in the surf, along with every imaginable bit of detritus that might be associated with a struggle of that magnitude.

After the first wave was reasonably well secured on the beaches, our group was relieved by other fighters. They took up our duties while we returned to our base in southern England near Stoney Cross to re-arm and refuel for another mission later in the morning. Our group flew eight missions in support of the effort that day. We were far more heavily engaged in the year following the invasion in pursuit of our support of Patton's 9th and 11th Armored divisions after the breakout at St. Lo. But nothing will ever replace the impression of the fury and intensity and the magnitude of the D-Day invasion on June 6, 1944.

INDEX

Military Units

305

People

Places